# Visual Merchandising

**Karin Zaghi**

B
U
P

In-store Communication
to Enhance Customer Value

Translation: Jill M. Connelly

Typesetting: Laura Panigara, Cesano Boscone (MI)

EGEA S.p.A.
Via Salasco, 5 - 20136 Milano
Tel. 02/5836.5751 – Fax 02/5836.5753
egea.edizioni@unibocconi.it – www.egeaeditore.it

First edition: January 2018

ISBN Domestic Edition 978-88-99902-25-4
ISBN International Edition 978-88-85486-41-6
ISBN Moby pocket edition 978-88-85486-43-2
ISBN Epub edition 978-88-85486-42-3

Print: Digital Print Service, Segrate (Milan)

*To my family*

# Table of Contents

# Acknowledgments

As with my first book (Zaghi, 2008), this work represents the compendium of many contributions from colleagues, professionals and companies: each one has added an invaluable component to the broad and complex discipline that is Visual Merchandising, enriching my long experience in the field and in the classroom on the topics of communication of the store and in the store.

The first contributors I want to thank are those who provided me with materials and interviews for the case studies: Mick Odelli and Micol Lorenzato at Senso Immersive Experience, Isabella Tonelli for Vivienne Westwood, Chiara Brancadoro for Lush, Elisa Contarini for Canon, and Alberto Aspesi at Aspesi.

Heartfelt thanks also go out to my colleagues, who spurred me on with their thought-provoking and insightful advice, especially Isabella Soscia and Gabriele Troilo who shared with me their professionalism and friendship.

For the English version of this book, I want to thank Jill Connelly, who patiently responded to all my requests, with a mixture of expertise, efficiency and affection.

Thanks also to Roberto Gamba and Cinzia Facchi at Egea who believed in the tremendous potential of this book on the international market from the start, without hesitation. Their support was vital in seeing this project through to the end.

All my love goes to my entire family, who teach me to live life with passion and dedication every day. And most of all, to my dearest friends, Alle, Gabriele, Irina, Isabella, Luisa, Manuela, Myriam and Stefania, whose gift to me is the joy of a timeless friendship, whose affection gives me strength even in the hardest times.

Finally, my thoughts are with my grandma Fernanda, who was the first person to teach me how to love, and to my mother who did her best to stay by my side. Both of these women will always be with me, in a special place in my heart. To my father who taught me never to take anything for granted. And to Giuseppe who took me by the hand to lead me step by step through the wonderful walk of life.

And last but not least to Guglielmo, life of my life, who has given me the immense joy of becoming a child again, to live life with tenderness and hope.

To all of you, *grazie*!

Karin Zaghi
Università L. Bocconi, Milan

# Introduction:
# What kind of visual merchandising?

I have warm memories of my undergraduate days in Luca Pellegrini's class. He was a Professor of Economics of Commercial Distribution at Bocconi University in Milan. Minute by minute, word by word, this gifted teacher opened up the world of modern distribution to me, a world still in its infancy in Italy, by sharing his passion for the study of the relationship between the customer and the store. This was a time when many saw distribution as simply representing one of the four marketing levers, when it was managed directly by industry to ensure that products would make it to the market efficiently and effectively.

At that time, most academic research asserted that the purchase decision was a top-down process. In other words, the assumption was that purchases were motivated by a need that materialized in the mind of the consumer, who would gather information and then weigh the alternatives to arrive at a final choice. In some cases, the process might end with an ex post assessment of the validity of the purchase. This conceptual framework was a powerful incentive for scholars and marketing researchers, fueling their enthusiasm for analyzing purchase intentions and brand associations with respect to the perceptive aspects of retailing.

This was back in the early 1990s, long before visual merchandising was considered a discipline in its own right, when it basically consisted of a set of techniques that served to maximize the productivity of retail space. Many years have gone by since then, but I can still hear the words of Luca Pellegrini introducing Visual Merchandising not so much as simply visual selling, but as an actual marketing discipline. In his view, distributors were meant to play an active part in the channel, with their own segmentation and positioning strategies.

Nowadays, the more highly evolved companies are well aware of the fact that nearly two-thirds of all purchases are impacted by in-store marketing activities. But more importantly, these companies see the store as a relational environment where they can integrate all available levers to manage that critical moment when the offering meets the market. In other words, the focus of attention is not necessarily the buyer, much less the consumer, but the customer. What's more, in an era when product visibility is priority in terms of impacting customer purchase behavior ("I see, therefore I buy"), decision-making is definitively interpreted as a bottom-up process, no longer a top-down one that's immune to the environmental stimuli of the display space.

Today, the decisions customers make in stores are often anything but rational.

First of all, although some segments of the purchase process take place at a subconscious level, the entire process has a similarly substantial impact on behavior. Added to this, we need to consider the enormous potential of all multisensory communication, visual messages above all since this aspect represents the most essential component of the external stimuli that shape the cognitive process at its most holistic and spontaneous.

So what seems clear is that to come to a better understanding of the effectiveness of various kinds of displays, the most essential aspect to bear in mind is the effect of environmental stimuli on emotions, and the resulting perceptions created by the context. Following this line of reasoning, we have to focus more on unconscious perceptive processes, as compared to rational ones. It's true that a more rational approach does emerge when consumers consider a new product, or an expensive item, or simply something interesting. But most of the decisions people make in the store come from force of habit, and fall into an automatic perceptive system that requires little effort.

Intercepting customers is essential to starting a conversation, in an attempt to encourage them to take into account the products in question. While evaluating various alternatives, the aim is to prompt customers to factor these options into their decision-making process. Put another way, the fact that people find a given item in the product assortment is no longer a guarantee that they will actually buy it. Instead, investments need to be made synergistically on all the visual merchandising levers to activate and enhance the offering, and the entire store as well.

So why do the studies on these topics still seem underrated? And more importantly, why do I still come across stores where the entire sales area is managed following a purely functional rationale, with the single aim of selling products? Stores where people only become customers if they buy something; if not they're simply visitors, and not very welcome ones at that. They're seen, perceived and experienced like a waste of time, pure and simple. How much longer will a store visit be considered entirely functional, with a largely utilitarian value? When, instead, will we see the store experience take on hedonistic value, morphing into an activity that generates emotional gratification, one that's only marginally associated with the benefits that derive from a possible (albeit not indispensable) purchase?

When these two situations arise there should be a continuum connecting them, not rendering them antithetical. This book begins here, developing the thematic foundations of my first book: Atmosfera e visual merchandising: ambienti, relazioni, esperienze [Atmosphere and Visual Merchandising: environments, relationships, and experiences] (Zaghi, 2008).

The educational, emotional and experiential dimensions of purchasing have become vital components in developing purchase behavior models, as customers more than ever before are looking for moments of engagement. Likewise, visual merchandising has evolved with respect to the traditional orientation of store management based solely on commercial concerns, which simplistically saw this discipline as a logistical tool serving exclusively to maximize the productivity of display spaces. Today more than ever before, visual merchandising is the very essence of store communication, spanning from the definition of a distribution concept to the launch of a new product.

This book represents a more enlightened response, in light of the potentialities inherent in this rich discipline. Far from solely providing an aesthetic framework, visual merchandising is the basic premise of the relationship between the customer and the offering. The store experience may not necessarily become a purchase, but is most certainly based on the relationship between the perceived space and the actual space.

In this context, when considering the communicative role of the store, we need to distinguish between the self-conceived identity created through the design of its commercial structure, and the communicative image that the customer perceives in concrete terms. Store identity is, in fact, innate in the format and the concept of distribution, and derives not only from design choices but also from the expectations of potential customers with respect to the offering of the competition. This identity is not static, nor is it the unilateral outcome of the original vision of the company. On the contrary, identity can be powerfully impacted by the evolution of the surrounding competitive context.

Instead, the image of the store derives from a bi-directional communication process, one that is strongly shaped by systems of value, contingencies and expectations of potential customers. In fact, as we'll discuss more fully in this book, the set of strategic and operational decisions (in terms of localization, external and internal design, layout and displays, and so forth) are analyzed and assimilated by customers following their own rational and experiential frames of reference. This is how they come up with a personal representation of the offering, which they interpret according to their own perceptions.

In other words, the identity of a store is unchanged, at least temporarily, because it is anchored to the design choices made by the company. By the same token, the image is constantly changing, as it derives from both the circumstances in which the communication flow takes place and the subjectivity of the interaction between the customer and the store.

So while it may be true that the store is assuming increasingly relevant status in the complex communication transmitted to the final market, this role can be only partially achieved by means of explicit and verbal linguistic codes (sales personnel, signage, and so on). These codes must be more broadly reinforced by non-verbal communication through choices affecting atmosphere, in terms of design and the multi sensory environment.

This is how the store itself becomes a product made up of messages, symbols and the values of the company, from one standpoint. And from another, the store rises in a figurative sense to the role of "communicated" "text," where, instead of objects, ideas are being sold, so an individual product is presented as the solution to a need.

What's more, there's a fuller awareness of the function of space as a means of communication and an instrument for activating relationships; this is progressively promoting the centrality of information. In this phase, high technology takes on a priority role, not only as a functional element, but also as a sensorial and perceptive one. The culmination comes in the design of hypermedia stores, where technology is not only an information tool and a purchase guide, but also a fundamental building block in constructing customer experience.

In addition to this, today more than ever before, designing and managing a store by taking a communication approach necessitates close collaboration among all the different stakeholders in the distribution channel.

In other words, in recent years visual merchandising has also become a question of channel relationships, even if industry and distribution still have little inclination to share their intentions in any meaningful way.

Looking to the future, optimizing investments in visual merchandising must go hand in hand with redefining the entire organizational process in terms of positions, roles and responsibilities. All the functions throughout the entire channel need to be clearly allocated, in a climate of more open collaboration not only with regard to sales, but also communication and enhancement of the product assortment.

Everyone will have to share a single objective: to create relational environments that are conceived, designed and managed so that they become, above all else, sources of pleasure and arousal. This ensures that the store and the purchase experience are not only replete with stimuli, but also offer an opportunity to consolidate relationships with products, brands, and the store itself.

Given these premises, this book begins by contemplating the atmosphere of a store as a preferential dimension of experience. Drawing a distinction between the proposed and the perceived atmosphere, the first chapter interprets the store environment as the result of a cognitive process where the object and the subject exist contemporaneously. This is implicit in the production of a space distinctly marked by mass media and mediatization.

Beginning with the determinants of atmosphere, we'll explore the spheres of action for customer/atmosphere interaction, to conclude that the items to purchase are found in a space imprinted with certain sensorial qualities which each individual only partially perceives in an entirely subjective way. These aspects act on his or her cognitive, affective and behavioral systems. In this sense, designing an experience represents a design philosophy that doesn't correspond to any specific profession. In fact, the idea is to upend the traditional perspective of the designer, which is far too influenced by an ideal, be it aesthetic, functional, or purely commercial. Instead, store design needs to reach the point where the conception of space centers on an experience in which customers themselves produce this space by inhabiting it.

Continuing on, the second chapter deals with the highly topical question of new communication artifacts, describing the most recent dimensions of communication in hi-tech interactive environments. We'll discuss how the store overcomes the boundaries of physical space and expands that space on a perceptive level, and we'll seek to understand whether all this drives store design toward systems of augmented reality (AR) and how it does so.

Studies demonstrate that technology shores up communication value by improving brand recall and enhancing brand recognition and awareness. In addition, although technology does boost demand, it isn't a substitute for traditional media. This seems to indicate that the biggest challenge in the future will be to maximize the combination of new channels with more traditional tools, while avoiding an exponential increase in the sophistication of materials with no thought to the concrete returns that will result.

Chapter 3 introduces the store concept, which represents the values and identity of the store. This concept takes shape through the complex combination of elements, depending on the approach of the designer and the different corporate philosophies. Since this topic is an extremely personal one, tying into the specific aims of each individual company, we won't be exploring the concept in depth. Instead, first we'll look at the process of store design. In the rapidly changing world of distribution, this process must respect the rules of speed and efficiency that apply, which often diverge substantially from other design sectors. This is followed by a definition of merchandising which highlights its limits and explains the need to expand the field of action of visual merchandising, i.e. marketing of the store, in the store, where industry and distribution can find mutually advantageous synergies.

In the subsequent chapters, the conception of the store is framed as a sequence of areas, each differing in terms of function and capacity to interact with customers in various stages of the purchase process. Chapters 4 through 7 address the relationship between the store environment and the cognitive, affective and behavioral systems of customers from the perspective of value creation. From the store façade to the external windows, from the layout to the focal point, from the display to the space allocation, from Point of Purchase (POP) communication to the design of all the relative material. Underpinning it all is the conviction that all the different levers of visual communication, both inside and outside the store, must be managed collectively. The basis for doing so is the fundamental realization that visual merchandising activity shouldn't be planned with short-term objectives in mind. Instead, this activity proves to be a priority component in implementing positioning strategies to qualify the image of the commercial offering.

Chapter 8 is dedicated to channel relationships, and more specifically the role that industry can play in the process of planning and managing visual merchandising activity. The main focus here is the two spheres that represent the foundations of visual merchandising of brands. The first (core technical-formal aspects) pertains to organizing space and finds its development context in an orientation toward productivity; the second (core values) offers a way to enrich objects on an emotional level. This is achieved through a constant and continual interchange between the information function and the suggestion function of messages that are founded synergistically on product communication and brand value orientations. Based on the key findings of a study I conducted (Zaghi, 2013), we'll explore three distinct strategic orientations: productivity of the space, communication of the product and value of the brand.

As far as approaches to interaction between industry and distribution, the analysis will turn to pertinent organizational models and interface roles. The final conclusion here is that exploiting potential areas of collaboration must be contingent on shifting attention from the product to the category and the area in the store. A continuum needs to materialize that can be ensured only by redefining roles, responsibilities and procedures relating to the entire process of planning and managing visual merchandising, using an integrated communication approach at a channel level.

While acknowledging the importance of adopting an experiential approach, the final chapter centers on the main attitudes that customers adopt while actually making a purchase, as well as the cognitive processes that they experience. To be specific, Chapter 9 delves into the use of space in stores, and the relative degree of occupation, differentiated between experienced space, perceived space and imagined space. In doing so, the main findings from observational analysis are presented from a study conducted in the Aspesi monobrand store in Milan. The priority here is to grasp the actual customer-product-space relationship, determining the effectiveness of visual merchandising activity in order to implement actions that aim to modify this relationship, either partially or entirely, wherever there are gaps with respect to corporate aims.

Last, a glossary will help readers understand the topics covered here, introducing and explaining the terms, acronyms and neologisms that are in common usage in visual merchandising.

That's all for now, and I hope you enjoy the book.

# 1 Store atmosphere as a preferential dimension of the store experience

## 1 The store as an emblematic experience

Through the years, the roles and functions of the store have gradually been expanding. Today, in fact, we've reached the point that the store is universally seen as the means that industry and distribution use to plan and manage the process of communication with consumers, and the place where this happens. Consumers, in turn, make their final choices by mediating a number of factors, both internal and external to the store, in a more or less conscious way: the physical impulses of the product (functional features, size, packaging, brand) where it's located (the store, the layout, the display) and how much it costs. All these aspects interact to influence the purchase decision process.

While recognizing the importance of external factors, the store can no longer be exclusively interpreted as a commercial sales tool. Indeed, it's through communication – the exchange of verbal and non-verbal messages – that customers adopt and modify their behaviors. Put another way, industry and distribution together establish a communication process with customers, with the store serving as the setting and the vehicle for this interaction. The primary aim is to communicate the value of the product assortment (Zaghi, 2013).

In fact, the store has great theoretical value, which parallels its concrete contribution to the consumption context: environment is the outcome of a cognitive process, not the product of an existing reality. People are the space that they perceive; better still, they produce that space by inhabiting it. This relationship, referred to as *enaction*, connotes a simultaneous exchange of subject and object, which only exists in perfect synchronicity.

In the circularity of perception and action, worlds are continually being produced by the knowing subject: a story of reciprocal coupling is being constructed between the world (or the reality that is being known) and the knowing subject. As we will explore further in this book, there is a seamless contemporaneity between subject and object, implicit in the "production" of space, space which is indelibly marked by mass media and mediatization.

Kotler (1973) was the first marketing management researcher to grasp the significance of the place where goods are purchased and consumed, in particular the atmosphere of this place. He pointed out that sales environments could be designed to influence purchase decisions, in some cases even more effectively than the product itself.

However, as we'll discuss in detail below, it was environmental psychology which set out to analyze the variables that create store atmosphere. More specifically, this discipline explores the capacity of all these different elements to influence emotional states, and consequently purchase behavior, and how this comes about.

Naturally, at a managerial level, store atmosphere is also recognized as a key ingredient for creating a purchase experience, and as such a differentiating factor. The growing number of firms coming from highly evolved distribution contexts, the rise of ecommerce, and an increasingly attentive and discriminating clientele: all these trends force stores to look for new sources of differentiation for their offerings and to find innovative alternatives for generating value and consolidating customer relations.

The literature on economics and marketing further underscores the critical nature of store atmosphere, while adopting an experiential viewpoint that accentuates multisensory perception. This approach highlights the fact that when individuals are faced with offerings of goods and services which they may often perceive as undifferentiated, the only route to securing competitive advantage is to give them a memorable purchase and/or consumption experience. To do so, all the senses must be activated (sight, smell, sound, taste and touch) to create the perception of positive emotions, which in turn lead to the behaviors that are advantageous to the company.

Summing up, then, space communicates, conveys and sells the image of the company. This image depends not only on the mix of services the store offers, but also on the atmosphere it provides. This is what shapes the perceptions that customers experience when they see the store from the outside and spend time inside. This atmosphere is what distinguishes the store's very personality.

People who go inside and explore this retail space have to be able to relate on a personal level to its style – a combination of the atmosphere and the communication of the values that customers aspire to. The store needs to express the possibility of living the experience of the brand/store identity, sparking emotions by being unique. If the environment represents an amalgamation of the values of the brand/store (equity), it will stimulate customers in a positive way, offering them a product that is the sum of all its tangible and intangible parts. Likewise, by adapting to decision-making criteria, the store environment can facilitate customer choices, rendering them more stimulating and pleasant from an experiential standpoint as well.

## 2    Store atmosphere

Given that atmosphere can help establish the image and competitive positioning of a store, we need to understand how this process works. The basic premise is very simple to define, but complex to manage. As we discussed before, customers perceive the atmosphere through their senses, not by evaluating the offering in rational or economic terms. In fact, store atmosphere is connoted with aspects spanning from aesthetics to emotions. Consequently, it's no simple thing to come up with an objective definition of atmosphere, based on unambiguous dimensions and clearcut characteristics. Atmosphere instead depends on subjective perceptions. It's the silent language of communication: an ever-present quality of the surrounding environment that can be described in sensorial terms. Specifically, these four senses are primarily involved:

- *sight*: color, lighting, size, shape;
- *hearing*: volume, tone;
- *smell*: scent, freshness; and
- *touch*: softness, smoothness, temperature.

Although taste is not directly associated with atmosphere, certain stimuli can elicit memories of particular flavors. From an operational standpoint, store atmosphere is the result of the combined effect of a series of tangible and intangible factors. These, along with assortment, price, and service policies, contribute to creating image. The components of store atmosphere can be grouped together in four areas (Zaghi, 2006, 2008):

1. *Exterior design* is everything that communicates with people before they enter the store. This encompasses the structural elements of the store that visual merchandising exploits: the façade, the store sign, the entrance, the store windows; the height, size and unique features of the building; and the parking area. Added to these are adjacent stores, along with the look of the surrounding area; taken together, all this characterizes the store setting.

2. *Interior design*, or the elements that characterize the internal environment in terms of flooring, lighting and air conditioning systems, perimeter walls, dressing rooms, elevators, stairs, furnishings, multimedia kiosks, children's play areas and uniforms for sales staff. Again, in the vein of multisensory communication, scents, music and colors also come into play here.

3. *Layout*, that is, visual merchandising decisions for organizing space in the store, which determine the size and position of the areas allocated for sales, displays, customer service and personnel. In mapping the internal traffic flow, the store layout also sets out the width of the aisles, the display fixtures and criteria for grouping merchandise, and the display sequence and management for each department.

4. *Interior displays* tie into visual merchandising activity relating to techniques and methods for displaying items, allocating display space to products, and in-store posters and signage.

5. *Point of Purchase (POP) communication*, which refers to support material for displays and sales provided by producers with the aim of guaranteeing a recognizable, preferential, exclusive space for their products and/or brands, to draw attention to them in the store (Zaghi, 2013).

So as we can see, atmosphere is a multi dimensional concept that comes from merging several factors, accentuating one or another depending on the distribution format in question.


## 3    Thematic universes

We've often reiterated the need to create a store identity that is clear and distinctive to customers thanks to a unique, unmistakable image. This is an invaluable source of sustainable competitive advantage grounded in differentiation. Developing a theme may pave the way to achieving this goal. In fact, a similar strategy is a way to act on customers' affective system, distinguishing the store by staging an original, evocative story that conveys an identity, a style, a life philosophy. "Theming" is an actual communication strategy reflecting the thematic development of the brand identity, and ultimately integrating with the interior retail space with an eye to creating a captivating environment that can immerse customers in the story that the store wants to tell.

Communication systems that revolve around themes are certainly one of the most investigated topics in the field of design. A theme might be based on a variety of languages variously associated with aspects such as: tradition, culture, entertainment, geography, history, technology, and many more. In concrete terms, the most common themes we find today are: status, tropical paradise, the Wild West, classical civilization, vintage, Arabian fantasy, urban, fortress/surveillance architecture, modernism, progress.

Whatever the theme, the key is to figure out what will actually fascinate and captivate consumers. Added to the pleasure of making a purchase and "playing store," which essentially is what shopping can be, the idea is to set the stage for product images with an eye to winning over customers. As players in a new multisensory culture, customers don't necessarily go into a store to buy. Instead they may also (or only) want to catch the latest trends, or take part in a collective performance, the dramatization of a lifestyle that they may or may not feel to be their own. More or less unconsciously, customers get a taste of the performance, the rite, the pantomime that is played out just for them, to seduce them and prompt them to buy.

So this approach to store design actually resembles set design, where the aim is to reconstruct an environment that encourages customers to become actors playing parts in a scene. On a design level, this means translating every single communication tool into a chosen theme, to make the expressive choices come together and the representational processes for each artifact converge, aligning with a repertoire of signs that blend in with or belong to the thematic universe of the store. Customers find themselves in a dramatized space where a world is constructed by working and acting on a representation, never a believable reality.

In order for all of this to occur, four guiding principles apply:

• An engaging theme has to alter visitors' sense of reality, removing them from their daily routines and establishing a new sense of place (Fig. 1).

*Figure* 1 – A country setting in a French pâtisserie.

- An all-encompassing backdrop must be created, combining space, time, and matter to form a compact, realistic whole (Fig. 2).
- The theme must be reinforced by offering a variety of "sets" in the same place (Fig. 3).
- The theme must be consistent, harmonizing with the identity of the company that stages the experience, as far as possible (Fig. 4).

Though by now theming is a common strategy in modern sales outlets, the concept store offers the most emblematic example of this trend. Beyond selling products, the main goal of this distribution format is selling a gratifying experience, one that's consistent with the corporate philosophy being dramatized.

Here the customer is a spectator first, and a buyer second. Being welcomed into the store and actually making a purchase become two complementary and conjoint moments in the same phase of customer service.

In every sector we find numerous companies that have opted for the concept store format. Some examples are pictured below: Agent Provocateur (Fig. 5), American Girl (Fig. 6), Disney (Fig. 7), M&M (Fig. 8), Nike (Fig. 9), Rainforest Café (Fig. 10), and Replay (Fig. 11).

*Figure* 2 – Stepping into the past in an English pastry shop.

*Figure* 3 – The bedroom in an apartment morphs into a store for 55 DSL.

*Figure* 4 – High Tech Milano has the look of a charming souk, where customers can wander around and be inspired by new ideas and motivations to make a purchase.

*Figure* 5 – The dressing room resembles an alcove in Agent Provocateur store in London.

*Figure* 6 – American Girl Place in New York welcomes children into the world of the famous dolls, without missing the opportunity to teach them a lesson in positive values.

*Figure* 7 – A detail of the magical atmosphere of a Disney Store, where enchanted castles and fantastical worlds, out of space and time, delight old and young customers alike.

*Figure* 8 – Millions of candies and giant M&Ms characters tower above customers at M&M's World in New York.

*Figure* 9 – Gigantic mannequins look like real-life basketball players striking incredibly dynamic poses that reinforce the positioning of the brand and craft a theatrical atmosphere at Nike Town in New York.

*Figure* 10 – The Rainforest Café in Chicago faithfully reproduces the theme of the chain: from indoor waterfalls that create torrential rainstorms, to aquariums, to tropical plants that create a frame for the exotic environment.

*Figure* 11 – At Replay in Milan customers can breathe in the country atmosphere thanks to natural materials glowing with special-effect lighting: from the wooden shelves and flooring to the resin tables, to porphyry and more wooden flooring, to vertical gardens – all this creates a highly theatrical scene.

In Italy, the undisputed pioneer of this philosophy is Elio Fiorucci with the concept store he invented in the mid-1960s, inspired by Carnaby Street in London, a temple of the youth culture of the times. The first Fiorucci department store, designed by the sculptor Amalia Del Ponte, opened in May 1967 in Milan's Galleria Passarella. The famous Italian singer Adriano Celentano performed at the grand opening of the store, which presented a style that was perfectly in tune with the spirit of the times: iconoclastic, free and carefree, full of color, sensual, seductive, unique.
Here's a description from the newspapers of the day: "The entire space is opaque white and shiny cornflower blue. It's the biggest, craziest, most extravagant store ever." The multisensory environment owes its success in part to a captivating dramatization based on the cultural values of love, imagination and irony. The Fiorucci store headlined as a newsworthy, cultural event that created media buzz simply due to its very existence.

## 4    Interaction between the atmosphere and the customer

Initial attempts to model the influence of atmosphere on customer reactions date back to Mehrabian and Russell's work (1974). Within the context of environmental psychology, these authors proposed a causal model to explain the relationship between environmental factors and individual behavior. Basing their study on the cognitivist paradigm, Stimulus-Organism-Response, Mehrabian and Russell proved that physical or social stimuli in a given environment, together with individual personality, directly impact people's emotional states and consequently their behavior. Specifically, four groups of variables constitute this model: environmental stimuli, personality variables, emotional states and response behaviors.

1. *Environmental stimuli.* The effect of the environment on individuals' emotional spheres is assessed by means of the information rate, i.e. the amount and intensity of information that people are capable of absorbing when they come in contact with various characteristics of the environment.
2. *Personality variables.* Individuals can express different orientations with respect to hedonism, which means they can be receptive in different ways to environmental stimuli. Specifically, the authors differentiate between *screeners* and *non-screeners*, pointing out that the latter are more inclined to use all their senses in combination.

3. *Emotional states.* We can use three categories in analyzing emotional reactions elicited by environment-generated stimuli which subsequently mediate behavior.
   - *Pleasure (P),* connoted with feelings of well-being, joy, happiness, or satisfaction;
   - *Arousal (A),* the level of stimulation and activation; and
   - *Dominance (D),* knowledge of and control over the environment; the freedom to act.
4. *Response variables.* All the behavioral responses of an individual can be classified as *approach* or *avoidance,* and are found in four possible situations:
   - a physical desire to stay or leave a given environment, associated with the intention to visit that place;
   - a desire to simply look around, in other words, not to interact; this relates to seeking out and coming in contact with environmental stimuli;
   - the desire to communicate with others, or to avoid interaction and ignore the chance to dialog with other customers or personnel; and
   - the increase or decrease in satisfaction with respect to expectations, relating to the frequency of store visits and the time and money spent there.

In 1980, a variation of Mehrabian and Russell's model was proposed by Pratt and Russell, who eliminated the dominance factor. In fact, their research demonstrated that pleasure and arousal were totally independent in all circumstances. On the contrary, dominance seemed to require cognitive interpretation by the subject in question, and as a result was dependent on the other two factors. The new bi-dimensional model specifically identified two related dimensions as the outcome of every interaction of pleasure and arousal, and generated eight descriptors for emotional reactions to environment: pleasant, arousing, exciting, distressing, unpleasant, gloomy, sleepy and relaxing.

The PAD Model (Pleasure, Arousal and Dominance), introduced by Mehrabian and Russell, was applied for the first time in a commercial context by Donovan and Rossiter (1982) to demonstrate the relationship between the physical environment, and emotional states and behaviors of customers in the store. These two researchers also showed that dominance did not seem directly related to any behavioral response. Their results suggested the need to re-conceptualize store atmosphere in light of its power of persuasion.

At a store level, the PAD model validates a series of observations made by Lillis, Markin and Narayana (1976) a few years prior, based on their exploratory study on the social and psychological significance of space. Here are their key considerations.

*Space is a key modeler and modifier of behavior.* The relationship between environment and behavior is increasingly clear: while people shape space, space in turn shapes people's behavior.

*As a delimited environment, the store impacts customer behavior through the psychology of stimulation.* The environment is capable of creating expectations and influencing behavior through stimulation. (For example, people lower their voices and stop smiling when they walk into a bank.) It follows, then, that store designers can evoke desired expectations by exploiting the psychology of stimulation. Generally speaking, a commercial setting is full of stimuli: innovations, the element of surprise, the quantity of information. Customers who are exposed to input from various design factors will experience a variety of emotional states which revolve around three major axes: pleasure/displeasure, excitement/boredom, influence/passivity. Behaviors spring from a combination of these emotional states based on attraction or repulsion. Attraction translates into a desire to inhabit the space, to spend time there, to explore, to interact with other people or objects in the space (via visual and/or physical contact). Attraction is also expressed by a desire to return to the same space again and again. Repulsion, instead, manifests in a feeling of discomfort and malaise that gives rise to anxiety, boredom, a disinclination to socialize, and lastly a desire to leave and never come back.

*The store impacts customer perceptions and attitudes.* Store design, the essence of atmosphere, is a source of information for customers. Store features can be designed to encourage intense sensorial involvement (lighting, department divisions, layout, displays, colors and so forth). Perception, instead, is a highly psychological activity relating to the process of converting sensorial input into meaningful data. Customers learn while they perceive, and what they learn influences what they perceive. A well-known fact is that reactions to physical space impact reactions to the shopping experience in a given retail environment. Behavior not only depends on perceptions, but on attitudes as well. Attitudes are commonly understood as states of readiness to act which, when triggered by appropriate stimuli, translate into action. Summing up, then, the environment, design, and structure of the sales outlet can not only supply the proper stimuli for turning intentions into behaviors, but can actually modify customers' attitudes and impact their final choices.

*The use of space and the design of the store can be planned to trigger desired customer reactions.* Like a Skinner Box, the sales outlet can be planned to reinforce customer behavior. The essence of store design can be summed up in: observing and analyzing the boundary between behavioral states, from an environmental and behavioral standpoint; defining alternative behavioral states; and controlling environment contingencies which engender and maintain the desired alternative state.

After the pioneering studies of the 1960s and 1970s, marketing literature on the topic of customer/environment interaction has been and continues to be particularly prolific. Following the stream of environmental psychology, a great deal of research has fully corroborated that every element of store design influences individual perceptions and behavior, either directly or indirectly, in terms of: final purchases, store image, perceived quality of service, time spent in the store, attitude toward the store, aesthetic and hedonistic pleasure, self-affirmation of individual identity, and consumption of personal transpositions, such as utopias.

From a methodological standpoint, some researchers considered the impact of single variables of atmosphere through laboratory studies; others, instead, dealt with atmosphere as a holistic concept. Despite their differing approaches, all academic investigation concurs in asserting that atmosphere, although unrelated to the product, is a critically important factor. In fact, atmosphere deeply impacts perceptive processes, and likewise the nature and intensity of the feelings consumers experience. These impressions are subsequently linked to an image of the store, and can reinforce or challenge the consumer choice.

So we can conclude that psychology also takes into account the affective and emotive component to explain customer behavior. The intensity of emotional reactions to a store is actually directly related to elements that are intrinsic to the perceived "form." To clarify, a store can release a lived experience; the image of a store is the product of a reaction between the customer experience and the components of the physical environment. In other words, the "form/design" exerts influence on consumer behavior, which also depends on the methods for perceiving and storing information: form is knowledge, emotion, and relation.

## 4.1   *Spheres of action*

There is a vital difference between proposed atmosphere and perceived atmosphere: the first is the set of sensorial qualities that the store designer tries to incorporate in a given space; the second, being the fruit of subjective perception, can vary greatly from customer to customer. In other words, merchandise is located in a space that has certain sensorial elements which are perceived only in part by each individual and in an entirely subjective fashion. These elements act on customers' cognitive and affective systems, influencing the information they note and their emotional state, and as a result, the probability that they will make a purchase.

Atmosphere can impact purchase behavior in three ways:

1. as a means for creating attention;
2. as a means for creating a message; and
3. as a means for creating perceptions.

In the first two cases, atmosphere actively intervenes on the decision to choose a given store by transmitting distinctive stimuli which might convey, for instance, the level of attention that customers will receive. This not only highlights the differences between distributors, but also supplies the basis for identifying the stores where they can make purchases.

In the third case, instead, atmosphere directly impacts the decision-making process in choosing a specific product, encouraging impulse purchases in particular. As regards this last aspect, the literature on psychology affirms that a pleasurable, comfortable sales environment elicits feelings of happiness and satisfaction that can enhance buying behavior, especially impulse purchases.

Specifically, research offers a series of empirical findings showing that a pleasant environment:

• engenders a positive state of mind which makes individuals feel inclined to reward themselves more generously, and act with greater energy, spontaneity and freedom;
• makes shopping more fun and fulfilling;

- prompts customers to stay in the store longer, spending more time browsing; and
- increases interaction between shoppers and sales staff.

Naturally, there is no such thing as an ideal atmosphere, because every market is made up of unique individuals. In light of this, we should keep in mind that in purchase decisions, the "situation" is important, that is, all environmental factors that determine the context in which a certain item is purchased in a given space and time. Five of these factors are key:

1. *Physical setting*, that is, the physical and spatial features of the environment;
2. *Social setting*, referring to anyone who interacts with customers while they're making their purchases, including sales staff and other people in the store at the time;
3. *Temporal perspective*, in other words, the amount of time customers have to make a purchase;
4. *Defining the task*, that is, the motivations behind the purchase; and
5. *Antecedent states*, or the temporary physiological states and moods of customers.

In light of our discussion above, what's clear is that atmosphere proves to be most important in highly competitive arenas, where other retailing tools have gradually been neutralized, and a strong homogeneity in distribution has emerged in terms of assortment and price. In such cases, atmosphere can play a key role in generating a differential advantage, becoming a useful tool for attaining a distinctive market positioning. Likewise, atmosphere is also vitally important when products are marketed by targeting specific social classes or customer categories with particular lifestyles. In these circumstances, atmosphere must be consistent with the market segment in question.

Therefore, to have a successful offering, planning the general atmosphere of the store is essential. In fact, firms must coordinate all the different ingredients of atmosphere, especially because they have very little time to capture customers' attention. Experts calculate, for example, that a store window has a mere eleven seconds on average to transmit its message, while inside the store, around twenty seconds is enough to shape customers' overall impressions.

Consequently, a sequential planning process must be followed that is extremely consistent across every phase.

More specifically:

- defining the store's target segment;
- understanding the profile of these customers (discovering whether or not they're interested in a purchase experience);
- pinpointing the variables of atmosphere that reinforce the emotional reactions that customers are looking for; and
- determining whether the resulting store atmosphere can compete effectively in the market.

In summary, what appears clearer than ever is the impossibility of competing by utilizing traditional marketing levers alone, such as product benefits. For example, today such benefits are beginning to all look alike due to the intense competition on consumer markets. So the key to differentiating products is to offer the emotion of an experience, integrating products into a new amalgamation that takes into account the complexities of the personality of each individual consumer. Experiences provide sensorial, emotional, cognitive, behavioral and relational values, which are exactly what brands can leverage to satisfy a need that has been emerging for some time: to build a true relationship with the consumer.

## 5    A unique experience

At this point we can draw a clear and incontrovertible conclusion: planning displays means, first and foremost, taking on the perspective of the customer. The aim in doing so is to observe, or better still, to live the entire customer experience firsthand, assessing all the opportunities for establishing a relationship between environment and behavior. If we begin with the assumption that environmental stimuli can create expectations and shape behavior, designing spaces and displaying products are activities that can be deliberately and consciously planned to trigger desired reactions in customers.

So the store must become a medium that has the capacity to excite emotions and engage customers in a gratifying experience. From a simple information collection point and a place to buy goods and services, the store has to turn into a place where people want to pass the time, where they find entertainment. The concept of a store is no longer simply the outcome of architectural choices; instead it represents a system in which design means realizing the distinctive elements of a brand/store based on emerging or consolidated aesthetic and communicative trends.

In other words, the store can and must stand out, reinforcing its identity by activating and nurturing an effective and immediate communication process, one that connects with customers in the final stage of their purchase decision process. This means guaranteeing a spectacular context that offers a unique experience in the very same moment in which customers are actually making their purchase. An engaging environment that sparks their interest, while spotlighting product functionality as a priority value: the setting in which all this unfolds represents an increasingly critical success factor. What's more, the store needs to be interpreted in recreational terms, so that customers derive satisfaction from the store visit itself; the possibility of a purchase is secondary. The store becomes place to live the experience of the brand/store identity, where people find pleasure spending time during their visit.

The economic crisis of recent years has redefined purchase models, making hedonistic needs even more pressing. The gradual increase in the weight of ecommerce can't help but reinforce this trend. The growing desire to satisfy needs that are educational, not only functional, makes the hedonistic approach to the store even more relevant today. When people go shopping they're looking for an experience that goes beyond the purchases they may make. More and more often, in fact, it is experience that represents a basic driver for the desire to visit a store. Customers aren't simply searching for a product; instead they're seeking a gratifying experience; the store visit itself becomes the ultimate goal of shopping.

Today more than ever, especially in light of the growing popularity of online commerce, the store must put on a show, beginning with the atmosphere it creates in the retail space. This space must be designed not only to sell, but also to communicate and enhance the offering, perhaps by organizing events to draw in customers, bringing them in contact with the offering and tempting them to try out the products. While it's true that customers more and more often buy a product for its unique, inherent connotations, the store must still enable them to evaluate the entire impalpable universe encapsulated in the values of that item. New concepts must be conceived and designed so that customers feel called on to live and share a multisensory experience, one that immerses them in a symbolic universe where they play an active part. They can also use sensory stimuli to intervene in an emotional sphere as well as a physical one.

In other words, once and for all the store must become a relational platform which tells a story that customers can live and enjoy, starting from the moment they make a purchase. The values of the commercial offering are described in a consistent context, where all the visual merchandising and multisensory communication levers are designed and managed to create and enhance desire, also through techniques leveraging emotions and sensory perceptions (Zaghi, 2013).

If this doesn't happen, then the question is not so much what the future of the store will be, but if there will be a future at all, in light of the changes underway in purchase behavior that are driving the dissemination of the showrooming phenomenon.

## 6    Cost-benefit analysis in an experiential approach

As we've said before, the experience strategy paves the way for innovation and competitive differentiation which are more difficult for competitors to imitate, especially if they are linked to territorial and environmental specificities. Nonetheless, the costs associated with this strategy may be greater than what a distributor would normally spend. These costs can be broken down into five categories:

1. *cost of planning and monitoring*, relating to creating and designing an experience, and later tracking results;
2. *cost of purchasing materials* to set the stage for the experience and create a unique atmosphere that can clearly stand out from the competition;
3. *cost of personnel* as far as training employees, and external personnel when needed to stage special events;
4. *cost of space*, meaning the opportunity cost of using space like a stage, or hosting events that substitute product displays; and
5. *cost of communications* linked to the need to give visibility and notoriety to the experiential positioning.

Beyond the possibility that some cost items might be overlooked when calculating profits, other risks inherent to experience-building strategies derive from neglecting to clearly define the expected benefits.

First, creating an experience can translate into a search for the *novelty effect*. In this case, there is a chance that the experience itself remains only fleeting and temporary, if its "staying power" isn't shored up by incrementally renewing key elements of the activity. The reasoning here is that the novelty effect tends to wear off quickly, leaving in its wake a passive attitude that won't generate significant medium-term results.

However, there is also risk associated with applying joint strategies which attempt to build experiences by utilizing complex atmospheres and integrating multiple communication tools. The danger is that they may give rise to a superfluous or ambiguous positioning. This would turn an opportunity for differentiation into a series of conflicting and confusing perceptions, leaving customers with a feeling of discomfort and without a clear understanding of the dimensions of the positioning. In these cases, the store can lose the centrality of the products in the offering, completely transforming the focus of its core activity, often without making a deliberate choice to do so, but as a consequence of a process that is not properly controlled.

## 7    The expert in quality relationships

Experience design isn't a discipline. It's about defining a design philosophy, a method for approaching design from a relational, holistic, evolutionary and complex perspective. There is no professional role that does all this; in other words, there's no such thing as an experience designer.

Designing an experience means reversing the traditional viewpoint of a designer, which is often too dependent on an aesthetic, functional or merely commercial ideal. It means taking the perspective of the user instead, or better still, the client: the person who will use the store as a step – a very small step – in a long and complex process. We need to remove the store from the purely subjective vision of designers, who work by following their creative sensibility and respecting their art, personalizing objects and situations with their own added value, with the value of the company. In other words, formulating individual, quality solutions.

The designer must take on a new role, conceiving space designed around experience, where the customers are the ones who produce the space by inhabiting it. Subject and object exist only in perfect synchronicity. This new role catalyzes and coordinates various professional figures, interfacing with all the stakeholders involved in the process. This new professional must understand, above all, how to satisfy the growing need for well-being, how to minimize the environmental impact of human activities, how to regenerate and enhance the quality of space from a social standpoint. At the same time, this role calls for engagement in creating settings of meaning and places for symbolic sharing.

In other words, even before the project takes shape, the designer must know how to visualize and materialize the relational qualities implicit in the architectural space of the store, a place where relationships are highly concentrated, where sharing is strong and the communication dynamic is intense. This role calls for skills that are more proactive and organizational, rather than creative, as far as interpreting the quality of exchanges. This is in a world where space for symbolic mediations is continually expanding.

## 8    New trends in store design

This brings us to the conclusion that in the years to come, stores will be more and more closely connoted with shared traits which are already emerging in the evolutionary trends of store design. This is a response to customers who are constantly evolving themselves in the ways they consume and make purchases.

The principle distinguishing features of the store of the future will be:

- open sales spaces with layouts that give the feeling of transparency and lightness;
- wider aisles, corridors and spaces for moving around in the store;
- light colors, pastels, white, ice;
- different types of flooring to differentiate sales areas;
- light, modular, highly specialized solutions;
- variable, adaptable lighting with points and bands of illumination to spotlight products;
- informational communication intensified by the use of images, colors, symbols;
- rest areas where customers can relax;
- consistent store image even in accessory service areas;
- non-invasive multimedia kiosks for customer assistance;
- integration between internal and external image, sales and service; and
- emphasis on the total integration of store environment and store/brand identity.

In the past, the protagonists of consumption were physical in nature, organic and structural characteristics, use values – all having to do with products. Today, and very likely in the future as well, consumption subscribes more and more to the logic of a game, to expressivity, well-being and pleasure; following instincts and not needs; driven more by aesthetics than by ethics. The intangible service component replaces the tangible one, in a context where market competition centers squarely on services, which are non-material and far more multidimensional in terms of perception and assessment.

Immersed in the great flow of change, postmodern consumers are flexible, and love to wander along meandering pathways, because their most distinctive traits are eclecticism and synchronism. They leave more room for emotions and sensoriality; they use consumption as a way to communicate, to signal their identity. They express greater autonomy in the world of production, and they want something out of the ordinary, something never seen before. In the purchase process they resort to creativity and imagination too, but more than that what they're looking for is a game, seeking pleasure in their exploratory approach to shopping.

# 2    Interactive environments:
## new dimensions in communication

## 1    Hypermedia stores

This a time when distinctive models for store design coexist and intertwine. In this context, rethinking the design dimension means reconsidering the sign production, the processes involved, and the entire systemic framework. Along with this comes a reflection on the changes brought about by the digital revolution. This means considering new media and the connections that these changes are generating in the field of communication, as well as how much they are contaminating the very conception of a communication system.

This also means evaluating how these changes intersect with competencies that traditionally belong to the fields of visual merchandising and retail design. In fact, it is from these very intersections and remixes activated by technology that new design responses are taking shape (albeit extremely slowly). But beyond this, what we are also seeing are new communication formats and tools, as well as new ways to interact.

For years, the use of modern information and communication technologies (ICTs) was linked to the notion that a store's information system was like a simple automated mechanism for performing repetitive activities with little added value. So relative investments aimed to maximize efficiency by automating a number of operations and optimizing things like stock rotation, shelf replenishment, fluctuations and peaks in demand – and in doing all this improving human resource management, too.

Initially, among mass market distributors and in self-serve big box stores in general, self-checkouts were installed next to traditional cash desks allowing customers to scan, bag, and pay for their purchases by themselves. Later came mobile self-scanning units, handheld optical readers which customers can use to scan product codes while they shop. This enabled retailers to collect information on the routes people took through the store during their visit, as well as the sequence of the purchases they made. In the most recent iteration, mobile optical readers have morphed into Personal Shopping Assistants (PSAs), capable of guiding customers from shelf to shelf so they can find all the items on their shopping list (which they email to the store). A full color display also gives descriptions of sale items.

Since 2010, some distributors have capitalized on the popularity of smartphones and tablets, which allow customers to scan product codes or Quick Read (QR) codes using special apps that can normally be downloaded from the store itself, thanks to access to free in-store Wi-Fi. Some retailers even provide tablets for their clientele, so they can view virtual window displays or even utilize payment tools via Near Field Communication integrated chips (NFCs).[1]

However, the implementation of interactive technology often gives rise to retail environments that are stripped down to the essentials, particularly in grocery stores. Here, creative and aesthetic elements have disappeared, replaced with a cold and rational laboratory-like approach to store design, where functionality and technological performance take priority over all else (Biffi and Salviotti, 2017).

Finally, a full awareness is materializing of the role of distribution as a tool for communicating and activating relationships, along with the realization that the information garnered at a store level constitutes the core of competitive strategies. In addition to the primary aim of generating information that serves to maximize store efficiency, there is an ever-greater desire to transform the purchase experience into a time for interaction, for give and take. This experience is also an opportunity to convey specific targeted information to customers, and to progressively adapt the offering system to their needs.

With the view of the store as a communication tool gaining ground, high technology takes on a leading role as a sensory and perceptive element as well as a functional one. What we're beginning to understand is

---

[1] NFC is a connectivity technology that enables bi-directional communication between two devices that are placed close to one another. This generates a peer-to-peer network that enables both devices to send and receive information.

that the inevitable dissemination of more sophisticated applications does not necessarily need to conflict with the aesthetic quality of the environment, or the desire to perfect it on an emotional level. Instead these technologies can play a part raising the degree of environmental sensoriality, as the public more and more often demands.

In other words, technology makes it possible to expand communication, moving beyond the more traditional methods, superseding canonical thresholds. For example, in-store interactive technology, with its relational touchpoints, can offer engaging entertainment. In doing so, it represents not only an information tool to guide customers as they make their purchases, but also a basic building block in constructing their overall in-store experience.

Starting from the exterior of the store, the communication function can play out through images projected on to the building, making use of architectural elements as supports: from columns and walls to sidewalks – even incorporating the space reserved for passersby into the communication flow. This creates a distraction, interrupting them as they go by and drawing a line of continuity between the exterior world (the street) and the interior one (the store). All this underscores once again the store's presence in the urban space.

An emblematic illustration is the Excelsior, a department store in Milan, where the store sign has turned into a video sign, preserving the link with the store's past as a cinema while magnifying the force of attraction. In fact, the video sign captures the attention of passersby with a cinematic marquee, and turns the upper portion of the window into the "silver screen" showing moving images (Fig. 1).

Naturally, by overcoming physical space and expanding that space on a perceptive level, design horizons open up in multiple directions, even within the store itself (Fig. 2).

For example, systems can be installed that link a single location with a wider network; or webcams and monitors can offer a complete view of the store showing different angles of the sales floor at once, bypassing the physical dimension and letting the customer get "the big picture" at a glance. And let's not forget shelf spot systems that activate a dialogue between packaging and displays thanks to a microchip embedded on the front of the shelf. This microchip, which can transmit video clips and send messages about products, represents a means for developing new formats for brief communication, as we'll discuss further on in this chapter.

*Figure* 1 – Excelsior Milano: the façade becomes a video sign and an eye-catching window display in continuous movement.

*Figure* 2 – A play area with screens for showing movies, along with interactive monitors appropriate for all ages, in the "magic kingdom" of Disney Stores.

## 2 Moving toward digital communication

The early 1990s saw the design of retail scenarios based on the assumption that consumer choices would be "made farther and farther away from the store, based on the potential impact of electronic images."[2] In this context, store designers anticipated "a progressive disconnect by consumers who, in front of their home computers screens, would be isolated from the concrete experience of physical contact with both the merchandise and with other consumers."[3] Yet despite the propagation of ecommerce, the physical store is still a clear point of reference in the overall process of communication and distribution of the product/brand.

That said, the current system contemplates the potentialities of the virtual store, seeking forms of integration between online and offline services, experimenting with migrating certain store functions onto the web, and calibrating online and onsite connections. All this is where the physical store finds its own space on the web, in the same way that the web has a place in the store, by providing a direct point of access to the store's website. With the web, for the first time product communication is beginning to coincide with distribution and sales. In other words, communication is no longer simply affirmative, describing products and telling stories, or even persuasive, convincing people to buy; instead communication has become operative, supporting the purchase function.

So we are seeing a progressive, albeit very gradual, dissemination of in-store digital communication that is undoubtedly more interactive and engaging, guaranteed to capture customers' attention with new and imaginative techniques. The integration of supports introduced by digital technology, along with the pulverization and proliferation of moments and events that create a personal communication network, engender widespread, fluid communication.

Clearly, multimediality generates effective channels for direct, focused – and above all non-invasive – communication. However, this gives rise to an urgent need to confront the contextual mutations that emerge as a result (including faster communication processes). We are experiencing the dissemination of identity systems that continuously update their instruments, honing them, modifying them in an adaptive way, and matching them to

[2] Codeluppi V. (1992), *I consumatori*, Franco Angeli, Milan, Italy, p. 75.
[3] Ibid.

the changing system as a whole and to the evolving cultures of communication. These identity systems are shaped by continually updated forms and formats in an unending process of change that is constantly fueled by the inadequacy of current languages and channels of communication.

It's as if the affirmation of new technologies implies new communicative coordinates which, through the development of new devices, transform the perception of the physical space of a location. Through the presence of new communicative artifacts (installations, videos, projections, and so forth) windows open up on other scenarios. Connections are created between distant universes, blurring the boundaries between interiors and exteriors with forms of immersion, engagement, emotion and interaction that go beyond what the objects on display would suggest (Mandelli and Accoto, 2012).

These become symbolic elements of a renewed means of communication to entertain the consumer in real and virtual space in tandem, with the aim of intensifying the seductive power of the store. This is the way to redefine the communicative system and the new communicative functions that accompany consumers, guiding them toward the product and spurring them to connect, to join in the world of the brand, to make a choice, to make a purchase. All this transforms temporal relationships and the links with the contents of the communication, as well as interactions among various artifacts and the spatial system.

## 2.1    *Digital screens: a battle to the last centimeter*

As we've already discussed in detail, the progressive intensification of competition among brand companies is spurring them to constantly boost their investments in stores. The aim is to enhance the offering and attract the attention of the customer, raising the conversion rate in a context where 80% of all purchase decisions are still made in the store itself (Zaghi, 2013). In light of this, the progressive dissemination of digital communication is rapidly broadening the horizons for on-shelf communication through the use of customized screens that can be attached directly to display modules.

Specifically, monitors project images and sounds through motion sensors that turn an audio feed on and off as customers pass by, and when the store opens and closes. These screens are equipped with remote monitoring systems, and installed for four to twelve weeks at a time. In addition to providing detailed information on products and ongoing sales promotions, they also measure traffic flow along the store shelves via built-in sensors.

Figs. 3 and 4 show some examples of digital monitors custom built by Pointmedia A/S. This Norwegian company, founded in 2010, develops new on-shelf communication platforms within the context of point-of-sale marketing.

*Figure* 3 – Quick and easy recipes using the products on this shelf (courtesy of Pointmedia).

*Figure* 4 – Video ads go with Nike shoes (courtesy of Pointmedia).

In 2012, Pointmedia was the recipient of the Annual Retail Marketing Award. According to recent studies run in Scandinavia, transmitting video content can boost sales results on average by anywhere from 49.4% (for generic clips) to 92.8% (for personalized videos).


## 3    Augmented reality

In this dynamic context, digital communication can evolve into augmented reality (AR) systems, offering the advantage of running instantaneous marketing tests in the store by collecting data in real time, and proposing sales initiatives that are geographically segmented (Friskney, 2007).

AR consists of enriching human sensory perception through information that would not be otherwise detectable with the five senses. This input is manipulated and electronically channeled by software with rendering and tracking capabilities. AR can also diminish the quantity of information normally perceived through the senses, again in order to present a scenario that is more clear, more useful or more entertaining. This type of technology identifies points that are fixed in space where devices track real shapes and objects, superimposing the desired virtual objects (images, videos, objects, 3D lettering and so on), and following every movement in real time. So AR is actually a variation on virtual reality (VR).

With Virtual Reality the user is immersed in an artificial environment where natural perceptions of most or all of the five senses seem to be totally absent; instead they are replaced by other perceptions. In AR, on the other hand, people continue to experience the real world while discovering virtual elements that enhance or manipulate this reality, overlapping with the physical environment. The line of demarcation between VR and AR seems to be an academic distinction: mediated reality can be seen as a continuum with the concepts of VR and AR sitting side by side, not at opposite ends.

The reality we already perceive can be augmented with 3D animation, video clips, audio tracks and multimedia integrations. These features are delivered via the following devices: handheld video cameras, viewers (VR eyeglasses), audio (headphones) or manipulation (VR gloves), a PC or Mac with a webcam or other sensors for vision enhancement/protection (glasses with built-in retina shields). Mediation normally happens in real time. Information from the real world becomes interactive, and users can digitally manipulate this input. Examining VR in greater detail, we can identify two main types:

1. On handheld devices, smartphones must be equipped with a global positioning system (GPS) and a magnetometer (compass), an Internet connection to receive online data, and an app for viewing a realtime video stream. The device frames the surrounding environment and overlays various levels of content in real time, from geolocalized points of interest (PDIs) to 3D elements.
2. On computers, markers are used (ARtags) with stylized black and white designs; these are picked up by the webcam, recognized by the computer, and then superimposed with multimedia content in real time (video, audio, 3D objects and so on). Normally AR applications run on Adobe Flash technology.

Looking back on the history of AR, the expression was first cited in the literature as early as the 1940s. However, AR eyeglasses first appeared in the 1960s in studies run by Ivan Sutherland at Harvard University and the University of Utah (Sutherland, 1968). In the subsequent two decades, further experimentation was conducted by NASA (Ames Research Center), the US Air Force (Armstrong Laboratory) and the University of North Carolina.

The first operational results emerging from relevant analysis date to the 1990s, when scientists at Boeing applied the technology on assembly lines producing mechanical components for airplanes. The more recent drop in the cost of VR hardware provided additional impetus for research not only on innovating VR methods, but also on improving performance. This resulted in a massification of AR technology, which can now be found in a wide range of contexts and sectors.

In the so-called *Post Social Era*, we are seeing a transition from Digital Convergence to Convergence Augmentation. The first refers to a combination of digital components such as voice, text, image, streaming media, and personalized services; the second is a new vision of convergence in which the digital environment meets the real world in the following ways:

1. Augmented Consumers, who are more stimulated by technology, better informed and more highly skilled, autonomous and quick in decision-making;
2. Augmented Products, designed to be associated with digital information; and

3. Augmented Reality, which emits digital components in the real world to create more engaging spaces.

The outcome of all this will be to consolidate certain trends that are currently taking shape, pertaining to:

- *Gamification,* or the dynamic interactive integration of games on websites, in services, in communities and in content provided by companies, as well as advertising campaigns to get consumers more engaged and active;
- *Smart Signs,* which are digital displays that integrate facial recognition technologies or RFID, capable of profiling customers based on demographics or emotional parameters; and
- *Augmented Retailing,* consisting of AR in the store.


## 4    Augmented retailing

With augmented retailing, the contribution of technology creates a catalyst that can be leveraged to experiment with remixing traditional means of communication and digital artifacts. Technological innovation materializes mainly in the richness of the information that stores can provide to customers: no more boring data on technical specifications or prices, but videos and far more detailed inputs are at customers' fingertips, with the press of a button or a touchscreen. Specifically, communication based on video players serves two key roles: to provide information on production methods, product features and functions, or to illustrate the product in use, while giving the public access to a modern tool. Audiovisuals represent a language that acts like a magnet for customer attention, livening up the retail environment at the same time.

Numerous theories on the effectiveness of communication based on moving images underscore the positive relationship between attention and movement. These theories assert that a moving information source has more potential to capture the attention of the public and to induce people to evaluate the message it conveys, as compared to a static information source. Indeed, monitors effectively serve to spatialize and temporalize communication, introducing a storytelling dimension in brand representation. This technique bypasses the usual of spheres of advertising, making room for innovations that can also evolve in the direction of information, in a dimension that can and must be functional too.

In any case, research on the design of new communicative artifacts, embedded in a brand/store identity system, cannot neglect to consider the physical and psychological needs of customers. In particular, the former can be satisfied by ensuring that the media in question is clearly visible, turning up the volume and slotting the video into a broader framework. Computer stations can then be added that offer virtual navigation, allowing customers to go beyond the place where they are, to get information on other stores in the network, and then decide where they want to go to make their purchases. Psychological needs, instead, are fulfilled by supplying customers with useful information intended to increase their attention, such as data on prices, promotions or coupons.

Thanks to its remarkable flexibility, digital communication makes it possible not only to send a certain message at a specific time and place via multimedia audiovisual content, but also to modify that communication very rapidly. In other words, this technique guarantees communication solutions that are highly evolved and dynamic. These solutions add value to products and brands, contribute to accelerating sales and boosting customer recall, and prove to be high impact determinants of customer satisfaction. Moreover, the transformation of places where people make purchases is leading to modifications in service tools which previously played no part in the system of communication. Today instead such tools are components in a communication circuit that is becoming more and more unified.

Consider for example the experiments being done over the past few years with mirrors. The role of these tools is changing, with mirrors beginning to play a part in a process designed to initiate an interactive circuit linking brand and customer. Some stores are replacing mirrors with reflective panels and video cameras which record customers from all angles so they can see themselves on a big screen and decide whether the clothing they're trying on actually suits them. At the same time infrared sensors take measurements and relay these data to a computer, so the system can offer recommendations, for instance on similar garments customers might like. Other new forms of communication are personalized digital business cards, which are password protected to access customer chat rooms.

All this is evidence of an evolutionary path that is progressively becoming: "A unified system of digitalized communication, in which ecommerce, traditional distribution channels, high-tech fitting rooms equipped with body scanners, digital business cards, and more come together in an experience in which the online universe and direct in-store experience in-

*Figure* 5 – An interactive touchscreen for the virtual catalogue of major appliances at the Assago Carrefour Planet in Milan.

tersect. The first allows customers with an internet connection to shop, surf the virtual store and try on clothing thanks to their personal avatars; the second, beyond the physical contact with merchandise, enriches their knowledge of products and brands, knowledge which must be loaded with new value – and service – related content"[4] (Fig. 5).

In summary, among the myriad advantages inherent to the high level of in-store interaction, we can cite some relevant results that emerged in recent studies:

• to expand the educational component, acting on the affective/emotional system to enrich the store experience;
• to inform customers on product availability;
• to control the order of content presentation;
• to garner positive attitudes toward the brand;
• to guarantee the same quality information in all locations at all times;
• to disseminate the same message throughout the retail network;
• to instruct customers;
• to boost intentions to purchase;

---

[4] Bucchetti V. (2004), "Segni e artefatti per lo shopping" in Bucchetti V. (ed.), *Design della comunicazione ed esperienze di acquisto*, Franco Angeli, Milan, Italy, p. 43.

- to determine the most popular offering;
- to promote certain products over others;
- to provide information on all the opportunities that complement a given product;
- to guarantee that key messages are conveyed even without the support of store personnel;
- to gain a better understanding of the customer profile of system users; and
- to measure actual customer satisfaction.

Summing up, the new challenge is to find the optimal way to combine these new channels with more traditional tools, without succumbing to technophilia, which leads to an exponential increase in the sophistication of materials without taking into account the concrete returns. An "ecstasy of interaction," centered purely in the pleasure of connecting and participating, to generate multimedia events that serve no purpose beyond communication, and which end up being completely sterile. Often the balance between communication/transfer of meaning and communication/interaction is a difficult one to achieve and maintain over time. In other words, far from being a channel, communication becomes an end in and of itself within the process of interaction.

In the past few years, more and more companies have been seeking the best possible balance between this new and captivating paradigm and the traditional one. In fact, history shows us that when new media are introduced, they are added on to existing channels. Specifically, according to recent studies on the industry, technology will contribute to the value of Point of Purchase communication by enhancing brand recall, recognition, awareness and boosting demand. But it will do all this without replacing more traditional media.

## 5 Anteprima Emotions by Senso

For Vogue Fashion's Night Out, Milan 2016, the Anteprima Boutique (Corso Como 9 in Milan) organized an exclusive event entitled Emotions. With the collaboration of Senso, an Italian company based in Padua, Anteprima presented innovative design solutions, creating immersive and interactive experiences. Throughout the week the store was transformed into a space for experimentation and innovation, using smart displays called *Teca* and *Scrigno* to realize Immersive Storytelling (Fig. 6).

*Figure* 6 – The standalone display patented by Senso and installed in the Anteprima boutique for Vogue Fashion's Night Out Milan 2016 (courtesy of Senso).

All this, combined with visual merchandising activities and new technologies, forged a captivating brand experience.

Specifically, the event spotlighted the Lucchetto, the iconic wirebag from the Anteprima collection. The Lucchetto came to life in the Teca, a standalone display with a technological spirit, symbol of the design and creativity of Made in Italy and patented by Senso.

Thanks to an ingenious system of hidden projectors, tailor-made for Anteprima, the Teca showcased the strong personality of the Lucchetto Bag. In an engaging video starring the Lucchetto itself, the bag's features were transformed in real time to tell the story of its chic and eccentric nature. A series of dynamic audiovisual clips were projected onto the Lucchetto, perfectly matching its shape and geometry (using micromapping), so customers could admire the bag in all its color variations. The end result was an immersive and magical customer journey of discovery into the universe of Anteprima.

Two Teca were actually used for the Night Out event. The first was displayed in the window to capture the attention of passersby and encourage them to enter into the boutique to discover the iconic bag, and along with it Anteprima's entire New Collection (Fig. 7).

A second Teca was set up inside the store to enrich the shopping experience, blending seamlessly with the boutique's elegant and minimal interior

*Figure* 7 – Teca in the window display (courtesy of Senso).

design. This Teca gave customers a closer look at the Lucchetto, offering a fascinating way to discover Anteprima products. During the week-long event, a smart countertop display called Scrigno was the perfect comple-ment to the Teca. With a compact size and an enticing design, Scrigno told the story of "Perpetua the Pencil" through a series of animated clips and infographics, using a patented projection system (Fig. 8).

With impressive expertise, the Perpetua Special Edition, created for An-teprima to celebrate Emotions, demonstrated how to convert intangible val-ues into tangible expressions thanks to smart displays like Teca and Scrigno.

## 6   Interactive store windows

Communication through visual storytelling moves beyond the descriptive dimension of the offering, beginning with the notions of boundaries and thresholds. All this gives rise to extensive experimentation involving store windows, with more and more intensive intermingling of digital commu-nication and AR (Fig. 9).

Interactive windows give customers the chance to connect directly with the merchandise on display, to mix and match items according to

*Figure* 8 – Scrigno: The countertop display patented by Senso and installed in the Anteprima boutique for Vogue Fashion's Night Out Milan 2016 (courtesy of Senso).

*Figure* 9 – An amusing Sephora window entirely taken up by a monitor where passersby can see images of themselves walking through falling snow.

their personal taste, and to consult a virtual catalogue, making purchases on touchscreens, which can also be found inside the store (Figs. 10 and 11).

*Figure* 10 – A balanced mix of aesthetic and product, innovation and tradition in these Furla windows.

*Figure* 11 – One of the first interactive windows at Salmoiraghi & Viganò in Piazza San Babila in Milan.

Interactive windows can have lights and colors that change as people walk by or as the number of customers in a given space fluctuates, thanks to special technologies with motion detectors (like Kinect), and integrated touch-free webcams. Two of the companies that have used this approach are Adidas and Nike.

Adidas launched interactive windows in Italy for its OBA campaign in 2011 (One Brand Anthem: Adidas is all in). This initiative, with its sophisticated interactive systems, allowed everyone who passed by to become an Adidas star. Beyond displaying photos of the brand universe, the windows were linked in a network and equipped with interactive touchscreens that let people take pictures and shoot videos. They could then see the images they created in the window and share them with the entire system of installations set up in participating locations in cities around the country.

The following year in Nuremberg, the company came up with interactive window with QR codes for fast sales leveraging multimedia technology. Computer-generated images of human mannequins were projected on a screen, and people passing by could move them or change their clothing, consult the catalogue, choose different styles or models, and interact with the "mannequins". What's more, simply by snapping a photo of the QR code and inserting the code/PIN, they could make instant purchases.

In July of 2012, Selfridges in London designed window displays for Nike using Kinect technology to interact with passersby. Some offered actual interactive games, and others changed shape, design and color when people approached the window (Fig. 12).

*Figure* 12 – In Selfridges, one of the Kinetic window displays for Nike, which tracks and follows the flow of passersby with moving balls.

# 3 From identity systems to visual merchandising

## 1 The visible domain

Our post-industrial society can be considered the domain of the visible, where visibility is an aesthetic based on the continual stimulation of people's perceptions. Yet only in the last two decades have we begun to pay particular attention to the aesthetic aspects of every facet of reality as we perceive it. Indeed, today we have developed a different view of the relationship between ourselves and our surroundings, with respect to the past.

This tendency to focus on aesthetics proves to be a powerful force in shaping the way consumers act, even to the point where the "spectacularity" of products is taking on far more relevance than their intrinsic quality. Now more than ever, image is everything. In fact, it is image that triggers the psychological and cultural mechanisms that come into play during people's purchase decisions. The product presentation and the retail setting create a framing effect, encouraging consumers to make a more attentive evaluation of the offering in question. They see a given item as a valid option only if the package is consistent with their perceptive canons and the product properly positioned in the store. What is lacking in aesthetic attractiveness, people do not even see (Morace *et al.*, 1990).

Today more than ever before, the persistent tendency to see the spectacular obstructs the simple perception of the object in question. This is why the role of the store is so critical. While it is true rationally speaking that buyers do not place much importance on design elements, at a subconscious level they clearly behave as if they do. If the product presentation is uninspiring, this creates a negative bias in the minds of consumers, giving them the impression that the item in question will not fully satisfy their needs. What is more, by paying attention to the display setting, consumers become experts in deciphering the symbolism and grasping the messages emanating from the store atmosphere. These messages are transmitted by external and internal design elements combined in various ways: everything from decoratives and props that are not for sale, which evocatively complement the products on offer, to the overall structure of the display.

The combined effect of all these signals is what enables consumers to intuitively construct the positioning of the products on sale in the store, and to make up their minds whether or not to purchase them. In other words, taking up once again a concept which we discussed extensively in the first chapter, communication between the retailer and the customer is gradually shifting from the verbal domain, based on dialogue and trust, to the sphere of image. In fact, it is through image that the consumer expects to capture the key concepts that inspire the industrial and commercial offering, by means of a sign system that can only be decoded by those who belong to the same cultural system. Some studies have even revealed that individuals respond to environmental factors in a way that is not arbitrary but learned, inherited and dependent on a series of characteristics, such as lifestyles.

## 2    From store identity to store concept

Taken to the extreme, the culture of image leads to the dissemination of stores that no longer display merchandise, but rather offer a synthesis of cultural models proposed by the designers and brands in the store assortment. This, in some cases, can trigger *post-purchase dissonance*. What this specifically refers to is when aesthetic and theatrical associations predominate over the functional and qualitative characteristics of an offering. The risk here is that most of the product's attractiveness dissipates the moment it leaves the store, because it is removed from its original commercial context, giving rise to a serious scenario of dissatisfaction. In this case, identity, founded on the offering's concrete features, is a far cry from image, which, on the contrary, can exist in an entirely evanescent dimension.

For years, businesses focused on store image. Recently, however, some have begun to realize that most prominent product a store has to offer is its identity. This concept can be equated to the outcome of the interplay of numerous forces, no longer the simple sum of the assortment, the price, and the aesthetic quality of the display. Store identity must necessarily be anchored on a global philosophy. Therefore, building store identity begins by pinpointing the profile of the target customer, and from there moving on to consider the overarching style to communicate, the kinds of products to propose and, most importantly, the corporate culture to adopt. All this adds up to the value that the company wants to offer to its customers.

Once the store identity is determined, following an integrated communication approach, the next critical step is to create the concept. This consists of clear, explicit, shared guidelines to delineate the context in which all the communication choices will converge: from external to internal design, from advertising to promotions, from brand packaging to displays. Everything must be designed and executed consistently, with an eye to differentiating the store from the competition in a unique and enduring way. This calls for an in-depth exploration of the company and the market, capturing indications from various sectors in order to lay down the rules for a new method of communication.

Consequently, the definition of the store concept can only come at the end of an analytical path that leads to the representation of the store's image in the eyes of its customers. Though this might find some basis in objective data (competitor analysis, market positioning), the concept is for the most part intuitive, the starting point being aesthetic considerations that can generate design innovation.

Store designers have a complex array of factors to consider:

- the values of the store and the most effective way to represent them;
- the target customers and the type of communication this audience will respond to; how competitors address the same target;
- where the store is located; and
- how much money is available in the budget and how much various communication options will cost. Only then can they decide on a store identity that is consistent with the competitive arena and in synch with the retail context, or, taking the opposite tack, strive to break away by choosing an innovative image in an alternative setting.

The success of a concept depends not only on the synergistic integration of all communication activities, but also on the total congruence of all the signs that are utilized. In other words, without a global project, there is no way to effectively communicate the company's store identity or to disseminate a consistent image. In light of these considerations, concept development should definitely be integrated in the process of strategic planning.

3    Centrality of a coordinated image, substantiating the brand,
     or communicating by subtraction?

Underpinning every identity system are the notions of difference and permanence. How these concepts should be reinterpreted on a project level is
the topic of heated debate, even today. At the heart of the discussion lies
the highly topical question of the centrality of a coordinated image.

Some companies (like Aprilia and United Colors of Benetton) opt for
a communication strategy that in some sense limits the weight of the
brand. They adopt a vision based on corporate style, circumventing the
rules of a coordinated image, at least in part. In these cases, the corporate brand makes room for other aspects, giving precedence to elements
that are more flexible and adjustable over time, making them more easily adaptable to the continual reactualization that this strategy requires
(Bucchetti, 2004).

When discussing the difference-permanence dichotomy, we cannot
neglect to note certain moves in the opposite direction made by major
international brands like Nike, the subject of these comments: "The identity of the Nike brand is also powerfully conveyed, as demonstrated by
the pervasiveness of the 'swoosh,' the graphic symbol of the brand, which
is everywhere – on product displays, in elevators, on door handles and
handrails. The swoosh is also duplicated and magnified through ellipti-
cal shapes that can be found throughout the store. Nonetheless, Schmitt
and Simonson are justified in wondering whether this excess of force and
consistency activated by the Nike brand in communicating its store might
ultimately run the risk of proving to be a form of 'aesthetic totalitarianism,'
a sort of 'communicative excess' that may in some sense hinder consumer
engagement."[1]

In direct contrast to these retail giants, systemically designing and
managing identity and flexing all their media muscles, we find cases of
*spontaneous neo-graphics*.

As Bucchetti explains:

This expression encompasses signs that emerge from a process of intensive
dissemination of a coordinated image involving the entire communication
system of the stores, through various methods and to differing degrees. This

---

[1] Codeluppi V. (2000), *Lo spettacolo della merce*, Bompiani, Milan, Italy, p. 91.

has also prompted small-scale retailers to come up with their own image program. More often than not a "program" simply consisting of transitioning from "name to font," a process which starts with choosing and digitalizing lettering, and ends with output that is primed to become the store identity. This perspective is very distant from a design perspective, and far removed from aesthetic or semantic sensitivity. Generally speaking, in more recent years this approach has characterized the entire sphere of the graphic project, which has descended into a phase of democratization. As a result, the graphic interpretation of the store name, which centers on putting a visual to the name, or we could say "spelling it out," is combined with the production of a logo-identity. This process has given rise to myriad signs for the market, signs that appear on the street and validate the presence of individual stores in their respective urban contexts[2].

Last comes the notion of *reduction,* a communication strategy based on creating a powerful identity enabling the company to act exclusively through the system's basic signs: the brand, the institutional colors and the sign system, applied to all the essential communication levers (such as the store sign, shopping bags, labels, displays and so forth). The store takes on a supporting role in the communication plan, letting the product, as the protagonist of the display space, take center stage. Seductive and informative aspects of communication are minimized (if not eliminated altogether), relegated to the website or product catalogue.

The store becomes a directionless space, with paths winding through it that are conceived to allow customers freedom of movement. The main focus is the spatial layout and product displays, and how they can be organized to best attract customers. In other words, the tendency is leaning toward super-minimalism where the spotlight is trained on the product, so the absence of anything else becomes a source of value. It is the product alone, presented in its essential aspect, that speaks to the customer.

In this case, instead of expanding, communication contracts, contrasting with the dominant model with its tendency toward communicative exuberance. Standardization, replicability, interpretability of solutions all come to the fore once again. The coordinated image system is again placed at the focal point, conveying the idea of stability, a constantly developing image over time, and a disconnect from continuously changing communication.

---

[2] Bucchetti V. (2004), "Segni e artefatti per lo shopping" in Bucchetti V. (ed.), *Design della comunicazione ed esperienze di acquisto,* Franco Angeli, Milan, Italy, p. 20.

## 4    Integration between the company and the store designers

The goal in designing a store is to develop a global project founded on the synergistic integration of positioning strategies and communication activities, ensuring perfect congruity among all signs. To do so, the first requirement is that the Marketing Department directors (a.k.a. *silent designers*) are fully aware of the impact of their actions on the design process.

Store designers are tasked with the initial design of the retail space. This means they must have marketing competencies and knowledge not only of the store's target, but also the factors that impact customer purchase decisions, competitor profiles, and company objectives for the design project. After initial contact with the company, store designers are already expected to formulate project guidelines through renderings, even though they may not necessarily have the determinants or the substance of the store identity in hand yet. What is more, although the Marketing Department and the store managers may have a voice in the store design, they only come to the table during the final stages of the design process. At that point, a clear direction has already been staked out by the architects and the store designers, with room for only minor deviations.

Unfortunately, although there are some signs that a gradual change is underway, a sharp cultural contrast still persists between managers and designers today. On one hand, managers find it difficult to weigh design decisions. In fact, their backgrounds and expertise are normally grounded in analytical, non-creative disciplines, making them ill-prepared to manage projects that involve concepts that they have little proficiency in, based on visual input that calls for entirely subjective assessments. It is no coincidence, then, that often managers tend to underestimate the critical role of design, and view it exclusively as a resource capable of infusing products with added value. Instead, design can contribute to attaining major corporate performance targets, on par with other communication investments.

Store designers, for their part, have little inclination to work within common managerial boundaries, or evaluate the outcomes of their choices in economic terms. Instead, they seek to promote overarching concepts like the desire to enhance the environment, educate the public as far as taste in the arts or even help foster social changes. After all, store designers are often judged on the basis of purely artistic parameters such as originality.

Summing up, then, it is true that managers and store designers come from worlds that are diametrically opposed, with cultures rooted in diverse educational backgrounds and personal skills. Yet clearly, given the critical nature of this stage, adopting a synergistic approach is indispensible. From the moment the store identity is determined to when the store concept is designed, economy and creativity must find a constructive combination.

Added to this is the fact that the store concept cannot by nature be static, but instead must be readapted (if not entirely revisited), keeping pace with the evolution of the competitive context, every five years at the most. During this period of time, it is absolutely essential to monitor the effects of the retail space, and the behavior and perception of customers. This calls for a periodic "atmosphere assessment," in other words, a detailed and systematic analysis of the sales environment in all its constituent elements. The aim here is to determine whether or not the current commercial atmosphere is still conveying the desired message to target customers: essentially, whether the store identity and store image continue to coincide.

There are a number of valid reasons to run this analysis on a regular basis. First, markets are constantly changing, and as people gradually accept some of these changes and reject others, new design trends emerge. What is more, new product launches on occasion necessitate modifications in the store's layout and displays. Also, some store fixtures might show signs of wear and tear caused by the flow of customers, as well as normal obsolescence. Lastly, business managers and store directors may not be able to objectively view certain unflattering aspects of the store which customers notice and have no qualms about criticizing.

Summing up, then, the atmosphere assessment also enables retailers to effectively evaluate if existing structures need revising, to what extent this should be done, and whether or not these changes will impact a few stores or the entire chain.


## 5   Developing the store design

As we have often reiterated, store design is a complex process. Although the final aim is to optimize corporate profits, the primary focus must remain unwaveringly on the customers, in an attempt to provide them with the most satisfying shopping experience possible. This combination of intents must harmonize with all the components of the design mix, in terms of:

- *performance*, closely linked to the effectiveness of marketing research in evaluating customer expectations, both functional and non-functional;
- *quality*, which determines the choice of materials and finishings, in order to accurately communicate store identity;
- *duration*, particularly in visual terms, to mitigate the risk of rapid obsolescence of the final project;
- *look*, linked to the unique forms and styles that come together for a pleasant, distinctive presentation that satisfies customer needs and at the same time stands out clearly from the competition; and
- *cost*, inevitably impacted by budget constraints, but also by estimates of the overall value of the project, which has to satisfy the needs of the customers who utilize it.

This said, we have often stressed the importance not only of in-depth market knowledge, but also constant interaction between the store designer and the company. Indeed, a soundly structured blueprint must be followed, from gathering and analyzing data to the more operative stages of developing and managing the project. This process must be broken down into distinct phases, activities, responsibilities and timelines. Below is a suggested plan:

1. preliminary stage;
2. project development;
3. awarding contracts and executing work; and
4. post store opening.

## 5.1    *The preliminary stage*

This stage centers on gathering and analyzing the technical data and information needed to develop the project. It normally lasts around two weeks, and involves the following activities:

1. *Meeting with the client*: the purpose here is to compile a brief, detailing the needs and expectations of the client company. This is when the store designer gathers commercial information regarding the image, aesthetics, and distribution format, as well as technical input relative to the product and the store operations (number of cash desks, size and physical features of the stockrooms, areas reserved for customers/staff, etc.)
2. *Visiting the site*: this is an opportunity to come up with the creative approach for the project, with an eye to the store's size, architectural features, and the surrounding context.

3. *Gathering technical information*: activities include analyzing the regulatory specifications for designing the store and assessing structural barriers and/or building code restrictions as well as accessibility issues.

## 5.2    *The project development stage*

This stage, lasting from four to six weeks, covers creative and technical development, continual progress checks and presentation of the project to the company, with relative activities broken down as follows:

1. *Developing the project*: deciding on the layout in terms of number and type of display systems, horizontal pathways, vertical links, the creative interpretation of the architecture, stable and mobile fixtures, materials, colors and finishings.
2. *Verifying the display capacity*: identifying the display criteria of product categories and lines, generally in collaboration with the Department of Visual Merchandising of the client-company.
3. *Designing the lighting system*: not only to illuminate the store, but also to spotlight specific areas and to draw attention to the features of the products on display.
4. *Presenting the project to the company*: ascertaining that project decisions coincide with the company's expectations by analyzing renderings.
5. *Compiling technical drawings*: illustrating the architecture of the spaces, the furnishings and the technical systems.

## 5.3    *Awarding contracts and executing work*

This stage lasts from eight to twelve weeks, and involves a number of people who all have a hand in organizing the construction site and the production of the fixtures and furnishings. The following activities are carried out:

1. *Requesting permits*: generally dealt with by a local architect, since relative requirements vary from country to country.
2. *Drawing up documents for the contracts*: with the collaboration of a local architect.
3. *Awarding the contracts and planning the work*: also with the participation of the store manager, in particular for handling orders (on behalf of the company) and controlling the production of the fixtures, decorative elements and finishings.

4. *Overseeing the work*: usually taken on by the local architect under the supervision of the store designer, especially with regard to any aspects that have a substantial impact on aesthetics.

5. *Supervising the production and installation of fixtures and furnishings*: here the store designer and local architect work together to ensure the timeline is respected for all stages in the project realization, to guarantee that the store opens on schedule.

6. *Visual merchandising*: relative to all display areas, both in-store and out-of-store, handled by the company's Visual Merchandising or Marketing Department, with assistance from external consultants. In this stage, the store designer takes on the role of coordinator to ensure that a proper balance is struck between the actual product and the "theatralization" of the product presentation.

## 5.4    *The post-opening stage*

After the store opening, the store designer has to make sure that everything is operational, and then draw up the final cost summary. This stage consists of:

1. *The punch list*: verification that each company involved in the project actually completed the work it was contracted to perform, checking for possible defects or inconsistencies with respect to the original project, calling on all participants to take responsibility for their work.

2. *Cost analysis*: summary of all expenses, to be compiled after work is finalized.

## 6    Implementing identity systems in a retail chain: from replicability to difference

If a store identity project encompasses a retail chain, the question arises as to whether each individual store should conform to the initiative and to what degree. As mentioned previously, today there is still widespread debate regarding difference and permanence, which underpin every identity system, and how to reinterpret these notions on a project level.

The rise of retail chains and franchising networks dates back to the 1970s. This trend led to the spread of the *corporate identity* as a communication format for the store, a notion which was then transformed into a shared set of standard practices. These in turn incorporated the rules of systematization from the model of reference, and refined and evolved the relevant tools that eventually gave rise to actual programs for identity consolidation. This is where the *visual book* comes into play, an operating manual containing the complete set of rules that apply to image management in the retail space over time.

In following this approach, some companies opt to set up pilot stores. These serve as testing ground for store designers working at company headquarters who need to come up with a format that will successively be cloned throughout the network. In this case, individual store directors are obliged to execute to the letter all the store design solutions to be implemented all along the chain. As a support tool, they are provided with a meticulously detailed visual book. This allows the central store to transfer downstream all the instructions needed to implement the entire project from a structural and managerial viewpoint, within the framework of visual merchandising (Zaghi, 2013): from internal and external architecture to fixtures, displays, posters, and in-store signage and more. The visual book, by elaborating all the various communication artifacts, illustrates possible variations on myriad operational tools, such as: documents, in-house publications, in-store wrapping and packaging, staff uniforms, means of transportation, to encompass the systemic design of the store.

The main advantage of creating such a meticulous mold for retail spaces is the guarantee of a coordinated image that is consistent with the store identity. Nonetheless, there are also a number of disadvantages. First of all, when the evolution of the competitive context triggers the need to restyle retail space, this intervention should apply to the entire network, an extremely costly undertaking for the company. Moreover, identical projects leads to excessive rigidity, which does not allow for the unique local features to emerge, linked to various areas of attraction within the network. The outcome is that approaching visual merchandising activity from a micro-marketing perspective becomes impossible. But as we will see further on, it is precisely this perspective which is a necessary condition for improving company performance and customer satisfaction. Likewise, the distance that separates store designers from local specificities means they have no way to comprehend fully, and more importantly in real time, the changing preferences and needs of customers.

In light of these limitations, many chains have opted to decentralize store design by turning to local designers; this enables the chain to offer a high degree of variety in the store concept at the network level. With this approach, designs are exclusively territorial, and utilize materials, decorations and, more generally, visual merchandising solutions that are highly contextualized. In other words, design solutions are articulated around creating and enhancing differences, so that every single store in the chain maintains an autonomous identity, while belonging to a single system. This approach takes into account the stability of the system itself, along with the dynamics and methods for updating and evolving the store. Difference and permanence, the notions underlying each identity system, are reinterpreted at a project level.

These two notions are addressed by Floch in his in-depth analyses of visual identity with regard to the question of controlled deviation. This author cites the Fiorucci case from the late 1960s as the benchmark project (Floch, 1995). The aim here is to enhance each store's power of attraction by equipping it to adapt more quickly and effectively to the local dynamics of demand and the unique preferences and needs of target customers. However, the main disadvantage here naturally lies in the total incongruity and inconsistency that emerges between the image of the individual stores in the retail chain and the overall store identity.

Finally, a combined approach represents an attempt to reconcile the advantages of the two solutions (total centralization versus total decentralization) while mitigating relative disadvantages. In fact, many companies are forced down this path due to a pre-existing lack of uniformity in the retail network. So, they become experts in creating a certain concept, and then modulating it in a wide range of assorted design solutions so they can adapt it to the different retail spaces that come available in the markets in question, on a case-by-case basis. This approach, albeit lacking in standardized design, guarantees a certain degree of consistency between the image of the network and the store identity.

Clearly, this should not represent a final compromise in a diversified path of store openings throughout the territory of reference. The optimal strategy, instead, is to divide the stores in the network into clusters, groups that share similar competitive contexts and customer profiles. That way concepts can be designed and revised as need be to respond to the specificities that emerge in local contexts. So rather than an ex post solution, this approach is more accurately described as the output of a process that is set up and run in a structured, ex ante fashion.

## 7   From merchandising to visual merchandising: definitions and scope

In operational terms, merchandising decisions actually represent the completion of the building phase for the store. Nonetheless, in light of the considerations above, what clearly emerges is the need to expand the scope of merchandising to the far broader fields of action of visual merchandising. To fully comprehend the opportunities that arise in doing so, the place to begin is by defining merchandising. Numerous interpretations have been proposed over the years, yet they all more or less converge on viewing merchandising as the set of methods that, taken together, give the product an active role in sales. This thanks to a proper product presentation and placement inside and outside the store.

Specifically, merchandising acts on the affective system of the customer, to achieve the following aims:

- to prompt customers to visit the entire store, in order to boost add-on purchases; and
- to optimize the profitability of the sales area, highlighting the products that generate greater profit margins.

To do this, various levers are activated, which in turn encompass several different activities that deal with:

- the layout of fixtures and shelving;
- the layout of the merchandise; and
- the display and allocation of display space.

First of all, the layout of store furnishings has to do with organizing retail space and choosing display fixtures, as well as positioning displays to mark the path that customers can follow throughout the entire store. The decisions that follow speak to all the aspects of merchandise layout, identifying the sequence of sectors and departments along the path mapped out in the first step. Once the layout is established, merchandising activity centers on selecting the displays and allocating display space by setting down the guidelines for display criteria and assigning space to products.

Despite its vital role in achieving optimum store management, merchandising alone risks generating negative repercussions on the store atmosphere because it cannot fully realize the innate potential of visual communication. To circumvent this obvious limitation, the growing tendency is toward expanding the scope of action to encompass all decisions pertaining to store architecture, the store sign, windows, entrance, the design of various sections of the store, directories, posters and signage, in addition to all of the point of purchase (POP) communication.

So we have finally come to the point of implementing an active tool for communicating the image of the store and the products it offers, as well as informing, suggesting, persuading and promoting sales. All this not only targets people in the store, but those who are outside as well. In this sense, visual merchandising can be defined as marketing of the store, in the store. This definition highlights the joint effects of all the visual communication techniques that optimize the profitability of the display space while simultaneously maximizing customer satisfaction. Specifically, visual merchandising is a multifunctional activity that requires competencies that go beyond marketing to include semiotics, design, architecture, painting, and social psychology. The primary aim is to exploit various skills to communicate with specific customer segments via the display space. To ensure that this happens, there must be a perfect fit between the codes utilized by store and by the customers: this is the only way to ensure that people clearly understand the meaning the store wants to convey.

In this regard, however, worth noting is the notion of cognitive distortion, that is, the semantic "noises" that alter the meaning of the message transmitted by the store. As far as assortment is concerned, in some stores this distortion cannot be entirely eliminated for structural reasons. In any case, to minimize cognitive distortion, communication tools are needed that can shape the associations between the physical traits of the products on display (content) and the message the store is trying to convey (concept). To this end, all visual merchandising tools can help reiterate the meaning of the assortment, so as to limit distortion.

## 7.1    *Visual merchandising and assisted selling*

Naturally, visual merchandising activity is not the exclusive prerogative of modern retailing. In fact it is a vital tool for traditional commerce as well, which leverages various combinations of assisted and visual selling techniques. Clearly, the function and the very nature of traditional commercial activity revolves around assisted selling, which, by definition, cannot occur without direct contact between customers and sales personnel, who activate an adaptive communication process. However, by integrating and coordinating assisted selling with visual merchandising, retailers can augment store functionality, not only boosting economic results but fostering customer loyalty as well, thanks to consistent, effective, and innovative communication.

Visual merchandising brings customers into direct contact with product assortment, giving them access to products even without the intervention of sales staff. Specifically, we refer to physical accessibility when customers learn about a product by picking it up and looking it over, considering its intrinsic and functional features to decide how well the item suits their needs. This accessibility may be limited to the visual aspect, in cases where a product is clearly visible and "legible," even if potential buyers have to ask for assistance from store personnel to gain physical access.

But physical and visual access to products are not enough to maximize the effectiveness of visual merchandising. Indeed, accessibility must extend to a psychological and intellectual level in order for visual merchandising to fulfill its role. In other words, customers have to feel comfortable with the product in question, and understand what it is, what purpose it serves, and how useful it can be. This means criteria must be established for aggregating merchandise in such a way as to guide customers toward the product lines that best suit their needs. Particularly effective are clear, easy-to-read directories, positioned at a proper distance from displays, to draw attention to product families and lines that customers may not have considered before.

Visual selling represents an additional service that requires special attention when organizing retail space and product displays. Specifically, retailers must not only exploit the autonomous capacity for communication and attraction intrinsic to each product. The positioning and presentation of the offering should also be organized to enable customers to choose autonomously, prompting them to make complementary, add-on purchases thanks to the logical and functional aggregation and sequencing of merchandise.

A concrete example is a hands-on display, which facilitates the interaction between customer and product, as well as between customer and surrounding space. In other words, visual merchandising offers an add-on service to the customer, who enjoys the opportunity to evaluate products independently, choosing more or less freely and using the time she spends waiting to be served to get a clearer idea of what she wants and to look for new stimuli.

At the same time, this type of display is a useful support tool for sales staff, who no longer need to give general information because the products can provide this themselves (if properly displayed). Instead, personnel can focus entirely on assisting customers in the more complex and critical stages of the purchase process. Through visual communication, stores can increase the commercial productivity of assisted selling, limiting the intervention of sales staff to the situations, customers, and products that need it most (Fig. 1).

*Figure* 1 – The sales service counter at Unieuro in Bergamo, Italy, stands out in the middle of the aisle, and presents a vast display of products that customers are free to handle so they can evaluate the offering by themselves.

## 8    Visual merchandising, purchase intentions and impulse purchases

The growing importance of visual merchandising activity is closely connected to the rise in unplanned purchases. If in fact all purchases were planned by consumers before they even entered a store, visual merchandising would not play such a decisive role in influencing their final choices. What is more, there is a general assumption that customers behave in a rational manner, and they only decide what to buy after considering various alternatives; yet this proves not to be the case in real life. On the contrary, the dynamics that actually drive purchase styles show a gradual escalation in the impulsive component, due mainly to the fact that people have more free time, enjoy greater mobility, and resort more often to consumer credit. Consolidating this trend even further is the broader distribution of products that can satisfy increasingly specific needs. An additional contributing factor is the intensification of in-store communication activity, which goes hand in hand with layouts and displays that are becoming more and more effective in prompting add-on purchases.

According to a 2007 study conducted by IRI, a market research company, 71% of consumers of mass market goods plan to purchase a specific product category before entering a store. Breaking down this figure, 56% have already decided on the brand to buy, while 15% make that choice while they are in the store. The remaining 29%, who had not even planned the product category, behave as follows: 8% buy a brand that they already had in mind while 21% act on pure impulse under the influence of promotional activity and visual merchandising. These factors trigger unplanned purchases and/or transfer the consumer choice to a replacement category to satisfy the relative product function.

Before examining impulse purchases, however, first we should explore purchase intentions. Regardless of the level of planning of a given purchase, during a store visit customers are exposed to environmental stimuli from the retail structure, the assortment, and the services on offer. All of these elements can transform purchase planning levels into different purchase behaviors. Looking more closely at this concept, we can identify five different purchase intentions:

1. *Planned product and brand* refers to a purchase that is arranged in minute detail before entering the store. This can lead the customer to three different outcomes: buying the product and brand decided on before the store visit; buying the product but not the brand (replacement purchase); not buying the product or the brand (no purchase).
2. *Planned product*, but planning does not extend to the brand; this scenario may evolve into an occasional or one-off purchase, or no purchase at all.
3. *Planned product category* implies that the customer decides to buy the category in question before entering the store, but only chooses the specific product and brand while actually visiting the store.
4. *Generically planned purchase* is when the consumer recognizes a need before visiting the store, but has not yet decided on the product category.

5. *No planning* is when the consumer does not recognize a need, which means it may be latent. In this case, the purchase decision is not only made entirely in the store, but it is also a rapid one (involving far less information and decision time, as compared to a "normal" purchase scenario). To be even more specific, the impulse purchase can be classified as experiential or non-experiential depending on whether it elicits certain emotional and/or cognitive reactions.

Continuing on the topic of impulse purchases, from a conceptual standpoint, this behavior entails decision-making directly in the store, when the consumer comes across a given item and acts in a sudden, spontaneous way, without reflecting first.

First of all, people make spontaneous purchases when they find a product that they were not actually looking for; in fact, they may simply have been browsing through the store with no intention of buying anything at all. In any case, the desire and the decision to buy come about only when the customer sees the product. However, although a necessary condition is spontaneity, it is not enough to place that behavior in the category of an unplanned activity.

In fact, in order to define a purchase as "impulse," a second requirement must be met: it cannot be the outcome of reflection, since it does not involve any evaluation. In other words, when people make impulse purchases, they do not consider consequences or weigh other options. Their attention is focused exclusively on the instant gratification that will come from the purchase, rather than the search for a product that satisfies a need and/or solves a problem. Lastly, following on from the considerations above, an impulse purchase is immediate. The time interval from the moment buyers see the product and when they decide to purchase it is minimal; chances are very slim that they will put off the purchase to gather more information, compare the offerings of competing stores, seek advice or simply avoid acting in the "heat of the moment".

To sum up, an impulse purchase is when the customer:

- sees the product and approaches it without hesitation;
- wants to possess the product at that very moment;
- thinks mainly about purchasing and possessing the product immediately, rather than the possible negative consequences that may derive from the purchase;

- feels very excited at the prospect of purchasing the product; and
- perceives a conflict between controlled and purely impulsive behavior.

Delving into greater detail, we can identify at least four different types of impulse purchases (Alagöz and Ekici, 2011):

1. A *pure impulse purchase* is when people have an intense, immediate desire to buy and possess a product or brand the moment they see it. Although this desire might not be clearly motivated, it derives from a combination of various stimuli which lead to an irrepressible need to buy.
2. A *remembered impulse purchase* happens when customers notice the product on display in the store, and they remember that they should have put it on their shopping list. This type of behavior is classified as an impulse purchase simply because customers make the decision to buy when they see the item. However, it is not a pure impulse purchase because it implies a certain level of predetermination. In fact, the product in this case is actually useful, and may even be an item the customers regularly buy.
3. A *suggested impulse purchase* occurs when the perception of a need is triggered exclusively upon seeing the product or brand in question, and not before. This scenario lies midway between the first two described above. In this case, consumers can explain their desire to buy as a need that suddenly emerged when they saw the item, although they had never thought to put it on their shopping list before.
4. A *planned impulse purchase* is when consumers decide to buy a different product than the one they had planned, because they are attracted by a certain brand and/or promotion. This type of impulse purchase represents the most "pondered" kind, because the motivation here is a rational one, even though the decision is entirely unanticipated.

Many studies have brought to light the fact that most people have an innate tendency to make impulse purchases. What is more, this buying behavior impacts all product categories and all distribution formats, albeit to varying degrees. In fact, primary instincts are what trigger impulse purchases. There are no products that can be defined as "impulse," but rather products that are purchased impulsively more often than others.

Generally speaking, almost all products can be purchased on impulse, even though there are some that more readily lend themselves to this type of behavior, such as:

- goods with a low unit value;

* good which are not necessities (luxury goods);
* perishable goods and/or goods with a short shelf life;
* small items; and
* stockable items.

Similarly, there are some distribution formats, in particular self-service stores, that prompt more impulse purchases thanks to their product displays. What we need to keep in mind, in any case, is that a product can take on different connotations depending on the type of buyer, who may have a different perception of its value and functionality compared to other consumers. Likewise, some customers may be more receptive to advice from the sales staff and less swayed by product displays. Even diverse attitudes toward shopping impact purchase planning. A recreational shopper who associates the activity with free time shows a greater inclination toward impulse purchases compared to a functional buyer, whose only aim is to make a purchase.

Other considerations that may carry weight pertain to so-called institutional variables, that is, familiarity with the store and availability of time and money. As for the first factor, studies show that when people do not know their way around a retail space very well, they are more likely to make impulse purchases. Since they are unfamiliar with the path running through the store, marked by the various departments, they tend to pay more attention to the information provided by the layout, displays and signage to find products and brands. Thanks to this increased exposure to environmental stimuli, there is a greater chance that latent needs will clearly surface. In addition, the more time people have on their hands, the more likely they are to make unplanned purchases. Obviously, when they rush through the store, they get less exposure to environmental stimuli, and have less time to correctly interpret the information given by displays and signage. Lastly, the amount and the variety of the items that people buy seem to have a positive impact on impulse purchases.

All this corroborates the fact that we cannot unequivocally define specific products or distribution formats as "impulse." Clearly, all the behaviors described above are only one component of a much more far-reaching and complex process. In almost every case, in fact, an impulse purchase is merely the final outcome of a series of thoughts and actions that begin much earlier. It is easy to see that aspects such as promotions and retailing policies impact the sales environment (in terms of atmosphere, visual merchandising, personnel and crowds), but these are not the only relevant factors in this process. Also critical in the retailing world is the role of visual merchandising through initiatives promoting activation and visibility.

## 9 Balancing conflicting needs

Based on what we discussed in the previous section, there is no doubt that visual merchandising should adopt a micro-marketing orientation. Indeed, we have established the fact that this is the only approach that allows companies to implement solutions tailored for individual stores, taking into account not only the retailing mix of competitors, but also the architectural characteristics of the retail space and the sociodemographic traits of target customers.

Clearly, the most effective visual merchandising solutions are the outcome of a judicious and delicate balance between the needs of supply and demand. As we know, on the supply side the priority is to maximize profitability, orienting the flow of customers along a path that augments the display area they see and facilitates their decision-making process, all while helping them maintain the proper mindset for making a purchase. But two other critical aims cannot be neglected: rationalizing replenishment activity and reducing inventory shrinkage. These commercial requirements tend to conflict with the needs of demand. In fact, customers are not only looking to save time and simplify the purchase process, they also want to gather information and at the same time feel gratification on a psychological level.

From all this we can draw the conclusion that visual merchandising activity undeniably follows a short-term orientation. This is closely connected to the capacity to shape customer purchasing behavior in order to maximize the profitability of the display spaces, to encourage impulse purchases, and to modify the structure of turnover to increase the weight of items with higher profit margins. However, the most successful visual merchandising projects adopt a long-term view as well, with an eye to creating and qualifying the corporate image, respecting customers' mental organization of their needs, improving the purchase experience by making it easier and more stimulating, and ultimately nurturing customer loyalty.

In other words, the most strategic approach to visual merchandising attempts to satisfy the need for information in order to offer solutions that are capable of reflecting the marketing orientation of the store, while creating added value for the customer at the same time. In this sense, for the store, visual merchandising contributes to the process of differentiation and identity creation. Summing up, it goes without saying that balancing the short-term aims of efficiency and long-term goals of service quality and customer loyalty is inextricably linked to the strategic positioning of the store and the marketing policies it pursues.

## 10    The profile of a visual merchandiser

As visual selling becomes increasingly critical, the competencies that visual merchandisers need are progressively multiplying. In fact, these professionals are tasked with creating sales environments that are both functional and pleasant. This calls for activities ranging from handling the organization of sales areas, mapping out paths through the store, and presenting merchandise on various display modules, to choosing appropriate colors and lighting. To do all this, the skill sets of visual merchandisers should include creativity, a sense of order, artistic talent, knowledge of visual techniques and notions of interior decorating. Equally vital are an understanding of customer buying behavior and working knowledge of crowd psychology. To be more precise, the specific competencies that visual merchandisers need depend on the context where they work and their level of involvement within the overall organizational structure. Some visual merchandising positions are highly specialized, for example window dressing or in-store signage; others instead call for more general know-how.

For larger businesses, visual merchandising projects are assigned to a team made up of architects, interior decorators, store designers, and graphic artists. All the team members are normally coordinated by a leader with expertise in visual merchandising who is responsible for supervising all the components of store atmosphere. This team answers directly to the General Manager and works closely with all the corporate functions, in particular communication. In fact, intense interaction between the visual merchandising team and the Communication Department is extremely constructive for identifying possible synergies as far as investments in external institutional communication, maximizing their effectiveness by means of a sales environment that meets customer expectations.

In contrast, in smaller companies, individual projects are taken on by external organizations which for the most part handle window dressing and implement techniques for in-store product presentation. This work is monitored by the Marketing Department of the customer-company, which participates in developing specific plans for store design. Lastly, an intermediate solution is an internal corporate body that deals with design and resorts to external consultants only for the realization of individual projects.

## 11  Virtual visual merchandising

Most visual merchandisers design the commercial complex and display schemes by drawing them in pencil by hand on graph paper. However, as we will discuss further in Chapter 6, technological innovation has long since become so highly specialized as to provide substantial support for these professionals in planning stores. Computer programs offer useful tools for more efficient and effective design and management of layout and display solutions. Specifically, by drawing up a virtual store plan, visual merchandisers can create walls and floor space to scale, and add customized color schemes as well. Then, they can build their own display fixtures or import these structures from supplier catalogues. Once they position the stands, shelves and tables, they can populate them with products (Morgan, 2011).

In the initial stage, programmers work together with the company to come up with a range of shelving modules broad enough to accommodate the offering, with fixtures, decorations, and other materials for store design such as flooring and wall coverings. Drag-and-drop technology makes it possible to choose from various shelving modules. The visual merchandiser works on both a 2D and 3D format to decide on the size and the configuration of the retail space, and to choose coverings for the floors, walls and ceiling. Every fixture contains a "connector" and/or "container" where the product assortment can be positioned. Connectors hang items on bars or hooks while containers automatically fold garments and place them on shelves or counters. Naturally, the software allows users to move merchandise from one area to another, and modify the number of units to display on the fixtures.

What is more, visual merchandisers can develop planograms for single fixtures and visualize in detail the articles to be displayed there and the position of each one. Finally, the software generates a statistical summary of the sales space, including details and commercial values on each item in electronic format, to estimate sales per square meter/foot and/or per linear meter/foot. All design directives are inputted onto a "visual storyboard" which is updated in real time; this shows the store layout on individual pages, effectively illustrating the development of the collections. The store design can be shown as a floor plan or a perspective drawing, inserted into a three-dimensional space that viewers can visit virtually. To achieve a more realistic effect, the intensity and the direction of the lighting can be regulated, and mannequins, signage and images can be added.

Today, a vast range of software is available for realizing a virtual store. Mock Shop is just one of the many versatile, albeit expensive, tools that can create a virtual store with a storyboard for key items, generating high-quality visual, digital, and hard copy documents. These can be sent to the Purchasing and Marketing Departments, and shared with the entire retail network, to communicate the design and visual merchandising directives, revised and updated according to the calendar of collection launches.

## 12   Innovative retail design as a strategic asset in luxury companies: the Vivienne Westwood case[3]

In the digital age, the store has taken on a preeminent role as a communicative space and a relational platform for luxury companies. To attract the right target to the store, brands have to propose concepts that are innovative, but at the same time aligned with the heritage and the genetic makeup of the company. The winning strategy detailed in this case consists of selling an in-store experience that is consistent with the history of the brand, and no longer simply about the products. A radical change in design that severs any link with the brand identity would thwart the natural connection between brand values and consumers that occurs inside the store, distancing them from the very idea that the brand represents and from the story it wants to

[3] The author wishes to thank Isabella Tonelli for the content of this case, which is based on her 2016 MBA dissertation in Fashion, Luxury & Made in Italy, at Bocconi University, entitled *Innovative Retail Design as a Strategic Asset for Luxury Companies*.

tell. This powerful interplay of history and tradition is what makes Vivienne Westwood a fascinating case for study and reflection.

### 12.1  *The Vivienne Westwood story: the transformation from punk to couturier to international designer*

Vivienne Westwood is an independent luxury fashion house with a British soul and an international scope. The company boasts a worldwide distribution network covering more than 80 countries, with 30 flagships and over 700 stores. Brand equity consists of an inimitable asset – designer Vivienne Westwood – who made her radical mark on the fashion world by introducing stylistic innovations and triggering an aesthetic turning point thanks to the Punk movement. To get a clearer picture of the fashion house we need to delve into the personal story of Dame Westwood. As her husband and co-designer Andreas Kronthaler says, *"We tell a story, that's why people pay attention. What we are doing, it is fashion like it used to be. Vivienne is constant. You recognize what we make because it is not fashion; it is a story about her, and her reaction to the world."[4]* (Fig. 2).

The designer's success began in 1970s London, at 430 King's Road in her **Let It Rock** shop, known today as **Worlds End**. That space was destined to become a meeting place for the youth culture of the day, the cradle of a movement which, for the first time ever, was conceived in a store and then spilled out onto the street. With the support of her partner and collaborator Malcolm McLaren (who was also the manager of the Sex Pistols), Westwood came up with the idea of cross-pollination between fashion, music, and graphic design, a phenomenon that contributed to a stylistic and cultural identity recognizable the world over as Punk. Now, like never before, clothes represented a segment of society, identifying London insiders and outsiders during a period of ethnic tensions, revolts against the establishment, and civil protests.

The expression "clothes that look like ruins" (Westwood and Kelly, 2014) sums up Westwood's desire to make a statement against the conservative British establishment. This led to the debut of new stylistic expedients in the world of fashion; materials are torn, worn, personalized, designed with no clear reference to gender, held together with pins and chains, sporting provocative slogans to make fashion the personification

---

[4] Westwood V. and Kelly I. (2014), *Vivienne Westwood*, Picador, London, UK, p. 20.

*Figure 2* – Vivienne Westwood (courtesy of Vivienne Westwood).

*Figure 3* – The Orb, the company logo, with the queen's crown, idealizing the past, and the Saturn-like ring, projecting into the future (courtesy of Vivienne Westwood).

of an idea, a means of communication, a link between politics and society, a weapon of liberation – no longer an ephemeral question of style.

The desire to rebel against taboos, against the status quo, continues to be a distinctive trait of the fashion house, which is true to its Punk identity even today. It's there on the catwalk, along with the themes that the designer holds dear, such as protecting the environment and battling political and civil injustice. The constant revolt against the present, which began in 1971, is the main source of inspiration for Dame Westwood, and meshes perfectly with the mission to bring tradition into the future. This concept crystallizes in the company logo, the Orb, shaped to resemble a queen's crown to idealize the past, with a Saturn-like ring projecting into the future (Fig. 3).

Rediscovering and reminiscing about the past: these are the visible connotations of the Westwood collections, from the Pirate Collection of 1981, moving up to high fashion shows on Paris catwalks, and later in Milan and London as well. Once again Westwood spotlights revamped period costumes, Baroque drapings and corsets, providing a new frame of reference for ideas from the past.

All this while never losing touch with a quintessentially British nature, celebrated with tartan fabrics, or an equally subversive and anti-iconoclast soul. Vivienne Westwood can be counted among the fashion houses that succeed in encapsulating storytelling as the centerpiece of their value proposition. This is the aspect that is most appreciated by loyal clients, who see themselves as custodians and messengers; this explains why they feel like they are a part of the story (Clarke and Holt, 2016). Since this is a critical success factor, it must be replicated in the store as well, to keep this intimate connection with Westwood clientele alive. The idea of the fashion house is to leverage culture and art, to bring styles that characterized the past into the present, so we don't forget what came before. This is consistent with the desire to have a positive influence on customers, spurring them to "take an active part in social life," promoting awareness and ethical behavior. The end result of this worldview is that a Westwood garment reflects a strong personality grounded in a thorough knowledge of the history of the brand.

## 12.2 *The evolution of the retail concept at 430 King's Road*

To capture the unique features and differences between the two Milan stores, at Corso Venezia 25 and Via Vincenzo Capelli 4, we need to keep in mind the overarching evolution of the retail concept. In 1971, the first store was opened at 430 King's Road, London. Christened *Let it Rock*, it looked more like an art installation than a store. The customers, London's Teddy Boys, found a selection of vintage rock memorabilia from the 1950s in a hangout that offered a combination of music and art. The following year, the jukebox and the pinup-covered walls gave way to a more anarchical look, where the product offering was based on a personalized, do-it-yourself approach. Later the space was completely transformed with *Too Fast to Live Too Young to Die*, a reference to James Dean. The store became a place where rock was deconstructed, where experimentation happened, where bondage was introduced.

In 1974, with the third iteration of the boutique's identity, SEX appeared in huge pink capital letters on the façade. This was the turning point when the provocative and intimidating became the focal point of the store concept. The collection embraced fetish connotations and the store interior followed suit, with walls covered in shocking graffiti. The evolution continued with the reopening of *Seditionaries*, the aim here being to dress the heroes of the street, giving rise to the concept which we can still find today at King's Road: *Worlds End*.

Beyond the heritage of the fashion house, the evolution of the retail concept is always a total revamp of the interior and exterior, consistent with the changing image and updated merchandise on offer. The space is modeled on ideas the store wanted to sell and the atmosphere it's striving to recreate. King's Road 430 maintains consistency and authenticity, with Vivienne Westwood playing the lead in innovative in-store communication that also impacts the way retail is done.

In continuing with this analysis, experiential storytelling becomes a central theme. While ensuring that Worlds End remains a London destination and a stand-alone line, with the opening of flagship stores the focus shifts to the story that the Vivienne Westwood brand wants to tell.

## 12.3   *Mapping the store: Corso Venezia 25*

We will analyze the Corso Venezia 25 store in detail on multiple levels: layout, interior design and displays. The first impression that customers get is a warm atmosphere, as if they are walking into a bedroom, intimate and welcoming. They immediately perceive the store's communicative expedient: iconography. The walls are a part of the story. (Fig. 4).

As in the *Let It Rock* boutique, framed prints, fabrics, and photographs are on sale, depicting the designer, iconic moments, company symbols and Westwood slogans. Additional props such as the Union Jack accentuate the company's British roots; various Orbs and references to the collections complete the accents in the decor. Other stimuli draw customers' attention, they are meant to feel comfortable, as if they were in their very own living room. The Victorian armchairs invite us to take a seat, and the rugs embossed with the company logo create an environment that almost feels like home.

*Figure* 4 – Framed prints, fabrics and embroidery, photographs and iconic images enrich the interior, making it warm and welcoming (courtesy of Vivienne Westwood).

Crossing through Area 1, customers do not immediately come in contact with the product. Instead they find a decompression zone behind the window. This is the crucial moment in their store visit: they can continue straight into the heart of the store or go downstairs to the men's department (Fig. 5).

*Figure* 5 – The floorplan of the store, highlighting areas based on customer traffic flow (courtesy of Vivienne Westwood).

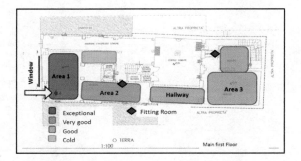

The area is considered an internal extension of the store window, exploited for visual merchandising with the placement of additional mannequins. In analyzing the traffic flow to pinpoint the zones of the store that get the most visitors, we can see that this area has the highest traffic. It's no coincidence that we find "grab and go" items here which can prompt impulse purchases or complete cross-selling: jewelry, perfumes and small leather goods. The racks near the entrance, on a rotating basis, display the top lines by Vivienne Westwood and Andreas Kronthaler for Vivienne Westwood, with powerful stylistic potential, as well as the Anglomania diffusion line.

The second line, with its lower positioning, eases the "entrance anxiety" customers may experience; if they see high-priced merchandise they may decide not to venture into the store. The aim is always to keep the two collections separate, to avoid any confusion. This means that if Vivienne Westwood is displayed in Areas 1 or 2, then Anglomania is placed in Area 3 and vice versa. Continuing through Area 2, near the cash desk, the product presentation is very carefully organized, utilizing drawer units resembling luxurious glass treasure chests, which also serve to protect merchandise (Fig. 6).

*Figure* 6 – To the right of the cash desk is a long, wide aisle with the entrance marked by mannequins, leaving room for both clothing hanging within reach of customers and items placed in display cases (courtesy of Vivienne Westwood).

The key transition point, both in terms of physical movement and in-store communication, is the aisle. Illuminated by natural lighting from an inner courtyard, the use of mannequins here borders on the theatrical, with an eye to exhibiting the full potential for wearability of Westwood pieces (which isn't entirely obvious when they are hanging on the rack). The effect is similar to an art gallery (Fig. 7).

Moving toward Area 3, we find a more private, almost reserved space. To avoid overwhelming customers, there are never too many pieces on display here, but easy access to the stockroom facilitates store personnel in replenishing the assortment. The coldest zone of the boutique is the men's floor, accessible via a stairway in Area 1 (Fig. 8).

To make customers aware of the men's collection and direct them to it, dedicated displays are positioned at the top of the stairs. This strategy enhances visibility and awareness, to compensate for the lower level of traffic. The display technique used here depends on the type of merchandise. While it's true that when items are hung on hangers, customers feel free to touch the garments, only mannequins allow them to appreciate the

*Figure* 7 – Mannequins emphasize the wearability of the clothing, offering ideas for purchase options (courtesy of Vivienne Westwood).

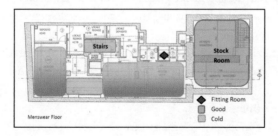

*Figure* 8 – The floorplan of the lower level of the store shows less customer traffic in the men's department, presented here (courtesy of Vivienne Westwood).

design of the high fashion pieces. Leather goods, instead, are presented on vertical displays (Fig. 9), which are higher than hat level in Area 3 (above 170 cm) (67 in). All four display levels can be found in the Corso Venezia boutique, beginning with ground level (from 20 to 60 cm off the floor) (8 to 24 in), then hand level (from 60 to 110 cm) (24 to 43 in), eye level (from 110 to 170 cm) (43 to 67 in) and again hat level.

*Figure* 9 – Displays are exploited at all levels, with the highest ones serving as focal points (courtesy of Vivienne Westwood).

Although retail theory associates the first two levels with greater profitability, since customers can interact more easily with the products, this store exploits the position of the wall as a focal point. In fact, since it can be seen from outside the store and inside Area 1, the wall creates a sense of depth. While the silent language of the interior design increases the propensity for impulse purchases, the décor complements and completes the sales environment.

Corso Venezia 25 primarily uses three contrasting materials: wooden floors, metal racks and displays, and glass. This creates a contrast with "tranquility pink" on the walls, combining materials from the past (wood) and the future (metal).

The only technological elements are the LED screens positioned behind the cash desk and on the men's floor featuring footage of the latest fashion show. This is part of the strategy to construct a multisensory in-store atmosphere, in this case stimulating the eye with the use of video in movement. As-Is store mapping, which offers a current snapshot of the store, also identifies other multisensory drivers. For instance, natural elements are placed on the cash desks such as vases of orchids, which create a balanced ecosystem and serve as a reminder of the designer's concern for the environment. The background music provides an accompaniment to the purchase experience without ever becoming overpowering. Finally, to entice the sense of smell, diffusers are used, scenting the air with the essence of Boudoir, an iconic Westwood perfume.

In general, Corso Venezia 25 aims to recreate and recount the Westwood story. This is reflected in the icons of the fashion house scattered throughout the store. The loyal customer can catch a glimpse of a number of nods to the heritage of the maison. The homey atmosphere harkens back to the original intention of establishing a gathering space, where customers feel at their ease, not oppressed by an obligation to make a purchase. The message that Dame Vivienne wants to send is that "nothing sells better than authenticity" and that "you can't be a designer without having ideas." This is why history and identity must be the cornerstones of the brand in all of its transpositions.

### 12.4  *Analyzing the new retail concept: Via Vincenzo Capelli 4*

November 30, 2015, marked the grand opening of the new Westwood concept store at Via Capelli 4, in the Porta Nuova zone of Milan. The strategic intent was to launch a new retail venue that reflected the international spirit of the continually expanding fashion house. So from the almost homey atmosphere at Corso Venezia 25, customers find a more modern, urban boutique with something approaching an industrial, minimalist style. This store isn't meant to be a boudoir, but an artist's workshop. Adding to a "work-in-progress" look is a picture leaning against the wall, not yet hung up, and screws that are visible in the wooden panels. However, while the old store told the Westwood story, here symbolism comes into play. Customers won't find any trace of Baroque-rock style; there are no Victorian armchairs or pictures of the designer. The minimal look of the interior design turns the focus on the products, which are accentuated by glass display cases and neon lights (Fig. 10).

Displays are almost entirely vertical, to offset the restricted floor space in the store. This has a negative impact on the direct customer-product relationship, as sales staff need to help clients reach higher shelves (Fig. 11). However, even if the store atmosphere may seem cold and lacking in strong associations with brand values, customers can look for signs that are hidden, but equally Westwood. For example, the fact that the décor is unfinished, destined to age with the store itself, can be considered Punk. All the wooden paneling on the walls is actually completely sustainable

*Figure* 10 – Glass display cases and neon lights accentuate the products in a modern and elegant setting in the new concept store (courtesy of Vivienne Westwood).

*Figure* 11 – Display fixtures made of cold materials are built on the vertical, with high shelves to fully exploit the sales space (courtesy of Vivienne Westwood).

*Figure* 12 – The unfinished décor highlights the net contrast with the modern materials (courtesy of Vivienne Westwood).

thanks to a partnership with Greenpeace, which guarantees that a tree is planted for each panel (Fig. 12). The theme of contrasting materials is reproposed, albeit in a futuristic vein. Customers find themselves in an environment that is rich with symbolism, and they have to make an effort to perceive enigmatic messages that are neither overt nor explicit. Seen in this light, in this case we can consider the store as the generator of a more intimate, profound and mature relationship with Westwood clientele.

The perceptive payoff here is undeniably different from Corso Venezia 25 in terms of layout, in-store atmosphere and displays. Since the connection is more introspective and subtle, without explanations from store personnel, loyal customers may get lost trying to codify the retail strategy. In fact, people who walk into the new concept store won't find any trace of the British essence of the brand, or the Punk origins of Westwood. Everything is left to the product, and the store becomes a simple container.

At the Corso Venezia boutique, customers are captivated by the storytelling that the interior design of the store nearly shouts out, but in the new format on Via Capelli they have to be seduced by the storytelling of the staff. This raises the question of whether or not Westwood clients are ready to interpret the hidden messages of the new concept store, quite a challenging proposition. After all, this is a fashion house with a unique history and a designer who is considered an icon in the fashion world. If clients fail to find any evidence of this history in the store, they may react by feeling a distance between themselves and this retail environment.

It's not a subjective question of affinity with a radically new retail format. Instead it's an attachment to the corporate identity which prompts customers to embark on an experience which, if positive, will culminate in a purchase. By nurturing visitors' emotional attachment to the brand, the company can shift the focus back onto the unique features of the physical store where what is actually being sold is a concept, conveyed through a multisensory, dynamic and authentic experience.

The Vivienne Westwood case inspires us to reflect on the importance of keeping innovative retail design consistent with brand values. Our analysis also highlights how the in-store experience can be influenced by the retail environment. The silent communication of a store enables customers to have a profound interaction with the brand. But if this is out of synch, the link with the clientele could be lost. Therefore, luxury companies must consider heritage as part of their interior design, as an invisible element that allows them to enrich and complete the in-store experience.

# 4  Visual merchandising and communication outside of the store

## 1  Interface design

The first point of application for the communication codes of visual merchandising is the exterior of the store, the mere presence of which transmits messages.

The constituent elements of external store design, when properly combined, add up to create a positive impression on the people passing by, making them pause, come closer, and then enter. And so begins their experience, as they embark on the perceptive pathway that leads them to interface with the very essence of the store.

From these very first moments, the design factors that activate the relationship with the store interact with the cognitive and emotional aspects of visitor perception. In light of this, our study of stores should focus on the symbolic elements that we all recognize at a collective level, our aim being to trigger mechanisms linked to sensorial and environmental memory.

Only a perfect blend of all the ingredients of exterior design can guarantee effective communication that represents and synthesizes the contents of the offering in an evocative way.

A message that conflicts with this formula tends to attract customers who are incapable of fully appreciating the offering. What's more, with no symbolic signals to entice them, the intended target won't be inspired to go into the store.

To put it simply, rather than exterior design, it would be more fitting to refer to *interface design*. "The interface is the filter, the thin membrane that is the point of contact between two different worlds... [The interface] organizes the perception, the vision, and determines the communicative context; [it] frames an experience."[1]

Product consumption is gradually becoming *visual consumption*. At the same time, the interfaces of this system, that is, moments of interaction, are shifting to more and more advanced and integrated thresholds. As a result of all this, companies increasingly seek to win positions of competitive advantage with respect to this filtered communication.

Here is a list of the design elements that form the basis of any intervention aimed at qualifying upgrading, and ultimately differentiating the store:

- the location, the position and the access points;
- the size, shape of the building and parking area;
- environmental features;
- materials;
- windows;
- awnings and ornamental overhangs;
- the threshold and the entrance doors;
- the atrium and entrance;
- the store sign; and
- lighting.

Below is a synopsis followed by an in-depth analysis of what has currently become the most critical areas to apply the principles of external visual communication: the store sign, the entrance and the windows.

We'll begin by pointing out that store designers can take part in assessing location options in terms of market potential, although as a rule they do not have a say in the final decision. Normally, this is simply an opportunity for the company to get an idea of how "in the know" they are about the commercial scene, and to consider their negative and positive impressions of a given location before making a final decision. Naturally, a meaningful and informed opinion is based on demographic and market research, along with information on the local ordinances that regulate the area.

As far as the retail space in question, store designers need to take into account vehicular access, the area surrounding the store, the entrance, the physical appearance, the parking area, lighting and signage. Retail areas

---

[1] Baule G. (2004), "Interfacce del consumo," in Bucchetti V. (ed), *Design della comunicazione ed esperienze di acquisto*, Franco Angeli, Milan, Italy p. 52.

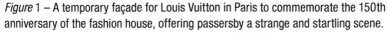

*Figure* 1 – A temporary façade for Louis Vuitton in Paris to commemorate the 150th anniversary of the fashion house, offering passersby a strange and startling scene.

can also come in different shapes and sizes, with unusual spaces often being more exciting for customers (Fig. 1).

Environmental features are also pertinent, such as topography, drainage, the conditions of the subsoil, zoning, utilities and environmental impact. A civil engineering firm can handle the technical factors, in collaboration with the store designer, to realize aesthetic objectives while complying with any relevant legal requirements.

In considering building materials, a combination of factors come into play, to include: cost, physical aspect, and availability, along with the local weather, compatibility with the host neighborhood, time and cost of delivery, and maintenance. Specifically, the choice of materials depends on the budget, as well as how much free rein the designer enjoys. How the materials are used, instead, depends on this person's creativity and ability to interpret and communicate the store concept (Figs. 2, 3a and 3b).

Awnings and decorative extensions, which can be made of a wide variety of materials, serve to protect customers and the products on display

*Figure* 2 – The external "dome" of New York's Apple Store – an icon of innovation and design.

from the weather (and direct sunlight). The name of the store might appear here, as a sort of store sign; in fact, often these store features are also purposed to guarantee a shared image to the entire retail network (Figs. 4 and 5).

Vestibules are used in areas that have severe weather conditions to protect visitors from wind, cold and rain. The flooring in this small room also collects dirt, water and snow, keeping the store interior clean. The lighting in the area surrounding a store impacts the store's image in a powerful way, satisfying various needs: safety, attractiveness, identification, decoration and unification. Ideally, store design should encompass lighting in a cohesive plan that is aesthetically pleasing to the eye.

*Figures* 3a and 3b – Louis Vuitton brings the Eiffel Tower to New York: the vinyl decal applied to this façade is a sensational reflection of the theme of the store windows.

*Figure* 4 – The overhang of Cool Britannia in Piccadilly Circus, London, makes this store "pop" in a high-density commercial area, creating the ideal stage for a spectacular entrance, complete with iconic and comical personalities.

*Figures* 5 – A simple awning gives a touch of refinement to the romantic window of the French concept-boutique Au Nom de la Rose, embellished by rose petals poetically scattered on the pavement.

As mentioned above, top priorities as far as the external attractiveness of the store, are the sign, the entrance and the windows, which we'll discuss in the following sections. These same communication tools are also present inside the store, at the access points to the different sectors, departments and shop in shops (where applicable), enticing the customer to enter in each individual portion of space.

Generally speaking, although it's not possible to formulate concrete rules for realizing commercial space, we can come up with clear, consistent guidelines that companies and designers should respect. First of all, building a commercial space begins not with architectural or design decisions, but instead with the choice of location (an urban setting, a city center, a suburb or on a main street, for example). Subsequent decisions include delineating the boundaries of the space, selecting the product offering, the target, the language of the market proposition and the store designer.

From this perspective, we can no longer consider the modern store as a space that springs up in a spontaneous way. Instead, a combination of competencies come into play: design, architecture, semiotics, marketing and social psychology. Leveraging on all these, we need to carefully examine the location, and meticulously analyze the façade, windows, areas of interaction between the street and the store – all this from an architectural, distributive and functional viewpoint.

To sum up, we have to explore in detail the "type" of image as it relates to the "type" of product offering and the customized architectural/graphic design propositions. Rigorous studies must also be conducted regarding the compositional connotations and the materials for the window dressing.

## 2    The store sign

The sign of the store and/or department is an essential component in the organization of the retail space, because it plays a key role in the communication of the store, indicating what the store offers, the quality of its products, and the customer segment it targets.

When designing a store sign, certain fundamentals need to be factored in, contingent on the urban configuration and the nearby retailers as well as the positioning of the store and the type of language it adopts to communicate with customers. Naturally, for stores in the city center especially, the architecture of the façade and the size of the street will influence the location and the dimensions of the store (Fig. 6).

For example, a rise in the number of store openings in the suburbs has led to the spread of gigantic signs that are visible from a distance. Perfect examples are petrol stations or fast food chains. To avoid interrupting the

*Figure* 6 – The sign for Mc Donald's on Broadway has a theatrical flair that blends in perfectly with the architectural style of the New York temples dedicated to musical theater.

recognizability of the architectural structure, the sign becomes an integral part of the whole, serving as a link between the graphics of the brand and the architectural system. It is up to the store designer to come up with the proper proportions for the sign, in relation to the size of the store façade. But more that the size of the sign, it's the value of the sign that sets the rules. The graphics, the size and the material it's made of are the marks of distinction; along with the corporate colors, symbols, and logos, they create a suggestive type of communication.

By combining all the signs the store uses in a coherent fashion, the store designer aims to symbolically represent both the offering and the commercial formula. This is what creates the force of attraction for the target of the store, establishing an initial point of visual contact and instilling the memory of the store in the minds of these customers.

Similarly, the store designer is expected to determine the proper number of logos inside the store (neither too few or too many), and decide where to place them.

The aim here is to shore up the positioning of the store and the brands it offers. For high-end stores, signs and logos are often very discreet in terms of size and number, to the point of nearly disappearing when the value and the reputation of the store is so strong as to render the sign unnecessary

*Figure* 7 – Reputation and a premium positioning explain why the sign for this High Tech store in Milan is almost invisible (not to mention the legal constraints that apply to the façades of historical buildings).

(Fig. 7). Less common are signs that are enlarged to the point of becoming unrecognizable and/or merging into the architectural features of the building itself (Fig. 8).

Diametrically opposed are stores that target the mass market, which typically make their logos and signs "shout out" by using loud, shiny materials and dazzling lighting effects.

Regardless of the positioning, when the logo is well known, the value of the sign diminishes to the point of disappearing altogether (Fig. 9).

*Figure* 8 – The sign of the first Eataly location stands out as a powerful visual element on this building in Turin.

*Figure* 9 – The iconic apple with a bite taken out says it all for Apple.

## 3    The façade and the entrance

The façade also represents a highly effective communication tool for consolidating the image of the store and conveying a message consistent with the commercial offering. When a store is housed in a building with a well-preserved façade, the image of a quality offering is far better than with a façade that is falling to pieces (Fig. 10).

In terms of design, the communicative potential of the façade makes it well worthwhile to explore every possible alternative to come up with innovative solutions as far as the design and the use of materials are concerned. But we must always be aware of possible restrictions that may apply, in particular with historical buildings (Fig. 11).

With regard to façades, there are three basic designs:

1. a façade underneath a portico or arcade;
2. a linear façade that runs parallel to the pavement; and
3. a corner façade.

*Figure* 10 – A seventeenth century building in perfect condition in the Alsatian village of Colmar provides a charming setting for a local biscuit shop; the façade is embellished with romantic decorations.

*Figure* 11 – The eye-catching design of this Renault dealership's façade on the Champs-Élysées in Paris provides the perfect framework for extemporary artistic and decorative installations.

A façade positioned underneath a portico or arcade typically leaves a wide space in front of the store, which allows passersby to look at the windows at their leisure (Fig. 12). Adopting this model, more than one store can be positioned in a circular layout, or in a more complex pattern with island windows or with concave or inclined glass panels.

A façade that runs parallel to the pavement is more linear and static. The monotony is broken up only by the entrance, which can be set back from the rest of the store while keeping all the architectural lines intact (Fig. 13).

The corner façade is similar to the linear model, but less monotonous, as it forms right angles with respect to the pavement, and may have asymmetric windows and entrances. Compared to the other options, here the traffic flow is more directly channeled toward the entrance, especially when there are deep recesses that allow passersby to slow down and stop, to window shop, without other pedestrians bumping into them (Fig. 14).

The sign generates awareness, sparks interest and spurs people to enter the store. The entrance, in turn, supports this moment of communication

*Figure* 12 – A façade beneath a portico.

*Figure* 13 – A façade running parallel to the pavement.

as it represents an actual filter, separating the urban space and the retail space. In other words, the entrance is the concrete materialization of the entire store experience. As such, it must serve as an invitation to enjoy the pleasure of a store visit, instilling confidence in customers that their purchase experience will be positive and worthwhile (Fig. 15).

*Figure* 14 – A corner façade.

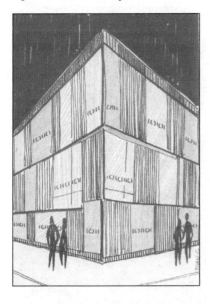

*Figure* 15 – The entrance to a small shop spills out into the street, giving passersby a taste of its scented and colorful blooming world.

So it comes as no surprise that the entrance is the symbolic element that has always captured the attention of store designers in their creative efforts. This is especially true for entrances to shopping centers, where the categorical imperative of visibility often necessitates monumental structures. All the choices that pertain to the entrance tie into aspects of design: whether the entrance is level with the pavement or there are steps leading up to it, how the entrance aligns with the flow of traffic, the width, the materials, the lighting, the possible obstacles nearby and how the entrance doors actually open (Fig. 16).

Once again, whatever the combination of choices the designer makes, the outcome must be consistent with the positioning of the store, and consequently with the exterior and interior design (Fig. 17). The entrance takes on special significance due to mechanical stimuli which trigger specific physiological and psychological responses (Fig. 18).

In relational terms, a closed door, which is often screened or tinted, can actually be a physical barrier that may even become a psychological one, making access particularly difficult for anyone who does not belong to the target in question. On the other hand, a store with an on-street façade with enormous automatic or manual doors that are transparent, wide open, practically not even there, underscores the in-

*Figure* 16 – A surprising pink elephant stands in the middle of the entrance, welcoming customers to the Gazzetta dello Sport store in Milan and never failing to attract attention among the crowds of passersby.

*Figure* 17 – "Free access to delight" is the enticing invitation to discover the Camomilla store in Milan.

*Figure* 18 – A contemporary art installation, part of Milan's Salone del Mobile, catches the eye, beyond the wide entrance to Sephora on Corso Vittorio Emanuele.

tention of targeting a mass market with an offering organized around a self-service format.

## 4    The window

The custom of displaying goods outside stores dates back to the very origins of trade, when the first merchants presented their wares out in the open. Even with the emergence of stores in fixed locations, the custom continues, with merchandise hanging on store fronts or in baskets outside for maximum visibility (Fig. 19).

For some time now, store windows have represented one of the symbols of societies based on free trade and unrestricted business initiative, but they also characterize urban decor and add to the aesthetics of city streets and squares. Seeing as the window is a space for proxemic relationships between the store and the public, in a matter of seconds it must capture the attention of the often-distracted passersby, piquing their curiosity and acting as an informational link between them and the store. All this while prompting people to actually go inside. In other words, the store window

*Figure* 19 – An eye-catching stand filled with soap cakes, or better still, soap in the shape of cakes, to entice passersby to stop in this natural cosmetics shop in France.

is much more than simply a physical space where a portion of the store's offering is put on display (Fig. 20).

Even more effectively than the sign and the entrance, the store window can accentuate the store's image by identifying its style and personality. In fact, the window gives an immediate overview of the store's format and the target, clarifying the needs it can satisfy, through what retail offering and which goods and services (Fig. 21).

In the setting that the window projects with its display, the merchandise plays a supporting role in the bigger story of the store itself. This provides the key that enables customers to discover and interpret the world of the store (Fig. 22). Because it serves to attract customers, the window should be designed and managed as a means of communication, not simply a sales tool (Fig. 23).

Once again interpreting exterior design as interface design, the perception and consumption of merchandise have evolved over the past century, and with them the forms and techniques for communication and exposition. The focus has gradually shifted to the level of transparency, ultimately wearing down the barrier of the interface, and creating instead

*Figure* 20 – Little boars curiously watch the people passing by, except for one who runs away in the opposite direction – asymmetry gives this window of a French butcher shop greater appeal.

*Figure* 21 – Swarovski windows seductively communicate a focus on the world of crystal jewelry and fashion accessories.

*Figure* 22 – The foodstuffs displayed in the window of Carluccio's delicatessen in London reflects this store's Mediterranean origins, as well as the quality and freshness of Mediterranean cuisine.

*Figure* 23 – The eye-catching and alluring scene in one of many theatrical Moschino store windows, with a sharp sense of characteristic self-deprecating humor.

a continuum between the external and internal store. This clearly underscores the desire for continuity, for *uninterrupted flow*.

Better materials, codified display techniques developed by visual merchandising and the evolution of sciences that study human behavior: all this can be leveraged to design and arrange display spaces that are aesthetically pleasing while at the same time effectively communicating with the customer, at a relatively low cost. Often, however, stores set up windows that are aesthetically beautiful, but have "nothing commercial to say" to prospective customers. A window can't simply be attractive or even striking, it has to generate traffic and enhance store image. So its beauty basically derives from realizing its commercial purpose in a way that is appealing to the target in question.

## 4.1   *Functions of the window*

Up to this point we've repeatedly underscored the extreme functionality that characterizes the window as a "tool". This characteristic is what enables us to transform it into a highly flexible and accessible medium for establishing a continuous dialogue with the street and the people passing

*Figures* 24 – These dynamic Benetton
shop windows reinforce the presence of
the store with images in movement.

by. In more concrete terms, the main objectives of a store window all tie
into to its basic, essential purpose, that is, to communicate, as detailed
below.

- *Communicate the presence of the store.* More often than we might imagine,
  people pay no attention at all to the stores on the street as they walk by.
  As a result, many store fronts are completely invisible to them in a continuum of architecture. So the window, first and foremost, must draw the
  attention of people who aren't familiar with the store, to open a dialogue
  that creates a point of reference for a future visit (Fig. 24).
- *Communicate the store identity* by reinforcing store positioning with a
  clear, distinctive image (Fig. 25).
- *Communicate the variety of the product assortment,* proposing/alternating
  various product categories and/or lines to accent the depth of the offering (Fig. 26); shoring up the links between the most characteristic products and the rest of the assortment, to trigger a domino effect;
  spotlighting the launch of new products or lines.
- *Communicate special initiatives,* such as promotions and events, to pique
  the curiosity of passersby, prompting them to go beyond the initial contact by offering an activity that adds to the pure product assortment;
  also to further reinforce store identity (Fig. 27).

*Figure* 25 – Santa Monica, California. An artistic display of the epitome of an iconic American product: Converse.

*Figure* 26 – An old but still highly innovative and appealing display with intense visual impact for a book launch in a Milanese bookshop.

*Figure 27* – An ear symbolizes the ability and the desire to listen to clients, emphatically representing the identity of a bank in this anniversary window display.

## 4.2    The open window

As we know, the store window is interpreted as the threshold of an interface, gradually disappearing in the communication that seamlessly flows between the space occupied by the public and the store/brand. More and more the latter is spilling out of the closed confines of the traditional store. An open window is one with no backdrop, showing the store, its interior atmosphere, the overall formula, and the mix of the offering and the display formats, beyond the individual items on offer. This window offers an imperceptible interface, with no visible frame or breaking point, where the interior and exterior blend continuously (Fig. 28).

Beyond a doubt the best option when proposing an offering organized by lifestyle and occasions for use, an open window also encourages contact with the store staff, who are an integral part of the store itself (Fig. 29).

Many small shops also prefer open windows, which allow people to see inside, creating the illusion of a larger sales space. Naturally, the window and the interior space must combine to create a unified display. This calls for carefully organizing the sales area, changing it up frequently, along with the product displays. Particularly critical here are the zones near the entrance which are the most visible from the outside. As people pass by, they can look around in several directions, so their attention may be drawn away from the products on display. To counteract this disadvantage, the key is to group together the items in a way that augments their visual

*Figure* 28 – An open window in the back of the bakery in a Iper hypermarket, in the residential neighborhood of Portello in Milan, reinforcing the message of fresh, quality service, perfect for daily purchases.

*Figure* 29 – The groundbreaking and by now famous open windows of Che Banca! underscore the innovative positioning of this credit institution.

*Figure* 30 – Two different internal displays for the same Swatch shop on Corso Vittorio Emanuele in Milan, very visible from the outside thanks to open windows.

weight, and in turn, the overall visibility of the window with respect to the surrounding space (Fig. 30).

In any case, eliminating the backdrop does not make the window disappear. Instead, it remains an essential space for product display and store communication. Although it might appear excessively haphazard, often the outcome is captivating (Fig. 31).

## 4.3    *The closed window*

A window that is closed off with a backdrop spotlights the product and its qualitative and stylistic content. This type of window also provides a stage for creating a theatrical product presentation, which can potentially be both attractive and distinctive (Fig. 32).

Passersby can immediately note the items that most resonate with their personal taste; this in turn intensifies their purchase motivations. What's more, a closed window lets people freely contemplate the merchandise on display, without feeling observed. In any case, compared to an open window, this option is limited in its ability to attract customers. The tendency here

*Figure* 31 – There is no communicative filter between the inside and the outside of this Scottish pastry shop in Inverness, in the Southern Highlands.

*Figure* 32 – A band and a moving ostrich in the animated window of the Printemps department store in Paris provide the choreography for Louis Vuitton suitcases, iconic products of the fashion house.

*Figure* 33 – Impactful communication
in a Lush window, where the offering
is replaced by traditional language with
an irreverent and suggestive tone, an
amusing feature of the chain's distinctive
style.

is to sell specific products (only the ones on display) instead of prompting passersby to enter the store and look at the entire assortment. In addition, since all the visual concentration is attuned to the products in the window, it is critical to avoid making any errors when setting up the display.

To this end, admittedly it is no simple task to make a few products communicate the commercial offering of a store in a clear, immediate, and exhaustive way. But by the same token, using too many products, in an attempt to exploit all the potential of the window as a sales tool, intensifies the feeling that the window actually contains the entire product assortment. This would dissuade people from entering who don't find what they're looking for in the window. So once again, the priority is not the quantity of products displayed in the window, but the quality of its overall communication (Fig. 33).

In light of this, a very effective approach to window dressing is to find a theme that echoes the same ones used inside the store. This makes the window quick and easy for passersby to read, and contributes at the same time to creating an image that is coordinated with the in-store displays (Fig. 34).

## 4.4    *The semi-closed window*

This option is a viable compromise: it has a backdrop, but one that doesn't completely obstruct the view of the inside of the store. A growing number of retailers are resorting to this hybrid solution, seeing as it offers the

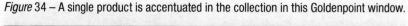

*Figure* 34 – A single product is accentuated in the collection in this Goldenpoint window.

chance to communicate via the window and at the same time the store itself. Clearly, the impact of a semi-closed window is highly contingent on the product displays inside the store. In any case, the more theatrical displays do not work well here, since they would create a confused and cluttered view of the store interior (Fig. 35).

## 4.5   *Managing the space*

The store window must be coordinated with the other communication tools and aligned with the image of the store. To do so, the window should reflect the same elements that go into the design of interior visual merchandising. These include:

1. the product assortment, grouped by function;
2. organization of the display space;
3. an organic product display;
4. the perceptive impact; and
5. the backdrop.

*Figure* 35 – A very effective Prada window, simple and easy to read, even though it presents an imposing theatrical display.

*Grouping the product assortment by function*

Key parameters in grouping together products in a store window are the needs of the target customers and their purchase processes, which perfectly align with what they will find inside the store. The first point to consider in designing the window display is the specific target; the aim here is to use the same linguistic codes, choosing the most appropriate channels of communication and subsequently verifying the effects of those choices. Following this approach, a multi-specialist store such as a department store can present a different retail section in each window, according to a shop-in-shop rationale. On the other end of the spectrum, a specialized store can differentiate windows by brand, style, end use or fashion trends, while respecting the same criteria for grouping products inside the store.

From a relational standpoint, differentiating windows is a way to attract different customer segments, while giving a quick, clear preview of what they'll find inside, and providing the key to reading the assortment even before entering the store. This means that the syntax of the displays, and the layout in general, need to arranged around one central theme. Products must be chosen that respect given criteria, to create a scenario that enhances the store's offering and to give the overall composition the clear functions of spatial organization necessary to make the logical structure emerge.

Various criteria can be applied to realize attractive displays which harmonize commercial needs and aesthetic aspects. Below is a list of some examples.

- The *commercial window*, based on product categories, shows one of the sectors covered by the store's offering, with a number of items on display which give a substantial idea of the product assortment (Fig. 36). There are various ways to classify products, such as by brand, category, theme, color, use etc. This type of window does not offer a powerful visual impact, since decorative elements are minimal, if not altogether absent.
- The *allegorical window* takes inspiration from a stage set, with a backdrop and lighting that create a theatrical atmosphere centered on a specific theme; here there are far more decorative elements than actual products (Fig 37). The window dressing can become even more enthralling by adding background music that is appropriate to the theme.
- The *advertising* or *brand window* is used to display a segment of the range of articles produced by a company. Normally the context brings to mind the current ad campaign by using posters and/or objects that underscore the product features, or reflect the external communication (Fig. 38).

*Figure* 36 – A shop window centering on the debut of a collection, organized by brand, in a Solaris store.

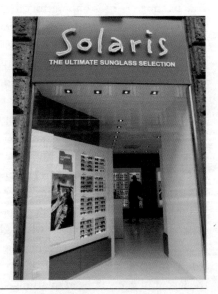

*Figure* 37 – An allegorical window in the Max Mara shop in Corso Vittorio Emanuele in Milan, featuring a display with theatrical flair.

*Figure* 38 – A mono-brand window at the FBL store in Via Torino, Milan.

- A *single-product window* can support a new product launch, consolidate the leadership of a best-seller or spotlight an item whose aesthetic features merit a solo exhibit (Fig. 39). There is more empty space than display fixtures here, so the support structures used for the merchandise must be refined and elegant (bust forms, mannequins, fixtures etc.). The space between the product, the accents and the window must be balanced.
- The *educational window* shores up specific informational campaigns, reminding passersby of the communicational message, even people who don't intend to enter the store (Fig. 40).

*Organizing the display space*

An essential aspect of the window is the layout, which should be designed keeping in mind the communication objectives that the store intends to achieve. In this case too planning is needed to synch the displays with the store's calendar of promotions. The window layout must respect the basic rules of visual composition: balance, proportion, rhythm and emphasis (Fig. 41).

The tool required here is a blueprint drawing up the layout design. This makes it possible to evaluate and plan the necessary materials and fix-

*Figure* 39 – An exceptionally expressive mass-market, mono-brand window.

*Figure* 40 – An informational window at a Salmoiraghi & Viganò store.

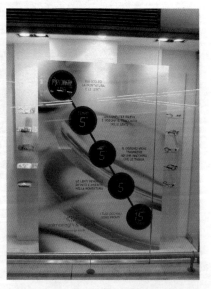

*Figure* 41 – Balance, rhythm and emphasis in the window display of this New York Nike store.

tures, and to verify that they are appropriate and effective in conveying the store's message. The products to be used in the window display also need to be collected, to minimize setup time between displays.

*An organic product display*

Consistency is the key to organizing and presenting the goods in the window, and is equally essential in terms of the display criteria. All this must be in synch with the expectations of target customers, their line of reasoning and their methods for reading the display.

This means that the window must be conceptualized as a geometric space with a focal point where customers will concentrate most of their attention. This area, right in the center of the window, is about one and a half meters (four feet) from the ground and has a visual diameter of around one meter (three feet). This point will shift slightly to the right for people approaching from the left, and vice versa. As a rule, when reading a window, the eye starts from the focal point and typically follows a counter-clockwise pattern (Fig. 42).

*Figure* 42 – Ideally, the store window is divided into sections, each with more or less impact on the public, indicated with a different percentage here; the center of the window is the focal point.

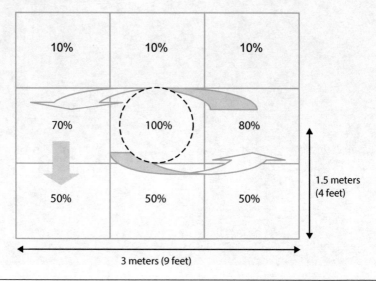

Given the greater visibility, the focal point should be reserved for the most important items or eye-catching decorations, which prompt passersby to look over the display as a whole. What's more, it's a good idea to create group compositions in this single point, and accentuate them with empty space all around. As we've mentioned before, this allows observers to rest their eyes, giving them more time to properly perceive the intended message (Fig. 43).

Likewise, the display fixtures in the window serve not only to support the products but also to communicate the image of the store. This explains why they should be similar to the in-store fixtures: functional, modular, flexible and adaptable to various types of merchandise.

In recent years, various methods have been developed to make store windows interactive. For example, window displays are transformed into theatrical productions with live models who pose as mannequins; heat sensors are positioned on the glass which activate lights or props; fragrance dispensers are built into displays (Fig. 44); small mechanisms play music or broadcast advertising messages (whispering windows). Last but certainly not least, digital technology is progressively transforming the store win-

*Figure* 43 – According to the template for reading a store window, products can be placed in a visual triangle, surrounded by plenty of empty space.

*Figure* 44 – The dispenser in this window releases a fragrance in the air to launch the new perfume by Marc Jacobs.

dow into a bi-directional medium with the introduction of touch screens. As we saw in Chapter 2, this technology enables customers to interact with the merchandise on display, allowing them to mix and match products to suit their personal needs, or to consult virtual product catalogues.

## The perceptive impact

A common window dressing mistake is to place too many items in a display. In general, a display should create a certain rhythm, alternating empty space with filled space in a harmonious fashion based on reflection and study, rejecting the temptation to fill up all the available space and every open surface in an indiscriminate and identical way. Simplicity and immediacy are the prerequisites that form the basis for all visual communication; they should always apply to every type of window to send clear, effective messages, and to avoid presenting a fragmented or disjointed series of products.

With few exceptions (Fig. 45), when too many articles are on display, this tends to downgrade the merchandise and convey an image of a mass

*Figure* 45 – Massification of the Fauchon window in Paris in no way tarnishes the store's image, instead it very adroitly enhances it.

market store with a low level of service. In addition, crowding merchandise translates into low visibility of the single items on display, and often leads to overlapping items that do not make up a unified offering (Fig. 46).

There are no hard and fast rules regarding the number of products that should be put in a given display area. But experience shows that to guarantee the maximum communicative effectiveness, products should only occupy 25% of the display space, leaving another 25% free to allow the eye to rest. The remaining 50% is for display fixtures and decorative accents.

Another guideline can be price. Every display area has a specific value, consisting of the cost of lighting, installation, unused space and so forth. So the rule of thumb would be that the cost of a given space must be covered by the profit generated by the sale of the products placed there. Following this line of reasoning, a super-luxury window can contain at most two products, along with advertising materials that enhance the value of the brand. An elegant window may display more items with less advertising material. In contrast, the window of a store that sells a range of bargain merchandise with low per-unit profit focuses entirely on assortment and price range. In this case, more products and product combinations should be displayed, seeing that high sales volumes are the only way to make the display space pay off.

*Figure* 46 – Close-up of the window of a traditional Milanese drug store, where product massification not only degrades the image, but limits the visibility as well.

Regardless of the number and variety of products, the window must present a display that ensures consistency with the overall store image, by exploiting the effective graphic and psychological impact that derives from the arrangement of the objects in question and the organization of the space around them. Naturally the purpose of the window is not exclusively to offer aesthetic elegance. In fact, excessive formality and refinement may actually intimidate some customers and drive them away. The key, therefore, is blending the requirements of commercial promotion, with displays providing a complete picture of the offering on one hand, and image and elegance on the other.

*The backdrop*

In a closed or semi-closed window, the backdrop takes on particular significance from a visual standpoint. Specifically, we can identify the following types of backdrop:

- *realistic*, where we recreate the scene and the proportions of a highly recognizable setting as accurately as possible; although this backdrop can be riveting, it may actually draw attention away from the products themselves (Fig. 47);

*Figure* 47 – Realistic backdrop for Brunello Abbigliamento.

- *environmental*, a type of realistic background where the products are part of the set (Fig. 48);
- *semi-realistic*, when only a few elements are presented (for reasons of budget or creativity), leaving the rest of the scene to be filled in by the imagination of the observer (Fig. 49);
- *fantasy*, with an accent on creativity and freedom of expression, with no restrictions (except budget) (Fig. 50); and
- *abstract*, consisting mainly of a composition of lines, forms, and panels (Fig. 51).

Whichever one we choose, as with displays themselves, the backdrop must use a language that is consistent in every way with the store's identity and commercial offering.

## 4.6    *Lighting*

To set up an impactful window, we need to plan the lighting, which should make the window visible from a distance of at least eight meters (24 feet), and render the message legible from two meters (six feet). Poor lighting

*Figure* 48 – Environmental backdrop for Max&Co.

*Figure* 49 – Semi-realistic backdrop for Camomilla.

*Figure* 50 – Fantasy backdrop for HSBC.

*Figure* 51 – Abstract backdrop
for La Rinascente in Milan.

*Figure* 52 – A good lighting project makes this hair stylist's window especially enticing, almost magic.

not only obscures the view of the products, it also discourages people from stopping, and creates a sense of neglect and carelessness that reflects on the image of the entire store.

Lighting can become a decorative element that captures the attention of passersby, piques their interest and spotlights the items on display, making them desirable in the eyes of potential customers. The ideal illumination is not always monochromatic; it can vary in intensity and color, depending on the display, the size of the window and the theme in question (Fig. 52).

Generally, planning the lighting for a window is useful for a number of reasons. Sharps contrasts can be produced between shadow and light, or colored lights are also viable options; to create well-defined bands of illumination, various types of light sources can be used. Lastly, the positioning of projectors and lighting devices should be carefully considered so as to satisfy specific needs.

The same is true for the effects that the creative use of directional lighting can produce. Here are three different techniques for the creative use of directional lighting.

- *Vertical from above* adds a dramatic touch to the display without creating shadows. In this case the light beam can either be concentrated in a narrow shaft to more effectively spotlight a specific space, or it can be enlarged to illuminate a wider area.
- *Horizontal from the front* provides better lighting for the observer's entire field of vision, avoiding the undesirable effect of flattening out the display.
- *Horizontal from the sides* reduces the distortions that can emerge from frontal lighting by skillfully exploiting the play of light and shadow; here blinds and shades help shield the eye from direct light.

As a rule, lights should be very bright outside and intense inside the window. Projectors are the best devices to use, as they can easily be combined with spotlights to produce more dynamic effects. For clothing stores, the overall lighting must be designed to avoid altering or distorting the colors and shades of the items on display; if a garment turns out to be a different color than the way it appeared in the window, customers may end up disappointed and dissatisfied. Halogen dichroic light bulbs are recommended, which create atmosphere and draw the eye to the products specifically and to the window in general.

## 4.7    Planning

What clearly emerges from our discussion above is that before providing the input for dressing a window, the people responsible need to be given all the fundamental components of the store's retailing approach. Simply knowing the principles and tools for visual communication is not enough. Visual merchandisers need to fully embrace the positioning strategies of the store in order to communicate them to the market in a clear and concise manner.

In addition, as we have often reiterated, the window needs to be planned and coordinated with points of movement and communication in the store (focal points, display points etc.), and with promotional initiatives as well. The message of all these communicational tools must be unequivocal and consistent. In other words, the window must reflect a clear communication idea, one which is studied, planned and tested (if possible) down to the smallest detail. The window should never be the outcome of random attempts to put together a display, which may be dictated more often than not simply by the need to move certain products.

*Figure* 53 – Rarely does the exception
to the rule produce a good result:
let the observer be the judge.

The conclusion we can draw, at this point, is that planning and organizing the window display is critical for minimizing the time it takes for setup and identifying and dealing with problems before they arise. This is why we need to draw up a general "window plan", coordinated with the sales calendar. Window displays should be renewed at regular intervals, depending on the retailing approach and the specific needs of the individual store. In any case, the recommended schedule ranges from every fifteen days to every week, depending on the traffic flow.

### 4.8   *Check list for an effective window*

An impactful window is the outcome of an expert mediation between commercial and aesthetic needs, respecting certain basic conditions that represent prerequisites for arranging and managing a space for communicating with the public (Fig. 53).

Naturally, the same taxonomy of expressive parameters can be applied to the internal and external display, but this should be done in the design stage, as well as during the ex post assessment, following this checklist:

1. visibility;
2. consistency;
3. simplicity;
4. originality;
5. variety; and
6. keep it clean!

1. *Visibility* is ensured when the display is clear and not overly cluttered with products; it's difficult to understand the message of a display when it's jumbled and overloaded. The rule is keep it light; build around a single theme (or two at most, if each one is clearly distinct); capture the customer by generating interest and desire. The only exception here is the discount store, when the message of a bargain jibes with the atmosphere of a market or a bazaar, where merchandise is haphazard, instead of being displayed in a clear and orderly way.

2. *Consistency* is created by grouping together items with similar (or at least convergent) characteristics as far as product use, that is, goods that satisfy the same needs. An example is a window display arranged by occasions of use, which is very powerful way to prompt combination purchases, and represents an easy criterion to follow.

3. *Simplicity* is another key aspect. The more a window emphasizes the product assortment, the clearer it is. This means we need to minimize the decorative elements that aren't essential to clarifying the meaning underpinning the visual communication. Superficial elements only load down the presentation, complicating the process of transmitting the message we want the public to receive. That said, we can't deny the importance of decorations, which are a good way to make a display dynamic and lively; the risk that we need to avoid is misusing them. Likewise, display fixtures should be limited, and easy to move, clean and modify, in light of the need to continually refresh the window. Specifically, the best materials to use for window displays are wood, connoted with nature and tradition, and aluminum, which conveys innovation and modern life.

4. *Originality* in a window manifests in differentiation, leveraging new products or communication themes, and/or display concepts, as well as spatial organization, decorative elements, display supports and color combinations. But originality shouldn't be an end to itself, a value to realize at all costs. Taken to this extreme, in fact, originality risks becoming eccen-

tricity, which on one hand can attract, but on the other can *dis*tract from the commercial message, or even elicit a sense of repulsion, driving people away from, not into, the store.

5. *Variety*, referring to how often the window display is renewed, is undoubtedly a relevant aspect of effectiveness. A window that never changes can't attract the attention of people who pass the store, since they become used to seeing it every time they walk by. Clearly, variety does not depend on products alone: we can also change a window with new arrangements or color combinations (tied into the seasons, for example), or decorations reflecting a plethora of themes.

6. *Keep the window clean*, not simply for the sake of aesthetics or hygiene. Instead this is a fundamental building block in constructing the store's image. Cleanliness is an index of clarity and innovation in products, continually in motion due to the changing demands of customers; cleanliness ultimately becomes an indirect sign of the store's success.

# 5    The layout: physical mobility
     to informational mobility

## 1    A theatrical production

A store is often compared to the theater, which it resembles in many ways. From the moment visitors step inside, the space unfolds before their eyes into two distinct parts: one for the audience (that is, for observation) and the other for the actors (for representation). No design project can neglect to incorporate this split nature of the store, with the backstage, the stage itself and the seating area. The first two belong to the retailer/actor, the third to the customer/spectator. On the stage itself, the retailer plays a part following a clearly codified rite that is at once linguistic, gestural, expressive and spatial. Likewise the customer takes part in the show too, following a more or less codified pattern. The selling ritual takes very little time, and almost without exception, everything happens with the "spectators" standing and "spectacle" playing out from a vertical perspective, at eye level.

The space in a store is accessible space, or better still, it possesses intrinsic accessibility: a space to be accessed. Put another way, the store becomes a place where architecture and design converge. The focus of the first is the study of horizontal space (movement, interpersonal relationships), while design develops along vertical lines (the scene, the product presentation). Interior design serves to create containers, lighting and all the other elements that stores need to arrange the offering, while visual design deals with how this offering is visualized, that is, the display.

This combination of elements makes store design, like stage design, extremely complex, with the backdrops, the scenery and the curtain – the entire project based on the principles of seduction. The preferential perceptive relationship lies in visibility, and the project is founded on the eloquence of the visual language, inevitably and continually upending the concept of "display" with an eye to attracting customers (Fig. 1).

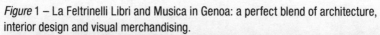

*Figure* 1 – La Feltrinelli Libri and Musica in Genoa: a perfect blend of architecture, interior design and visual merchandising.

## 2    The customer's perceptive pathway through the store

The overarching aims of any product offering are profitability and differentiation. Keeping this in mind, the necessary starting point for planning in-store visual merchandising activities is an assessment of both the real needs of the customers (which means analyzing how they engage in purchase activities) and the criteria they use when making purchase decisions. The aim is to help customers as much as possible while they weigh their options and select which products to buy.

As we know, the nexus of the customer-product-space relationship is the involvement of customers in that relationship. This is what we need to know to understand the ways in which the environment shapes purchase behaviors. In other words, how customers choose to participate in the relationship determines the degree of environmental activation, their receptiveness to environmental stimuli and, consequently, their behavioral responses.

Customer involvement, as we have often reiterated, can be rational or emotional. In the latter case, people shop for the sake of shopping; visiting a store is a way to fulfill personal needs such as self-gratification, pleasure, and enjoyment that comes from the in-store experience. So the store's necessary prerogative is to satisfy a variety of customer demands, not just the need to buy. This is why *open environments* have emerged where people have myriad purchase alternatives, and move in complete autonomy, without any outside interference or control. On the other end of the spectrum is purely rational customer involvement, when the sole purpose of a store visit is to buy products, maximizing economic benefits while minimizing costs (both monetary and non-monetary). In this case, as soon as customers step inside the store they want to know exactly where to find the items on their list, and to do so quickly without having to face too many setbacks along the way (Fig. 2).

They want to take their time to consider their options, handling products freely, and when need be, gathering information that helps them make the best choice, either on their own and/or while they're waiting for assistance from sales staff. Clearly the better equipped the store is to satisfy these needs, the bigger the boost to business volume. In other words, when customers understand quickly and clearly what the store offers (where, how

*Figure* 2 – To guide customers while they visit, Eataly often uses visual communication that's not just useful, it's fun.

and how much) without having to contend with any other structural obstacles that deter them from finalizing their purchase: this is when "the product speaks for itself." So everything depends on product appeal, which explains why here the preference goes to *closed environments*, where customer behavior is almost completely shaped and controlled by external levers.

Summing up, then, in view of the different levels of customer involvement, different approaches need to be adopted as far as the relationship between customers and space, to arrive at the relationship between customers and products: from accessing the space, to viewing it, to weighing the alternatives, to making a purchase. Everything must be strategically set up so that products can play their role to their full potential.

This being the case, in-store visual merchandising activities take inspiration from the organizational structure of the offering, i.e. the classification of the merchandise, which is subsequently reflected in the product layout. This constitutes the format for the visual presentation of the product assortment, the synthesis of the contents of the product offering and how it responds to customers' purchase motivations. Put another way, how the offering is organized represents how customers are meant to perceive it, how they interact with the set of products on offer. All visual merchandising tools serve to support the objective that results in this initial merchandise categorization.

As discussed in Chapter 3, traditionally the first sphere of action for visual merchandising encompasses the following:

- *layout of store fixtures*, i.e. the logical organization of sales space, as well as what display fixtures are used and how they are arranged; all this impacts the way customers move through the store;
- *layout of merchandise*, i.e. the rationale behind the way product families are grouped together; the aim here is to trigger possible associations among items to purchase;
- *the display*, i.e. the criteria for arranging products in the different sectors of sales area to maximize visibility and comparability; and
- *space allocation of individual products*, i.e. methods for optimizing the yield of linear display based in part on the space elasticity of each item.

Sequentially speaking, clearly decisions on how to arrange products according to sales capacity, like choices on how often to restock shelves, dictate decisions on how to exploit display capacity, as far as allocating quantity and quality of available space.

Only after these questions are answered, does visual merchandising step in. Working with the space dedicated to individual product groupings, the specific goal is to motivate customers to visit the entire store, drawing attention to the less visible areas too. To do so, the same tools are used inside the store as outside, adapted to the specificities of the individual sectors: the sign (*focal point*), the entrance and the internal window (*display point*).

Lastly, we mustn't forget all the Point of Purchase (PoP) communication. This involves designing and managing material that supports displays and sales, provided by producers to stake out space that is high-visibility, recognizable and exclusive to the product and/or brand that is being spotlighted in the store.

This chapter will detail various options for store layout. In Chapters 6 and 7 we will analyze the other levers for in-store visual merchandising.


## 3    Functions of the layout

The top priority of the layout is to put the highest possible number of products in the hands of the highest possible number of customers. Based on this premise, the layout serves a series of functions with the scope of optimizing profitability of the retail space without neglecting customer needs:

- to facilitate overall flow and circulation, rationalizing pathways through the store to ensure that all displays enjoy the same degree of visibility;
- to make the best possible use of sales space and display fixtures to present the entire offering, encouraging customers to visit the whole store;
- to promote planned purchases and spur impulse purchases;
- to optimize the mix of sales and margins, marking out in-store routes so as to achieve equal levels of productivity;
- to expedite access to/traffic flow in promotional areas;
- to reserve as much space as possible for customers, not only for sales;
- to correctly balance the spaces dedicated to customers, responding not only to various opportunities to socialize, but also moments for privacy;
- to support the work of the sales staff;
- to simplify activities involving replenishment, control, reorders and promotions; and
- to limit the costs of handling merchandise, managing displays and serving customers.

In other words, the store must guarantee a high level of structural flexibility, which simplifies any interventions that are needed to improve the effectiveness and efficiency of commercial activities, such as inserting new products or offering new promotions.

A decisive factor in store design is the sales floor plan, or the configuration of available retail space. Choosing the proper plan is ultimately about guaranteeing the maximum permeability without creating any hidden or hard-to-reach areas. This means that the priority in designing the floor plan is to avoid any recesses or blind spots, whenever possible. The retail space should expand in width rather than depth, to immediately accentuate the potential of the offering at the entrance of the store.

Likewise, identifying the access point on the floor plan of large retail spaces is an equally critical decision, because the entrance clearly marks the beginning of the path through the store. From here, as recent studies have shown, customers tend to move toward the center of the sales space, working their way around counter-clockwise. To favor this natural flow, it's best to place the entry point to the right of the structure, to make it easier for the customers to move around and to minimize the time they spend in cold zones where traffic is minimal.

Actually, the access point is what divides the store between hot and cold zones. The first are all the areas that extend from the entrance along the natural path that customers follow, including the main access route, the transition points in front of display counters, and the entry points to various sectors. In other words, hot zones are where the traffic flow is most intense, regardless of the products located there, which means that these spaces can be exploited to display the items that retailers want to move. Cold zones, instead, lie far away from the main flow of traffic. These areas are ideal for displaying strong sellers, that is, items that represent planned purchases, or have a high turnover rate, or powerful promotional impact. The position and size of relative displays depends primarily on the type of layout used in the store.

In other words, the store layout must be structured to allow customers to access every area, eliminating obstacles or bottlenecks. At the same time, profitability is a must for each and every square meter/foot of space, whether it is used to display products or to left open for customer access. In fact, the space in the store is not homogeneous in value or weight in relation to turnover. This means that an equilibrium must be created between areas where people enter the store, where they browse, wait, or transit, and their expectations with regard to the spaces actually earmarked for displaying the product assortment. Theme-based areas can also be set up along the pathways through the store, to slow customers down and increase the likelihood that they will make add-on purchases. Very briefly, the layout has to enable the customer to access the store's offering visually, physically, psychologically and intellectually. This makes it easier to manage displays and allocate space, activities that build on prior choices.

### 3.1  *Crowding*

Customers never want to find themselves in the middle of a crowded store. When a space shrinks to an extreme because too many people are crowded into it: this sensation would clearly make any customer uncomfortable, in turn generating anxiety and frustration, ultimately compromising the pleasure of the store experience, even before making a purchase. People's reaction to a crowded space is immediate: more than anything they want to resolve that feeling of discomfort, to leave the store and perhaps come back another time. Obviously, whether or not they actually return depends a great deal on how loyal they are to the store.

Even when customers decide to brave the crowds and go into a busy store anyway to make a purchase, they'll only stay as long as absolutely necessary, and they'll only buy what they actually need, without detouring to any other areas of the store. What's more, they won't interact with sales staff to ask for additional information on other related products they might want to combine with their purchase.

The result at this point is obvious: less time in the store and fewer purchases, due in part to less interaction with store personnel. But what counts even more is that customers will have a strong feeling of dissatisfaction about the entire store visit. As numerous studies have demonstrated, crowding in a store is the primary cause of stress, along with waiting in line.

Choosing the right layout requires weighing the potential impact on customer flow, and the possible risk of crowding that may result. But in some cases this is not enough. At this point a distinction must be drawn between density and crowding: the first is a physical condition defined by spatial parameters; the second is a psychological experience marked by a feeling of anxiety. Put another way, density depends on the size of the area in question and the number of people in it. Crowding, instead, refers to the stress we experience when we are surrounded by too many people.

Specifically, three types of density can be found in a store:

1. *objective*, based on the actual number of elements (people, objects, environmental stimuli);
2. *perceptive*, deriving from the customer's personal assessment regarding the objective density; this can vary from person to person and from place to place; and
3. *emotional*, resulting from a subjective comparison between the perceived density and the desired or expected density; this can give customers a sense of crowding when they perceive that the place that they find themselves in is too dense.

This triple distinction allows us to make a more precise evaluation of the situation, the motivating factors, and possible improvements that can be made.

Naturally, the easiest condition to modify is objective density. In this case, store designers need to set up and manage the layout lever in such a way as to limit the areas where too many people might congregate, in particular during peak times.

As we'll see, once the store project is implemented, we need to make constant and methodical observations on how customers actually use the retail space. This makes it possible to promptly pick up on any deviations in the route they take, or alterations in the time it takes them to move through the store. These changes have the potential to generate negative fallout not only on objective density, but also desired density, and even more importantly, emotional density.

Unfortunately, to evaluate these two cases of subjective density, it's no longer enough to simply observe customer behaviors and actions. We need to activate additional qualitative analysis through ethnographic interviews, which serve to emerge the emotions that customers experience during their visit to the store, in relation to the variety of expectations they may have. Ethnographic interviews explore customer opinions, values, convictions and beliefs along with other cultural aspects that can't be analyzed with other techniques, such as observation. In particular, such interviews make it possible to collect and process information on previously observed actions in the store, to understand them more clearly and to delve more deeply into the reasons behind them.

## 4 Planning the layout of display fixtures

As we've already said, the layout of display fixtures centers on planning horizontal space and vertical mobility (the latter through systems of stairs, escalators, and elevators). The layout marks the pathways through the store, channeling the flow of customers and shaping the mechanical and physical aspects of purchase behavior. To find the best approach to developing the layout, we must first to fully comprehend how customers relate to the store. In other words, we need to ask what their motivations are for visiting the store to correctly gauge the size of different sectors and departments.

To begin with, the store's floor plan is divided up into a series of spaces allotted to displays, sales, personnel, and customer services. Once each specific area is purposed, the next step is to calculate the *Coefficient of Occupied Space* or the ratio of the linear display to the total sales floor:

$$\text{COS} = \frac{\text{linear units of display} \times 100}{\text{square units of sales area}}$$

For example, stores that seek to stand out by focusing greater attention on customer needs will tend to have a very low coefficient, to appear less dense, which in turn is a way to enhance customer service. Regardless of the objectives, all choices pertaining to organizing space in the store are limited by several technical restrictions. Below is a list of some examples.

- The building which houses the store determines not only the size, but also the shape of the sales area, which impacts the arrangement and length of the display fixtures.
- The positioning of store entrances and exits channel the flow of customers in a specific direction.
- The location of cash desks and information/hospitality points may be obligatory.
- The stock room should be near heavy or fast-selling products, to reduce the time and effort needed to restock displays.
- Prepping areas need to be near the corresponding store sectors.
- Visibility varies from zone to zone on the sales floor, which means sectors that are high-risk for shoplifting must be positioned in easy-to-monitor places.

But the arrangement of display fixtures does not depend exclusively on technical constraints. Instead, this decision represents the ultimate compromise between the limitations of the floor space, the commercial aims (to circulate traffic throughout the entire store), and service aims (to help customers find what they're looking for as quickly as possible). Finally, during peak store hours, the display layout has to ensure that in-store traffic keeps flowing smoothly.[1]

## 4.1    *Balancing the dynamics of supply and demand*

It is impossible to come up with an optimal procedure for standardizing the layout of display fixtures in stores because floor plans vary widely, as do distribution formats, product assortments and retailing techniques. But here is one rule that always holds true: striking the proper balance between the dynamics of supply and demand is a must.

On one hand, the distributor wants to move merchandise as seamlessly as possible, and to maximize profitability per square meter/foot of floor space or linear meter/foot of display. Following this approach alone, the productivity of the display layout would depend exclusively on the size of the sales floor and the ability to create a flow of customers who see the entire assortment. To achieve optimal efficiency, displays would grow to cover nearly all available floor space, condensing any areas to a minimum that are not exclusively purposed for sales (cash desks, info points, recreational activities, store rooms, offices etc.).

On the other hand, however, customers want to be able to move freely through the store, without feeling herded along a set path or having to contend with physical obstacles that prevent them from reading the offering easily. What's more, they want to take care of their planned purchases as quickly as they can. When developing the layout for display fixtures, therefore, we need to weigh the trade-off between the two opposite approaches as far as customers' freedom of movement in the store. We can either:

---

[1] Innovative technology can simplify the analysis of in-store traffic flow, monitoring the areas that attract the most customers for the longest time. The system known as RFID (Radio Frequency Identification) consists of equipping shopping carts with an electronic device that records customer movements in the store (for further details, see Chapter 2).

- restrict it, in the hopes that customers will buy more; or
- unleash it, enhancing the enjoyment of the store visit and, in turn, potentially shoring up customer loyalty.

Regardless of the approach we choose, the final plan should stimulate smooth in-store circulation. To do so, the size of the traffic areas must be gauged to allow customers to move around without feeling crowded or stressed while they are browsing through the store, contemplating what to buy.

One smart solution is to create a central corridor, marked out by the arrangement of display fixtures, aisles, and open spaces. Then, this "Main Street" can be intersected by side streets, consisting of passageways winding through the different areas of the store. Another useful plan might be to map out alternative routes or "fast tracks" for customers who are pressed for time and need to "grab and go." Finally, a sure way to make the store visit pleasant is to create to a perceptive rhythm of lights, colors, materials and products that elicit moments of sharp focus interspersed with intervals of "down time" and relaxation.

To illustrate these aspects in a real store setting, Géant Magellant, from the French *Casino* chain, pioneered the concept of free circulation in hypermarkets. In light of the different needs the store serves for different customers, the chain opted to create three separate entrances that would lead on to three distinct "routes:" the main entrance for planned purchases, the supermarket entrance for daily purchases and the "free time" entrance for fun purchases (Fig. 3).

*Figure 3* – The floor plan of a hypermarket in the French chain Géant Casino, with three entrances, each one designed to satisfy a different need served by the store.

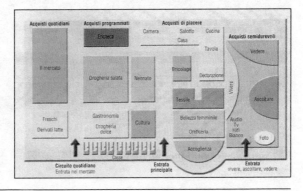

## 4.2    *A good start: the decompression zone*

The area just inside the entrance to the store plays a vital role in triggering certain physical and mental responses visitors. Ideally, people should feel a warm welcome, which can be achieved with soft lines, warm colors and materials, and open spaces (Fig. 4).

As a rule, first impressions shape future choices. This is particularly true when it comes to store image, where the initial impact also corresponds to a particularly delicate moment in the psychological and physical state of customers (Fig. 5).

In fact, at the entrance to the store, customers experience emotional tension, so they need a transitional space where they can adapt to their new environment. This involves a shift either toward a state of higher well-being (a positive emotion that draws customers in, engendering acceptance) or malaise (a negative emotion that drives customers away, generating refusal). The responses of an organism trigger visible physiological reactions as well (for example, people may blink less, sweat more, and have an increased heart rate) (Fig. 6).

*Figure* 4 – Christmas at Printemps department store in Paris is the perfect occasion to "deck the halls" of the decompression zone with a magical scene on a distinctly theatrical note, inspiring a sense of wonder in adults and children alike.

*Figure* 5 – Pave in Barcellona targets people with a passion for bicycles, greeting them with a spacious decompression zone.

*Figure* 6 – A Nespresso store opens into a richly decorated space with ornamental plants, glowing lighting and captivating images, creating a very warm and welcoming atmosphere.

This means that when designing the decompression zone, we need to exploit the elements that interact with the emotional state that customers experience in that place and in that moment. Again, this is the role of visual communication, which puts customers at ease, and gives them the feeling that they are in the right place at the right time (Figs. 7 and 8).

As we will discuss further in the observational analysis in Chapter 9, the decompression zone covers around six to seven meters (20 to 23 feet) just inside the store entrance. This is where customers look for reassuring points of reference, that is, elements that spark a specific memory such as a familiar product or brand.

We must keep this in mind when designing the layout, to optimize the displays in relation to the perception of the products. Put another way, the decompression zone is an adaptation area. Although the profitability of the display here is negligible, this space is critical for enacting the principles of comfort, emotion and communication that define store atmosphere. Again, this zone marks the starting point of the perceptive path that customers will follow, the source of the stimuli that will prompt them to browse through the entire store, rather than rushing to make their purchases as quickly as they can.

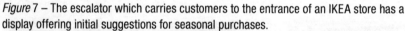

*Figure 7* – The escalator which carries customers to the entrance of an IKEA store has a display offering initial suggestions for seasonal purchases.

*Figure* 8 – La Feltrinelli Libri and Musica in Piazza Piemonte in Milan welcomes customers with a spacious decompression area that opens onto eye-catching wall displays highlighting new releases.

## 5    Display fixtures

Display fixtures must constitute the foundation for exhibiting products, creating an environment that enhances them and encouraging people to buy them. But displays should never overwhelm products by undermining their visual importance. Specifically, all display fixtures must serve three distinct purposes:

- to increase the value of the store section or department, leveraging the symbolic dimension of the product assortment;
- to create a clear classification of product categories and families, reinforcing the distinction between them; and
- to adapt to products with customizable components.

As for this last point, we need to reach an effective compromise between display solutions that favor standardization (albeit with flexible modules that can be adapted to different departments), and customized fixtures suited to the specific features and communication characteristics of the products on display. In fact, displays should be adapted to the product assortment, and not viceversa (as is more often the case) (Fig. 9).

*Figura* 9 – In small neighborhood supermarkets, the French chain Casino Shopping implements a store fixture specially designed for displaying cosmetics which allows customers test out products.

But this approach hasn't been widely adopted, despite the clear performance edge it provides for store departments, because of the cost. What doesn't help matters is the still-pervasive conviction that marked heterogeneity in product presentation represents a drawback rather than a benefit. The argument here is that to prevent boredom during the purchase process, retailers would have to reconsider design choices for all the display fixtures, with an eye to creating more movement in the sales areas and making the store more dynamic.

That said, there is no longer any doubt that personalizing – and consequently differentiating – display fixtures is crucial in terms of communication and values. At the very least this applies for areas offering special items such as pastries, wines, or perfumes (Figs. 10 and 11). Moreover, it's obvious that big retail chains have to build modules that are standardized, flexible, and adaptable to various departments, but there is no logical reason why these display fixtures all need to be identical.

In fact, as detailed in the following section, the rapid dissemination of layouts based on islands, if not actual in-store boutiques, clearly demonstrates that the situation is slowly but surely changing.

An interesting aspect to mention here is food displays, special spaces that send the message of fresh, genuine products at convenient prices, or reflect these values symbolically. This is done by presenting items in a way that stimulates the senses of taste, smell and sight, accentuating the components of pleasure that are innate to food. These displays also bring to mind the tradi-

*Figure* 10 – An innovative, elegant layout design for high-end wines in the Carrefour Planet hypermarket in Milan Assago.

*Figure* 11 – Special displays with design and colors that are particularly appropriate and attractive for the customers of Kidz, the children's section at la Feltrinelli, inside Feltrinelli Libri and Musica in Piazza Piemonte in Milan.

*Figure* 12 – The dark gray gondolas in the underwear section of a Carrefour Planet hypermarket effectively highlight the style of the products and place more emphasis on product presentation.

tion of buying food in specialized food stores (the bakery, the delicatessen, the butcher). The connotations that arise here include trust and food safety.

Some companies have even color coded their displays. At the Carrefour Planet hypermarkets, for example, all the gondolas for items in the non-food "shopping universes" are dark gray. Although the lighting needs to be brighter, the result is still highly effective thanks to the sharp contrast between the products and the background, highlighting the goods displayed on the shelves even more (Fig. 12).

One final consideration concerns the layout options for grocery stores,[2] where bonds with customers are built by letting them see food items as they are being prepared. Separating the customers from the store personnel are large glass partitions; in some cases there are no barriers at all except the counters displaying the different food items (Fig. 13). In various departments customers can actually see store personnel prepare food products, so these activities should be done preferably during peak store hours, to allow customers to participate in a multisensorial product experience.

---

[2] "Grocery" technically refers to the product assortment typically found in stores that offer both mass market goods and foodstuffs (possibly including fresh and super-fresh foods, in some cases prepared on-site), as well as non-food items, mainly personal hygiene and cleaning products. In larger stores such as hypermarkets and superstores, the product assortment covers other non-food categories, in particular perfumes, household items, clothing and textiles, white goods and brown goods.

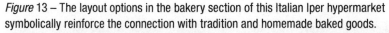

*Figure* 13 – The layout options in the bakery section of this Italian Iper hypermarket symbolically reinforce the connection with tradition and homemade baked goods.

## 6    Types of layouts for in-store displays

As far as the positioning of displays in the store, one or more of the following models can be adopted:

1. *grid*, with displays set out in linear paths and aisles;
2. *herringbone*, fixtures placed diagonally with respect to traffic flow;
3. *circular*, with a central ring meant to resemble the market square;
4. *island* or *free flow*, an asymmetric arrangement; and
5. *boutique*, designating separate areas for each product group, set apart from the other displays.

Of course, each model has a different effect on how in-store traffic flows. But whatever the choice of layout, the strategic objective remains the same: to avoid creating hard-to-reach areas.

As we've already pointed out, a determining factor in store design is the sales floor plan, that is, the configuration of the available sales area. This is the platform to build on, developing the sales space in relation to width rather than depth. From the moment customers step into the store, they should be able to see as much product as possible; this is the way to best serve their needs. Tight spaces and narrow passageways, along with hidden corners and cold spots, should be limited or eliminated altogether, enhancing product visibility.

### 6.1   *The grid layout*

With this layout there are long rows of shelves which create obligatory or semi-obligatory thoroughfares through the store (Fig. 14).

Almost all the supermarkets that were first opened in Italy during the '60s and '70s were designed to create a one-way system for customer traffic. The space was arranged like one single display, forcing customers to follow a pre-set path. The shelving units sat on the floor, perpendicular to the entrance, forming corners and aisles positioned at right angles. As modern distribution developed, the same massive displays of product assortment represented a very effective way to reinforce the message of a nearly infinite offering, piquing the curiosity of customers. But their store visit was de-personalized, offering no chance to detour from the route mapped out for them, except perhaps to retrace their steps a short distance in the opposite direction. The immense assortment was the primary competitive lever, while little or no attention was paid to any other aspects of the in-store experience, least of all customer enjoyment. In keeping with this approach, the displays were also highly standardized, with flexible modules adaptable to any store section, accentuating the abundance of the offering even more.

The growth of modern distribution has had an enormous impact on standard store layouts, introducing the variation of semi-obligatory thor-

*Figure* 14 – The grid layout model.

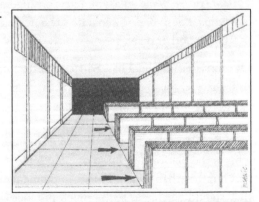

oughfares. In fact, not only have stores expanded in size, but also in the number of product categories, with the addition of outdoor areas, discount zones and bazaars (especially in hypermarkets). To prevent customers from feeling frustrated or uncomfortable, which would feed into a general sense of dissatisfaction, distribution has gradually enlarged their maneuvering room. Stores have added horizontal and vertical access aisles while maintaining a more rigid structure, typical of the obligatory pathway, inside different sectors and/or departments (Fig. 15).

Actually, nowadays we find totally pre-defined, obligatory routes almost exclusively in small to medium-sized stores with sales areas of less than 700 square meters (7,500 square feet). Examples include some discount stores and small supermarkets, as well as retail outlets located on highways, such as the *Autogrill* chain. With respect to the traditional layout model with a pre-established traffic flow, a semi-obligatory route entails creating a main circuit and then a series of integrative intersecting crossroads. This gives customers greater freedom of movement without one-way restrictions.

Here the "recommended" route is clearly mapped out from the entrance to the exit, with some breaks/links between key departments. This makes it possible to create adjacencies which couldn't be exploited otherwise. More importantly, customers can use shortcuts if they don't want to walk through the entire store. Specifically, by breaking up gondolas that are more than 10 to 12 modules long, stores can create alternative pathways flanked by end caps, often dedicated to promotions. These displays attract the attention of customers, prompting them to visit individual aisles instead of simply following the main route. For a perfect example we can look to IKEA, with its shortcuts and switchbacks winding through the store.

*Figure* 15 – A grid layout, very effectively illustrated on a map in a Coop supermarket, facilitates the visitor flow.

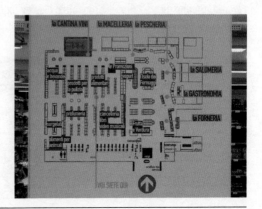

The grid layout, in the semi-obligatory version of the in-store traffic route, is the most popular model in self-serve grocery stores thanks to the numerous advantages it offers. Above all, the display capacity of a grid layout ensures an excellent yield per meter/foot of shelf space, even with products that generate low to medium margins. Grocery store shelves are normally at least 180 centimeters (71 inches) high and fairly deep, with five display levels; this guarantees an advantageous ratio of linear meters/feet of shelving to total sales floor area.

In addition, the durability of the materials used to build shelves makes them highly economical, and reduces the costs of installation and maintenance dramatically. Two more factors worth mentioning are the notable simplicity in arranging pathways through the store, and the perceptible increase in product visibility. This makes the assortment more legible and at the same time diminishes the different levels of inventory.

Although there are several advantages to a grid layout, we mustn't ignore the equally evident disadvantages. Specifically, a grid creates a product display that is far too uniform and monotonous, unappealing to people who prefer more variety and "spice." In addition, studies show that when customers leave the main aisle they rarely backtrack. This would suggest that the number of intersecting aisles should be limited, despite the fact that these are useful to break up the tedium of long gondolas that run from the back of the store all the way to the cash desks. The grid is also a format for spatial organization that is much more functional from a supply standpoint, with the focus on maximizing productivity and cutting the cost of logistics. One final consideration is that retailers who use a grid need to carefully gauge both the length and the width of the aisles (Figs. 16a and 16b).

*Figures* 16a and 16b – Curved, ergonomic display fixtures that are the right height (not too tall), and set at the proper distance, make this little Casino Shopping store easy to navigate.

At this point we need to draw a distinction between penetration aisles, which serve as boundaries for the different departments and represent the structural frame of the store, and secondary aisles which connect these departments. Unlike penetration aisles, which are generally very broad, the width of secondary aisles is usually less than three shopping carts placed side by side. Ideally, this measurement should vary depending on the department and the traffic flow. It's not simply a question of visitor density, but rather making the purchase process easy and convenient. If an aisle is too wide, people only look at the displays on one side; if it's too narrow, they'll move through it more quickly because it's too crowded.

## 6.2   *The herringbone layout*

With a herringbone layout the display fixtures are arranged to create a central flow of traffic from the entrance toward the rear of the store. On each side displays are placed diagonally with respect to the main aisle (Fig. 17). The main advantage of this model is the broad central aisle leading to the end of the department, or toward the next penetration area. The idea here is to exploit the tendency of customers to move safely and comfortably through open areas, where a slow pace guarantees the maximum yield per square meter/foot compared with all the other areas of the store. A diagonal arrangement of the display fixtures offers a quick view of all the different sectors simultaneously. At the same time, customers can see the inner-most items on each display. So a herringbone layout not only makes planned purchases quick and easy, it also encourages impulse purchases thanks to the greater visibility it creates for the entire offering.

*Figure* 17 – The herringbone layout model.

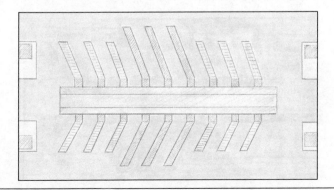

## 6.3    *The circular layout*

This model consists of a large central ring resembling a market square, the traditional place for buying goods. From here all the paths radiate out toward the perimeter of the sales floor, rather than running perpendicular to the entrance (Fig. 18).

This type of layout is an excellent solution for spotlighting certain store sections by positioning them near the center of the store. Since customers now enjoy full freedom of movement, we need to reflect very carefully on how to arrange the different departments in terms of product layout. The starting point is dividing up product categories, and then grouping together the ones that secure margins (routine categories) and reinforce image (destination categories), with respect to items that complete the offering (service categories).

The main square represents the beating heart of the whole store, with an accent on the architectural setting and an atmosphere that appeals to all the senses. This is the entire high-value area (which in a grocery store would be the fresh produce section). Here we find low display fixtures that allow customers a horizontal view of all the other sections radiating out from the center (Fig. 19). By setting up the central "piazza" in this way, we place the architectural and design components of the store in the spotlight, center stage, leaving the customers with ample room to move around. On the downside, however, the sections located around the perimeter of the store risk becoming dangerous dead zones, with little power of attraction. The Dutch supermarket chain Albert Heijn was a ground-breaker in redefining retail space by taking the circular layout approach, with 1998 remodel

*Figure* 18 – The circular layout model.

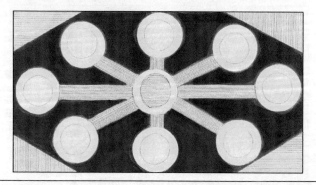

*Figure* 19 – A circular layout in a Nike display area where the central structure emerges architecturally and visually on an external ring.

of the store in Purmerend. Examining this model in greater detail, the main innovation here consisted of introducing a layout made up of concentric circles, which allowed shoppers to combine purchases not only in terms of product categories, but also sales formats based on different purchase processes. The store reflects the concept of a village high street, placing a discount store, a supermarket, a specialty shop and a cafeteria all under one roof. Along most of the store's perimeter, which would correspond to the suburbs, customers can find commodities and discount products. The entrance to the discount zone is clearly marked to separate it from the grocery area, with different flooring, lighting, and display fixtures.

Moving away from the periphery, the atmosphere changes and product value rises, till visitors reach the very center of the store, which is called *L'Aventure*. Here are the sections staffed by sales assistants, kid zones and a relaxation area with several tables where people can enjoy the food and beverages they've purchased in the kiosks and the café opposite. Following the main aisle, the store sections duplicate the sequence of the nutritional rhythms of the day. So upon entering the store, the customer first comes across a totem listing all the promotional activities; next is the breakfast section, followed by the lunch and dinner areas and finally the non-food departments, completing the product assortment. Last of all, beyond the cash desks, there are additional product categories supplemented with other activities to further expand the offering, such as cooking classes. The first such layout was implemented in Italy in 2000 at the Coop Lombardia in the Opera Superstore, with gondolas radiating out from a central area hosting fresh produce.

## 6.4    *The island layout*

With an island layout, display fixtures are arranged asymmetrically without any formal order, creating a totally free flow of movement (Fig. 20).

With no clearly marked paths to follow, customers tend to wander wherever they please. To limit any unpleasant sensations or disagreeable situations caused by the inevitable sense of disorientation, the shelving units in the central areas are no more than one and a half meters (four feet) high, making it easy for customers to see the entire sales floor. Along the outer walls, instead, there are higher display fixtures that serve as effective visual signposts guiding customers from one department to another (Fig. 21).

Until recently the island layout was most often found in non-food specialty stores, or in large department stores. But today this format is a valid alternative for the food sector as well, where it can be applied throughout the store or only in certain areas, in combination with a traditional grid layout. Specifically, in more innovative formats, self-serve areas displaying packaged products and eating areas and/or fresh food counters are situated side by side, as if they were market stalls; in some cases service is also provided (Fig. 22).

*Figure* 20 – The island layout model.

*Figure* 21 – La Rinascente in Milan: the classical and functional housewares section, designed by Aldo Cibic following a traditional island layout.

*Figure* 22 – The island of French cheeses, clearly visible even from a distance thanks to the curtain and the national cockades, beckoning to customers, inviting them to go to the deli of the Portello Iper store in Milan.

Generally speaking, an island layout is purposed more effectively for demand, because it does not force customers to follow pre-set paths, giving them total freedom of movement. The atmosphere that emerges is certainly more relaxing and pleasant compared to the grid layout. For this reason, customers tend to spend more time in the store, and make more impulse purchases. Along the store perimeter the displays are slightly taller, with a more visible product assortment which clearly conveys the store image.

Despite all this, a more spacious, comfortable environment also presents certain drawbacks. First and foremost, available display space shrinks, which means there are fewer display fixtures; the obvious result of this is a negative impact on yield per square meter/foot in relation to the sales floor area of the store. Also, as mentioned above, to facilitate customer flow – and more importantly to provide a sense of direction in the store – displays cannot be too high, to allow customers to get an overall view of the horizontal space (Fig. 23).

Added to this is the fact that the island model can only be used in stores of a certain size (no bigger than 1,000 square meters/11,000 square feet). In larger stores, this layout would create an unpleasant sense of disorientation. What's more, the display fixtures are more expensive and less stan-

*Figure* 23 – At Feltrinelli Libri e Musica in Milan, the island layout facilitates horizontal communication and makes the retail spaces comfortable and homey.

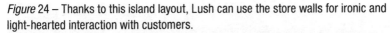

*Figure 24* – Thanks to this island layout, Lush can use the store walls for ironic and light-hearted interaction with customers.

dardizable, due to both the more costly materials and the display design, created to fit specific product types. Lastly, the displays themselves contain fewer products, which means higher logistical costs for more frequent restocking. In any case, with an island layout communication plays a more vital role, both with regard to signage and all the activities involved in setting out a stimulating perceptive pathway (Fig. 24).

Interaction with the layout also takes on critical importance. In fact, the criteria used for grouping together products must be renewed more frequently, even if only partially. This serves to pique the curiosity of the customers, encouraging them to browse around in the different sections of the store.

## 6.5 *The boutique layout*

An alternative to the model above is the boutique layout. Here the retail space is broken up into areas that are designed around a certain group of products or a brand; each boutique is clearly separate from the rest of the display area (Fig. 25).

*Figure* 25 – The boutique layout.

The separation can be total or partial. In the first case, the dedicated area is closed off by very high walls, which can even become displays themselves, with a special entrance that leads into a space with an atmosphere that is markedly different from the rest of the store in terms of design, layout, and fixtures. The end result of the boutique technique it that the sales floor is actually divided into myriad specialty stores following a shop-in-shop approach (Fig. 26).

*Figure* 26 – In the Design Supermarket at La Rinascente in Milan, the area dedicated to lighting design is structurally separate from the central piazza. Project by Studio 1+1=1 Claudio Silvestrin Giuliana Salmaso Architects.

*Figure* 27 – The elegant and accessible Ground Floor of La Rinascente in Milan, designed by India Mahadavi, houses personalized brand showcases with the most famous international brands of cosmetics and jewelry.

Another option is to create only a partial separation between the dedicated area and the rest of the retail space. Similar areas can also be called brand showcases and are often used by producers to realize a preferential space to optimize their in-store communication, compared to the store's standard. The priority aim of this format is to "isolate" the brand in order to consolidate a specific – hence differentiated – identity (Fig. 27).

A hybrid version of the boutique layout is becoming more and more popular with grocery stores. The aim here is to create highly differentiated areas, each with its own unique atmosphere, clearly reflecting the most symbolic contents of the assortment (Fig. 28).

A perfect example is the new concept by Carrefour: Planet Hypermarkets. The layout is divided into purchase "universes", distinctly identified and equally clearly communicated both with hanging wayfinding panels in color-coded plexiglass, and diverse flooring materials (Fig. 29).

*Figure* 28 – The Wine Cellar in this Iper hypermarket in Milan's Portello district evokes a striking sense of traditional, specialized trade, with old-fashioned displays.

*Figure* 29 – The multimedia department sign in Carrefour Planet in Milan Assago marks a space that is already clearly delineated by distinctive layouts and flooring materials.

## 7   Organizing the store by specializations and trades

What clearly emerges in the previous description of the trends in display layouts is the gradual transition that is underway. The store is transforming from a space defined exclusively in terms of assortment into a place that is created for the customer and enriched by the pure and simple language of the products. So the first step in properly designing a display system is to acquire an in-depth understanding of the physical features of the items on offer in order to assess the ergonomic implications. Even products that belong to the same family require differentiated displays, in keeping with their real and perceived value, the type of customer they target and the purpose they are designed to serve.

For example, let's take the product "shoe". This item can be presented and sold in a variety of ways: vertical floor-to-ceiling displays work well for technical footwear or sports shoes (Fig. 30); low tables or shelves, with an average product density, are appropriate for medium to high range shoes (Fig. 31); lastly, a few shoes can be placed in display cases, creating an almost museum-like effect for luxury footwear (Fig. 32).

*Figure* 30 – An entire wall dedicated to jogging shoes in this New York Nike Store.

*Figure* 31 – A snapshot of the biggest space in Italy specialized in fashion and luxury footwear, located on the third floor of La Rinascente in Milan.

*Figure* 32 – Two central display cases are set in between the elegant lighted shelves of a wall dedicated to classic men's shoes in the prestigious Ferragamo boutique in Via Montenapoleone, Milan.

What counts most is that anonymous impersonal retail outlets are on their way out. Gone are the stores that force visitors to travel one-way paths, flanked by displays on flat surfaces at the same standard height, the same flooring throughout, where lighting creates a uniform daytime effect, without spotlighting any single point or focusing attention on one area over another.

The decline of the store conceived according to a linear logic is giving way to the rise in retail spaces that are highly differentiated and differentiating, regardless of their size.

This is leading to a new store design organized by "specializations and trades". Through the shop-in-shop conception, the store has turned into one big piazza, with any number of small specialized boutiques that liven up the atmosphere with colors, scents and flavors.

In other words, a concept of the store is gaining ground that tends to re-qualify the environment by transitioning from a general store formula to a multi-specialist format. Hypermarkets were the first to implement this solution, but now smaller stores with limited product assortments have followed suit, modifying and mutating the basic principles such as legibility of the offering, and the idea of specialization, achieving an improved level of service.

Naturally there is no single rule that universally applies. There is simply a need for new spatial archetypes that deviate from the conventional segmented rectangle. As we already know, asymmetrical or concentric layout solutions are becoming more common, populated with highly symbolic points, interrupting the homogeneous continuity of the merchandise. While this continuity used to be reassuring to customers, underscoring how abundant the offering was, today they find it disorienting, even exasperating.

Likewise, store design is moving away from a grid or linear format and implementing other geometrical shapes (circles, diamonds, trapezoids) or natural forms (stars, spirals) that are better suited to creating a strong spatial identity while allowing a rational division of the store. Generally speaking, the variety of display techniques adopted in the same store is gradually rising too, with differentiation based on product families, customer targets and the setting the store wants to recreate.

In response to a growing need for modularity, there is a drive to adopt reversible fixtures that allow retailers to quickly transform the department in light of the offering, the season, and variations in lifestyles of target users. Shelving is lighter, brightly colored, ergonomic, in some cases stackable, equipped with wheels or tilted shelves to place the accent on the products.

The aisles that channel the traffic flow through the store are designed to help customers find the products they're looking for. This means that sizing the aisles properly is a delicate task that can determine the success or failure of the store, due to the relative psychological connotations. Indeed, aisle width and length have a major impact on the customer's perception; as always, the key is to find the best compromise. While it's true that widening aisles enhance the image of the store, beyond a certain threshold this can lead to a risky drop in profitability due to the corresponding reduction in sales space. By the same token, making aisles too narrow can create a strong feeling of unease and displeasure.

Regardless of the layout model, as we've reiterated several times, display projects increasingly aim to improve on the horizontal dimension of the visual perspective by exploiting the height and depth of the shelving to make sure customers can see the entire sales floor. In other words, the tendency is to move beyond the vertical horizon, giving clients the chance to get their bearings just like they would normally do in a small store (Fig. 33).

Once segmented by aisles, the spatial perception now encompasses the entire retail space, as if we were standing in village square: our view and our orientation become two essential elements that enrich our understanding of the sales area (Fig. 34).

*Figure* 33 – The mixed layout model.

*Figure* 34 – The Ambasciatori bookshop in Bologna offers customers a very warm welcome. The bookshelves are arranged in a grid layout, interspersed with lower structures and illuminated with warm table lamps. The central zone opens up on a horizontal arrangement and enhances the perception of the surrounding space, striking the right balance between architectural essentials and communicative theatrics.

## 8    Organizing the product layout

Along the path marked out by the display fixtures, the product layout establishes the sequence of departments (for example, women) or sectors (clothing), categories (formalwear), product families (skirts) and specific lines (long skirts). This is the final touch in the overall store layout. Finding the right product layout is all about traffic flow, because customers naturally tend to skip over certain areas and spend more time in others (unless they're forced to follow a specific path). So the key to an effective product layout is to encourage people to visit the entire store, without overtly obliging them to do so.

Obviously, the sales floor of a store offers a variety of values and weights with regard to product layout. This means that when we decide where to position various items, we need to strike the best possible balance, capturing and keeping the attention of the customer, who often tends to become distracted.

In concrete terms, organizing the product layout involves:

- grouping products;
- zoning and positioning departments, sectors, categories and families within the allocated display space; and
- sizing various areas.

## 8.1    *Criteria for grouping products*

The product offering should be organized in a way that facilitates the purchase process while inspiring customers to visit the entire store. This necessitates organizing the assortment so that it visually responds to all the customers' questions in a logical sequence, in order of priority. Product classification constitutes the template for the visual representation of a product assortment, the synthesis of all possible responses to the customer's purchase motivations. In other words, it's the way we want the customer to perceive and to interact with the set of products we offer.

Clearly, when retailers build a product assortment, it's based on a rational analysis of market segments where they want to operate, and the methods they want to adopt to compete there. Specifically, this last decision takes on enormous weight because the same product categories can be presented in a variety of ways, qualifying and differentiating the various forms of distribution, whatever the store image or décor may be.

In other words, how the merchandise is assembled and presented shapes the offering, steering it toward different needs, even when targeting the same customer segment. So product layout represents the choice of the best methods to use to compete on the market, on a case-by-case basis. A product classification also provides a set of qualitative and quantitative information. The first makes it possible to identify logical links between the various display groupings that guide and shape choices pertaining to the physical arrangement of the sales area. The second serves to size the groupings, determining the number of items and the quantity of each one. Once again, choosing the most appropriate criterion depends not only on the product features of the offering, but also on the needs of the customers, as well as the competitive arena of the target the store seeks to serve. Below is a list of possible classification criteria (and there are many more besides), followed by a brief description of each one:

1. product affinity;
2. complementary categories;
3. price;

4. brand;
5. occasions for use;
6. lifestyle;
7. target;
8. theme; and
9. movement.

1. *Product affinity.* This, the simplest and most common method, consists of setting up a sequence of departments based on origin (such as ethnic goods), nature (diet foods) or conservation method (frozen foods). We typically find this product grouping criterion in stores that seek to emphasize the product offering rather than a coordinated assortment. Thanks to the high information content, this type of classification is well suited to highly specialized offerings. On the plus side, it facilitates the decision making process and allows customers to find merchandise easily, so it works well for planned purchases. By the same token, this layout is more effective for products with low fashion content as its "power of suggestion" is limited. Lastly, no complex marketing analysis is needed, and at the same time there is a logical and coherent connection with the offering.

2. *Complementary categories.* By grouping together products that complement one another in satisfying needs, stores turn the focus on the customer, with the aim of improving the quality of customer service. The point here is to come up with a model based on how various products are commonly used, and interpret these items as input for meeting broader needs. (An example is the world of entertainment, where computers, books, and audio-visuals and other products converge.)

Following this line of reasoning regarding displays, the product affinity criterion brings together items that would have otherwise been placed in separate sections, often far apart. Clearly, in this case the display is more functional in serving customer needs, acting not only an effective shopping list of sorts, but as an additional stimulus for add-on and impulse purchases as well.

3. *Price.* This criterion is a valid option when the store wants to accentuate its economical offering, grouping items together based on price range (Fig. 35), possibly correlated to specific product category or distribution format. An example here is the one-price store. Generally the price criterion is more often linked to special events, such as sales, promotions, or price cuts.

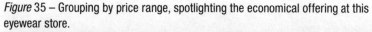

*Figure* 35 – Grouping by price range, spotlighting the economical offering at this eyewear store.

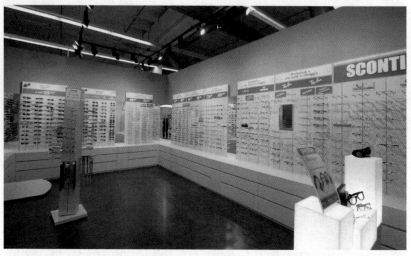

4. *Brand*. The brand can be a valid criterion for product presentation when it's the main motivator and/or the biggest attraction for consumers. In these cases, spotlighting the brand reinforces its communicative impact, creating a very positive ripple effect on the positioning of the store itself.

A perfect example is Salmoiraghi & Viganò in Milan's Piazza San Babila. In 2013, this store completely revamped its grouping criteria, shifting the accent to the brand by setting up specially dedicated brand walls, with an eye to design and using materials chosen ad hoc with suppliers (Fig. 36). This format has proven to be a successful one, but has only been extended to more elegant locations.

5. *Occasions for use*. This grouping criterion is very effective in highlighting an assortment focused on a single lifestyle but intended to satisfy customers with differing needs. An interesting example here is Chai, a French wine shop that proposes a product classification based on occasions in which people normally drink wine (wines for meditation, wines with friends, aperitif wines, wines for special occasions, wines for women). By doing so, the store offers its customers added value thanks to the information provided by the displays, simplifying the purchase process enormously.

A famous case of a total reconfiguration of sales space is Finiper with its "Universes". This was one of the first companies in Italy to redefine retail

*Figure* 36 – Salmoiraghi & Viganò reorganized its offering by brand in its Milan store in Piazza San Babila with personalized walls, responding to the currently trending purchase criterion for eyewear.

space in its Iper hypermarkets according to consumption processes, grouping together sets of product categories corresponding to several end-uses. Starting from the basics of category management, the new structure aimed to facilitate customers on their ideal purchase path, following a line of reasoning based on sequential choices dictated by their consumption needs.

The retailer identified six theme-based islands, marked with distinctive names and colors, accentuated by large banners placed high up on walls, visible from any part of the store: the pleasure of fresh food (brown), the pleasure of good food (yellow), the pleasure of dressing well (pink), the pleasure of living well (blue), the pleasure of having fun (light blue), the pleasure of the season (white). The primary aim was to transform the store into a relational environment. Here customers are no longer forced to move along a rigid route, staked out by high shelving made of cheap materials, with flat lighting and visual merchandising pushing promotions above all else.

Instead, for the first time in non-food sectors, the grid layout was converted into a free space, made up of a hierarchy of aisles leading to various types of products, placing the accent on the wide variety of purchase proposals. Here brand showcases are a favorite display option, marking the poles of attraction in the store. With the distinctive width and depth of their product assortment, these displays are characterized not only by ad hoc lighting systems, but specially designed and impactful visual merchandising as well.

Summing up, then, by applying certain fundamental principles of semiotics, the merchandise is more accessible thanks to a more effective product display, a proper combination of colors, a suitable setting and a better system for regulating the flow of visitors. For example, the Iper chain launched the Cà project: a single department hosting products related to the home, divided by the rooms in the house: the kitchen, living room, bedroom, bathroom, in addition to accents for home decor. All this is set apart from the other sections of the store thanks to a highly distinctive setting, and the entrance that reflects the different worlds of Cà (Fig. 37).

Aside from individual case studies, the new models for organizing retail space according to consumption universes have brought about a reconfiguration of display fixtures, which have become more modern, flexible systems. Specifically, there is an increase in the variety of the display methods adopted in a single retail store, differentiated by product family, target consumers, and the atmosphere the retailer is trying to recreate.

*Figure* 37 – The monumental entrance to Cà, clearly visible in the Iper store in Varese, where an offering emerges that proposes ideas and combinations of products for purchase.

6. *Lifestyle*. This type of classification takes into account the way customers live, how they look, and how they behave; lifestyle might be formal, casual, sporty, classic, and so forth. In this case merchandise is grouped together according to coordinates and themes. The aim is to satisfy customers' needs in terms of appearance, as well as purchase motivations, which center almost exclusively on putting their personal status on display, demonstrating their membership in a social group, or expressing their personality. The lifestyle criterion tends to boost complementary sales and play down the prices of individual items. This classification is used primarily to display clothing and accessories in fashion stores and high-end boutiques (Fig. 38).

A typical example here is the department store. In this context, once the product assortment is established, the product segmentation is reproduced at a structural level by creating different areas delineated with mobile panels. The end result should give the store a distinctive character. Spaces are more and more often portioned into specialized zones, rather than large merchandise groupings. Focal points of the store become the products groups themselves, organized according to a format based on "worlds of consequential interests" prompting customers to visit all the sections of the store.

*Figure* 38 – Topshop in London dedicates an entire department to all things denim.

7. *Target.* This product classification can be extremely effective in sectors such as toys and clothing, where age and gender represent the main categorization criteria. By focusing on the target, stores can quickly and intuitively steer customers towards the areas where they'll find the products they're looking for. This goes a long way in giving customers the feeling that they are in charge, accelerating impulse purchases. Generally speaking, the target criterion is combined with occasions for use (point 5 above).

An interesting case to illustrate this model is the Italian toy store chain Città del Sole, which groups together its offering by age brackets (0-3, 3-6, 6-9, 9-14). Then, within each range, there is an additional classification based on occasion for use. For instance, toys for three- to six-year-olds are divided up as follows: building, pretending, playing together, creating and imagining, putting on a show (Fig. 39). Also interesting to note are the words used to label the product categories, using typical language of the target – children. This message obviously doesn't reach the end users themselves, but the people making the purchases, eliciting a positive feeling of empathy.

*Figure* 39 – Città del Sole divides the sections of the store into age groups, making it quick and easy to read the product assortment.

8. *Theme.* This is a very popular layout criterion, especially among clothing stores, but it is also highly effective in other sectors such as housewares as well. A theme-based product layout is particularly useful for accentuating items that can be combined according to materials, colors or functions. Essentially, the store places goods together that work well together, offering customers inspiring ideas for multiple purchases (Fig. 40).

9. *Movement.* The final option presented here for merchandise layout revolves around creating a dynamic display, introducing elements that break up the uniformity and liven up the store (such as adding a section dedicated to plants in the fresh produce department). The aim here, as the term suggests, is to minimize the monotony of a display that is too linear, establishing product groupings that can prompt impulse purchases without making the search too difficult. Put another way, movement means not following a single criterion among those listed above, but opting instead to combine them depending on the traffic flow the store wants to generate.

*Figure* 40 – A harmonious theme-based table display set up in the Cà department of the Iper store in Varese, Italy.

## 8.2    *Zoning and allocating display space: some empirical rules*

Zoning, as the term suggests, means breaking down the sales floor into zones, and then positioning in each one the various departments, sectors, product categories, and families. This activity often involves a compromise between contrasting objectives. Once again, on one hand, commercial aims focus on getting the customer to visit the entire store. But on the other, service aims seek to reduce the time that customers need to spend there, with rapid "rotation", especially on high-traffic days, to ensure that visitor traffic flows smoothly. Here are some additional conditions that impact zoning:

- the size and structure of the display spaces, which dictate not only the orientation and size of the displays themselves (such as the gondolas), but also the location of entrances and cash desks;
- the position of the storeroom, which affects both the placement of bulky, heavy items, as well as the time it takes for restocking;
- the location of the refrigerated displays and prep areas, which need to be near relative products; and
- the placement of the information desk, customer service areas and cash desks.

Taking into account all these impacting factors, an ideal solution seems unattainable. In fact, only some of the many restrictions can be avoided by strategically assigning the areas based on buying behavior with respect to different types of products. As far as the internal structure of a store, there will never be easy access to every single area; zones that have low traffic and consequently comparatively low profit – are inevitable. In any case, as we have often repeated, to find the product layout that comes closest to the ideal solution, a series of empirical rules should be followed.

1. *In a multi-level store, position the best-selling product categories far from the ground floor.* The quality of sales space is not the same on every floor, in fact, the farther away from the entrance, the less visitor traffic there is. That means the products that trigger impulse purchases should be placed near the entrance, to take advantage of the highest traffic intensity. Instead the most popular products go on the floors that are farthest away, since they have the power to attract customers regardless of where they are placed.

2. *Communicate the positioning of the store at the entrance.* Once each floor is allocated, the next step is deciding the position of the sector and/or department on that floor, with respect to the top of the stairs, the elevators, and/or escalators as well as customer service areas. In one-floor stores, it is especially critical to earmark the areas near the entrance for sectors that effectively convey the store positioning.

For example, if the clientele is mainly interested in saving money, they should begin their store visit in an area dedicated to promotions and/or best-price items. On the opposite end of the spectrum, if quality and service are top priority, it's recommended to position highly specialized categories in this entry area. It's certainly no coincidence that supermarkets often place fresh produce near the entrance with attractive displays and vivacious colors; this serves as an excellent "calling card", sending customers an immediate message of freshness and quality. Likewise, the entrance area in hypermarkets is typically allocated to theme-based/seasonal promotions (such as a fresh food fair) or price cuts. Another option is to use this space during specific times of the year to shore up the displays in nearby departments which might need extra space; this would apply to school supplies in the autumn or toys at Christmas.

3. *Attract traffic with the store entrance.* Another astute way to exploit the store entrance is to place sections with the highest traffic and product rotation here, so customers can find some items on their lists right away; this puts them in a positive frame of mind to continue their store visit.

4. *Facilitate combination purchases with display adjacencies.* By displaying product adjacencies, stores can leverage complementary relationships and facilitate the purchase process. Naturally, the ultimate aim is not only to improve service quality, making planned purchases faster, but also to boost add-on purchases by satisfying the need for information. Specifically, adjacencies (i.e. the boundaries between different product categories) help create a logical order for the store visit, encouraging aggregations at a conceptual level, not only a product level. (An example is opting to display baby food near baby care items and baby clothes.)

5. *Scatter the most attractive product categories throughout the entire sales area.* By taking categories with a high potential to attract customers and spreading them out across the entire sales area, the chances are better that customers will visit the entire store. Generally speaking, all the best-sellers

with high rotation rates should be displayed in the less busy areas, to equil-
ibrate the flow of the store visit between hot and cold zones. But despite
sales performance, there are certain product categories that naturally represent *poles of attraction*.

- *Perishables* are high-frequency purchases.
- *Planned purchases*, for everyday use, earn high brand loyalty.
- *Promotional products* attract attention effectively when displayed in
  low-traffic areas.
- *Loss leaders* have high brand loyalty which translates into powerful com-
  municational value in terms of the store's price image.

In supermarkets and hypermarkets in particular, fresh food items are generally located at the back of the store, far from the entrance, so most of
the customers are drawn to this less-visible area. Prep stations are situated along the back wall, just behind the relative display cases. Naturally,
non-perishable food items (such as beverages, biscuits, cereal and tinned
goods) are displayed next to fresh items.

6. *Put impulse purchase categories in the spotlight.* Impulse purchases are
highly sensitive to display space. This means that relative items should
be placed along the main traffic routes, near strong selling lines and in
waiting areas – in other words, where the traffic flow is most concentrated. Clearly the quality of the space differs according to the visibility and
accessibility of the space in question. The possibility of customer contact
also varies with different positions in different areas of the store, depending on the visitor flow. For example, in supermarkets and hypermarkets,
general goods, cosmetics and perfumes, accessories and the like can be
positioned either among the planned purchases in the back of the store
(with the perishables), or in the center behind the food section and in front
of clothing, as people move toward the cash desks. In fact, once customers
have purchased all their necessities, they'll feel relaxed and psychologically
more inclined to browse through the impulse purchase areas.

However, before making this type of evaluation, the hot zones that see
high traffic intensity must be clearly identified (for example, the entrance
area, the perimeter of the sales floor, the cash desks). The same is true for
the cold zones (such as central aisles). Clearly there is a strong correlation
between the layout of the displays and the display quality of various areas,
seeing as the visibility and accessibility of these spaces depend on the layout models implemented in the store.

7. *Place planned product categories far from the main traffic flow.* A good rule is to isolate the departments where customers need time to reflect on their purchases from the main traffic flow, to avoid creating traffic jams. Since normally careful planning goes into this type of purchase, customers will look for the department they need, and will appreciate being out of the way of the crowds if this allows them to ponder their options at their leisure. In some cases, however, store designers prefer to set up obstacles to traffic flow right at the entrance, so that customers can see the store sections in this area clearly. This is called the *traffic jam technique*: placing products that customers need to carefully evaluate right near the access point. In this case, the aim is to realize a profit from the high-margin departments before customers fill up their carts with other less profitable items.

8. *Shift departments around periodically.* As we know, the more unfamiliar a store is, the more likely the customer will make an unplanned purchase. The explanation for is that when people don't know their way around, they tend to resort to information in the store, specifically on displays, to find the items they're looking for. So more exposure to stimuli means greater probability of making impulse purchases. Based on this premise, in some cases varying the product layout can be a good way to avoid customers becoming accustomed to too much of the same thing. Naturally, these modifications should not be extreme or customers will feel overly disoriented; if they can't easily and quickly find the products they've planned to purchase, they may decide to give up on the store and never come back.

The positioning of the sectors and departments, along with the relative impact on the interactions between product categories, are extremely topical questions. The starting point is the aim of enhancing the attractiveness of the path that customers follow through the store, which in turn boosts their purchase potential. Clearly, adopting the positioning criteria described above in no way guarantees that customers will visit the entire store. If this is the priority, the only solution is to set up an obligatory route by using different flooring materials, or placing display fixtures perpendicular to the entrance, forming corners and aisles at right angles, and creating gaps and passageways that customers will instinctively follow. In the most restrictive layouts, gondolas are arranged in such a way that customers are forced to walk by each one: up the first aisle and then back down the next. By the time they get to the cash desks, they've seen the entire product offering.

The decision of which of the two different methods to adopt has a powerful impact on the strategic marketing approach of the store. For instance, when there is a pathway clearly mapped out on the floor, it isn't possible to make rapid modifications in the content or the organizational structure of the different product groupings. In other words, display areas are rigidly demarcated. So the "obligatory route" technique is only appropriate when demand remains mostly stable over time. When long-term planning is not possible for the product assortment in question, the best option is to build an in-store route marked out by the arrangement of the displays.

Another consideration when setting up pathways through stores is the psychological side of customer habits. A route marked out on the floor is common in big box self-service stores, with average product quality in the assortment and little to no exclusivity. Instead, stores with different positioning should create in-store paths with display fixtures. In any case, the end result is the same: the experience loses all personalization for customers, since they are unable or unwilling to detour from their habitual path.

While exploiting space to the maximum, and offering a highly advantageous ratio of sales space to linear meters/feet of display, the rigidity of the model can present risks, especially in larger stores. When an obligatory path is too broad, customers get a growing feeling that they are pressed for time, so they lose interest in the display and their attention wanders. In other words, they no longer see the products as they're walking by. In light of all this, we can conclude that the best type of stores for the obligatory layout model are small to medium sized, such as discount stores, convenience stores and small supermarkets no larger than 700 square meters (7,500 square feet).

## 8.3    *Sizing the areas of the store*

The next step is to determine how much space to assign to each product category. The basic premise here is that this portion of space should not depend on the percentage of turnover, but the average per unit margin of the product category in question, prioritizing departments with above-average margins. This gives rise to the need to build a marketing system based on the classification of merchandise groupings. This serves to formulate sales projections that are clear and consistent, and to monitor the productivity of the groupings to verify that the sales space is properly allocated. Clearly, the method in question only provides general guidelines, so resulting space allocation decisions need to be optimized using logical corrections in light of the physical features of the products, among other things.

The key here is to avoid giving too much – or too little – space to a single category. In fact, studies show that when products are penalized by getting a quantity of linear meters/feet below a certain threshold, sales volumes drop below acceptable limits. By the same token, there is an optimal level for displaying a product, and beyond this point sales will rise, but less rapidly; in other words, any investment in additional marginal units of space will not pay off. Aside from the models and criteria we adopt, to create an efficient and effective product layout we need to consider a number of factors, such as:

- past data on previous layouts in the same store or in other stores in the same chain, which have similar architectural characteristics and target consumers;
- expectations regarding market evolution, in particular what merchandise has the greatest potential, estimated in terms of turnover;
- comparison with the competition, be it direct or indirect, taking into account stores that use different formats and/or operate in other geographical markets or other sectors; and
- data from purchase behavior research that can be conducted in the store.

In this regard, growing intensity in competition in modern distribution has major impact on the approach to product layout. Less and less often store layouts will be designed solely to optimize cost effectiveness, by creating semi-obligatory (or strongly recommended) pathways lined by displays that simply sell objects. Gradually stores will adopt a free circulation approach instead, which will boost the customer tendency to purchase; displays will not be limited to simply selling items but ideas, proposing product combinations and coordinates.

## 9    The focal point

The focal point acts like a magnet creating a powerful force of attraction and communication. It captures customers' attention thanks to its positioning, at an intersection or some other strategic location with respect to traffic flow and customers' field of vision (Fig. 41).

This means that it is not so much the choice of focal point that counts. (It could be an object, mannequin, a lavish composition representing the product assortment, an image reflecting the item on display, a splash of

*Figure* 41 – The focal point.

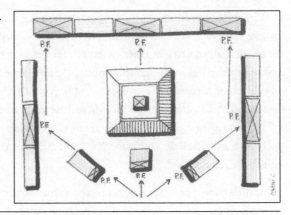

color, etc.) What does counts is the ability to distract the customers from the path they are following, steering them off on a detour through other areas in the store. To create a focal point, we need to find the optimal spot, one that is naturally most visible to customers, taking into account their vantage point and the customary path they take, as well as the physical structure of the store and the specific characteristics of the display fixtures. Visual merchandising develops the intrinsic opportunities of natural focal points, leveraging them through structural interventions and displays, or even devising them outright, if need be (Fig. 42).

Put another way, the focal point represents a means of communication and a source of vitality, energizing the store. Like any in-store signage, it

*Figure* 42 – The focal point captures the attention of the customers as they move along the normal pathway through the store.

enhances product visibility and highlights individual merchandise groupings, sparking attention and interest (Fig. 43).

A focal point has to draw people toward the store perimeter and break
up display monotony. To do so effectively, it must be readily legible and
visible from a distance (Fig. 44).

The focal point needs to be distinctive with respect to the other displays
in the department in question. The lighting on the products here also has
to be more intense, making this point stand out from the surrounding
area. Another key factor is the product theme, which must be immediately
clear. Decorative accents and complementary items can elicit customer interest, but they should not detract in any way from the visibility of the actual products, which are always center stage. In light of this, a series timely
themes, planned on an annual or seasonal basis and updated frequently,
can effectively contribute to refreshing the store image while giving the
sense of a highly dynamic handling of the product assortment.

The entrances to store sections warrant special attention; here display
fixtures should be arranged in a particular pattern to mark out secondary
penetration corridors that make it easier for customers to leave the main
thoroughfare and access the areas reserved for individual product groupings. These secondary aisles must be wide enough to be seen as actual

*Figure* 43 – Focal point or tropical flower?

*Figure* 44 – Leroy Merlin makes it easy
for customers to find their way around
by using gigantic products mounted on
perimeter walls.

in-store routes, rather than simply short cuts leading from section to section. To facilitate the flow of traffic here even more, internal windows are particularly useful, also known as display points.

## 10    The display point

The aim of a display point is to attract the attention of customers, drawing them into a specific sales area. This is realized with specially designed fixtures arranged along the path through the store in front of every product grouping. The aim here is to indicate to customers which products they can find nearby without blocking traffic flow (Fig. 45).

Regardless of what props and materials are used (from a simple mannequin set on a dais to an ad hoc display structure), these spaces need to be treated like actual store windows. As such they present all the distinctive elements of external windows, as previously described (Fig. 46).

There is very intricate interplay between focal points and display points. The communication of the focal point attracts customers to specific departments, where they can find all the products that are presented in the display point. In other words, the display point emphasizes and elucidates

*Figure* 45 – The display point.

*Figure* 46 – The composition of a display point can simulate a store window to present the product assortment of a specific department.

the communication of the product offering realized in the focal point, echoing and detailing the same theme, but not necessarily with the same merchandise. In general, the message conveyed by the focal points and display points should reflect the external store windows, highlighting the unique style and the commercial communication of the store.

## 11    Physical mobility and communicative mobility: graphics and signage

Many stores, especially those with a rigid grid layout, develop within the confines of a perceptive space that is completely enclosed on the vertical plane. When customers walk in, they can't view the entire sales area, so they're forced to depend on their physical mobility to move around from section to section to find what they've planned to purchase. Moreover, the route they follow is often obligatory, for them and for everyone else. This limits the possibility to move freely among the products on display. These circumstances call for a paradigm shift, an about-face in the approach to store design: it's not the customer who has to reach the product; instead the product should reach the customer thanks to continuous flows of information. In other words, physical mobility must make way for communicative mobility.

This aim can be achieved not only by opening up the customers' view of the store on the horizontal plane, but also by using proper signage that adequately exploits the extended perception of the sales area. Informational communication in the store must become a basic service that gives customers a complete picture of the routes they can take and the points of interest they can find, as soon as they step inside. This necessitates the use of innovative informational formats that are no longer simply local and analytical (communicating only with customers who have already reached the department in question), but synthetic and global as well.

There are a variety of ways to go about this, but graphics and signage are certainly the most effective. Graphics encompass all images that are displayed inside and outside the store (whether they are drawn, photographed, painted, carved, lithographed and so on). The advantages of graphics are the universality of the message they convey, as well as the ease and speed of comprehension for the viewer. What's more, graphics can readily reflect a lifestyle: images that illustrate events, situations or atmospheres are very effective in eliciting a sense of belonging in customers (Fig. 47). In other words, the environment that graphics can create is one where customers would like to be (Fig. 48).

Yet the purpose of graphics goes far beyond this. First, they don't simply make a display more dynamic, they also contribute to preserving a strong communicative consistency. To this end, graphics boost the impact of commercial initiatives aimed at sales promotions.

*Figure* 47 – The wall next to the staircase represents the urban context of street art, sign of the times for the lifestyle of H&M's target.

*Figure* 48 – The Maxi Sport photo of a pickup basketball game on an outdoor court reflects the typically American street sport experience.

For instance, in the field of fashion, store displays often combine images with mannequins, conjuring up clothing combinations that help customers make their choices. What's more, in-store advertising graphics encourage sales by reinforcing brand image (Fig. 49). Graphics also provide visual signals indicating the locations of various store departments (Fig. 50).

Signage, on the other hand, includes all written messages addressed to customers. It's normally most effective when combined with graphics to accentuate and clarify the message of the images. Often signage is the ideal tool for imprinting a photo, drawing or painting onto the collective memory. From a commercial standpoint, signage can be divided into three macro categories:

1. sales signage informing customers about a promotion;
2. category signage indicating a specific product family, a store department and/or a brand; and
3. institutional signage communicating pre- and post-sales services.

*Figure* 49 – The photo of the Prada collection constitutes a powerful visual element in the Salmoiraghi & Viganò store in Piazza San Babila, Milan.

*Figure* 50 – Images loaded with symbolic content reinforce the positioning of the "& Other Stories" chain with respect to the lifestyle of the retailer's target, a charming way to attract attention to the nail polish section.

*Figure* 51 – A hanging sign that is easy to see and to read, introducing customers to the main characteristics of the apple varieties on sale in the fruit section of an Iper hypermarket.

As with graphics, if properly positioned, signage can guide customers through the store, enabling them to find what they're looking for more quickly, and helping them gather more information on store services and product assortment (Fig. 51).

Techniques and materials that serve to create graphics and signage are countless. Here are just a few: posters (wayfinding wall signs for store departments, product signs, hanging signs, above- and below-shelf clip strips, institutional and promotional posters), lighted signs with sophisticated graphics, which are easy to memorize and clearly visible from a distance, strategically located information screens, slide show displays on monitors, large panels with or without backlighting, floor graphics (made of vinyl and applied on the floor on top of a transparent protective layer).

Among all the techniques listed above, one warrants a closer look: perimeter panels, which run horizontally along the store walls, in the space below the ceiling and above the top of the displays. Visible from any point on the sales floor, this space serves to communicate a continuous theme running through the entire store. It also helps customers find their way around, thanks to signage that points the way to each department, along with photos and graphics. In some cases, these panels can actually be turned into windows, placed high up on store walls, displaying objects that reflect a certain lifestyle (Fig. 52). Other stores fill these spaces with decor accents with a theatrical flair; an example here might be pictures hung on walls in waiting areas.

Naturally, stores that strongly identify with luxury and prestige will use more refined images, objects and materials, as opposed to the more simple and economical items on offer in stores with a discount image. The bottom line is that whatever the method or the instrument, what has to change is the approach to graphics and signage, since they can no longer be considered simple sales support tools. In this sense, there are certain common mistakes worth mentioning in design and information management.

To begin with, information materials and technologies too often tend to overwhelm the products and weigh down the retail environment. In

*Figure* 52 – Another photo of Leroy Merlin, where walls are used to display windows, also very effective in drawing attention to the perimeter walls while promoting product combinations to purchase.

these cases, the overall view of the store is limited by an excessive number of unnecessary elements compared to the merchandise on display. Added to this is the consideration that the signage often conveys scarce symbolic expression and little useful information, the latter creating no small degree of confusion.

To strike the proper balance between architectural essentials and communicative theatrics means to come up with signage that transmits information that is symbolic, synthetic and universally legible. Solutions that favor electronic technologies over material and paper-based support tools, with lighted images that take into account the visual-emotional links connecting different thematic areas of the store – all this will make transitions from section to section less abrupt and more seamless.

# 6    The display and space allocation

## 1    Visual attention

Many studies on visual merchandising activities are based on the premise that "*unseen is unsold*." In fact, when choosing which brand to buy, more often than not consumers are in the store. But here they actually take into consideration only a tiny portion of the products on offer (Inman *et al.*, 2009). In other words, in-store activities that elicit greater attention from customers should have a major impact on their behavior. While this is actually the case, it holds true only to a point. In fact, some studies show that enhancing customer attention in the store isn't enough, because not all of this attention ultimately leads to the final decision to make a purchase.

To understand this more clearly, think about how customers pay attention to certain products and evaluate them when making a purchase. But remember that in-store stimuli aren't alone in garnering customer attention – out-of-store factors do the same (Chandon *et al.*, 2009).

Specific examples of the latter encompass:

- the consumer, as far as motivations, buying habits, and demographics;
- the brand, in terms of market share; and
- the relationship between the consumer and the brand, with regard to consumption experience.

What is unique about external factors is that they can shape buying behavior if – and only if – they can trigger the consumer's memory during a visit to the store. In-store factors, instead, are determinants that can affect behavior exclusively when the phenomenon of visual attention takes place here.

These factors include:

- the number of facings, that is, visible units of product positioned on a linear display or a shelf, a measure of the quantity of space allotted to a product;
- the position on the shelf (vertical or horizontal), a measure of the quality of that space; and
- the average price, which serves as an indicator of product quality.

Basically, in-store factors represent choices retailers make as far as setting up displays and allocating space to SKUs within the specific area assigned to a given product category. The action of in-store factors triggers reactions from customers in the form of visual attention and evaluation. But the two are not necessarily related. Specifically, visual attention means noticing a product and re-examining it; evaluation, instead can be broken down into activities such as considering, choosing, and recalling.

Both in- and out-of-store factors influence the attention, consideration and choices of consumers. To be more specific, in-store levers act primarily on the latter two. For example, the number of facings has a major impact (albeit marginally diminishing) on visual attention and in turn on product evaluation. In fact, customers are led to believe that the leading brands and products are usually placed in more prominent positions on the store shelf. As a result, a high number of facings can have a direct positive effect on customer evaluation.

Delving into more detail, we can refer to two models for facings:

1. *Linear facing* refers to SKUs lined up on a shelf or on hangers, depending on the quantity and type of product. In this case, the *facing capacity* is the number of items on display in a sales area in a single facing, taking into account shelf depth and the vertical distance between shelves. For a product with a facing that is three deep and stacked two high, the facing capacity is six. So if that product is displayed with four facings, the facing capacity is 24.
2. *Non-linear facing* relates to products placed in baskets, bins, or on pallets or special stands.

Regardless of the model, the facing has a positive impact on purchases, in particular with younger, more educated, and more opportunistic buyers. But this is due not so much to differences in attention. (Actually, the degree of attention and the impact of marketing activities tend to be similar among various types of customers.) Instead these consumers are more inclined to take into consideration products that are brought to their attention through visual merchandising activities.

Likewise, the shelf position of a particular brand/product is a powerful stimulus for visual attention. Yet unlike the effect of a high number of facings, this attention doesn't necessarily lead to more evaluation. The reason for this is that the shelf position of a product, especially on the vertical, has a direct influence on evaluation. This in turn magnifies the impact of greater attention, for better (higher shelves) or for worse (mid-level shelves).

By the same token, it seems that visual attention alone is not enough to prompt a final purchase. For instance, although studies confirm that middle to high level displays are more effective in attracting attention compared to lower ones, only the highest placements lead to actual product evaluation.

As we would naturally assume, in-store factors play a bigger role in visual attention than out-of-store factors. But in contrast the latter have a greater impact on evaluation, which is only minimally affected by visual attention. To sum up, the most recent studies highlight the fact that in-store factors have a major influence on attention, which reverberates onto product evaluation in a significant, albeit limited, way. These limited effects consolidate over time and contribute to reinforcing specific out-of-store factors.

Among these, the consumption experience also has a positive effect on attention. This phenomenon is a relevant one in light of the fact that without attention, product/brand preference will never lead to consideration and ultimately choice. What is worth noting here is that consumption experience not only shapes expectations as far as product utility, but also cuts search costs and enhances the effectiveness of visual merchandising activities. These in turn interact with expected utility to drive consideration and choice, setting off a ripple effect.

This means that to assess brand equity accurately, beyond the traditional analytical metrics, such as recall and brand preference in scenarios of forced exposure, alternative research methods should also be implemented to appraise the actual impact in terms of visual attention. More generally speaking, when we want to come up with metrics to evaluate in-store behaviors, we need to remember that these can be grouped in two macro-categories based on:

- *attention*, measured through eye tracking, which reveals when and how customers notice and re-examine product assortment; and

- *evaluation*, assessed through individual interviews, to find out how customers recall visual attention, consideration, and choice.

Although the word "recall" relates to attention, it shouldn't be used as a proxy for *visual* attention for two reasons. First, when customers recall products, they disregard around two-thirds of the ones that they actually intended to buy. Second, and more importantly, recall discriminates in favor of the brands that customers prefer. This means that calculating visual attention based on recall could be dangerously misleading. For instance, highly educated customers might remember several brand names, but notice fewer brands on the store shelves. This goes to show yet again that companies should measure not only product evaluation, but attention as well by researching how customers "read" shelves through eye tracking.


## 2   The display

The display sets the scene for retailers to organize and present their products, which they group together as the store layout allows. The aim is to represent the offering with a visual impact that elicits emotions and maximizes sales. Here too the sales floor and the product displays have to be set up so as to make the offering as easy as to read as possible. An effective display presents the product assortment attractively and highlights adjacencies among various items that belong to the same product family, accentuating the commercial value while proposing new ideas.

To put it simply, the display should:

- attract the customer;
- elicit emotion;
- convey information;
- create a product culture;
- simplify planned purchases; and
- encourage combination purchases and impulse purchases.

Creating and managing displays, and synchronizing displays with the dynamics of other levers of visual merchandising: these are no simple tasks. A good display does not simply grab the attention of customers who pass by: it has to make them to stop and evaluate the merchandise. The optimal type and size display changes on a case-by-case basis.

## 2.1    Methods for displaying products

Depending on the relevant commercial and communication objectives, different methods can be used for displaying products. At this point the following display classification is useful:

- trial display;
- permanent display;
- seasonal display; and
- promotional display.

The *trial display*, the initial model used in a store when it first opens for business, is based on strategic choices regarding segmentation and positioning. The aim here is to test initial customer reactions and then revisit some or all of these choices, in light of sales performance and customer satisfaction.

The *permanent display* is the model used to propose and illustrate the store's entire product assortment on an ongoing basis. This display consistently reflects the distinctive features and the very essence of the offering, in other words, what makes it stand out from the competition. How this display is managed depends largely on what kind of merchandise the store sells. For instance, with fashion or fresh food, the fact that these goods are seasonal means space for permanent presentation will be kept to a minimum (Fig. 1). But in stores or departments that are less subject to fashion trends or seasons, linear displays are changed with far less frequency.

*Figure 1* – A massive, high-impact permanent display for the produce section in Whole Foods, a California supermarket chain.

*Figure* 2 – The daily special draws the
eye, encourages impulse purchases and
suggests product combinations in an Iper
hypermarket.

A *seasonal display*, as the name suggests, is used for products with seasonal
sales cycles. This kind of display must be high impact both in terms of size
and visual intensity (dramatic effect and informative communication). The
priority in setting up a seasonal display is coming up with an innovative
way to accentuate the product in question, spotlighting its aesthetic and/or
functional features. What's more, signage and product information should
be designed and managed to provide an added enticement to attract customers' attention while informing and educating them on the characteristics of the offering (Fig. 2).

The *promotional* or *special display* accentuates the novelty and innovation
of the product and/or brand, or emphasizes convenient pricing of the assortment, or draws attention to special offers. This kind of display is normally enormous, to guarantee both the maximum visibility in the store as
well as a sufficient stock of merchandise (Fig. 3). With respect to this last
point, the store should limit the risk of stockout to avoid leaving customers
frustrated and dissatisfied when there's no more product left to buy. In this
sense, running a product promotion means planning, designing and organizing the overall sales campaign at a store level to maximize the overall
efficiency and effectiveness of the initiative.

*Figure* 3 – A pyramid-shaped display
of bananas, with a wooden tree trunk
and packing crates serving as the base.
The overall effect is an open-air market,
evoking memories of a tropical vacation
right in the middle of a central aisle in the
product section of an Iper hypermarket.

## 2.2   *Display techniques*

From a technical standpoint, there are various ways to display products:

1. on shelves;
2. on hangers;
3. on hooks;
4. on tables;
5. folded;
6. in baskets or bins; and
7. on mannequins or bust forms.

*Shelf displays*

Whether they are part of free-standing displays or built in to wall units, shelves are a flexible, easy-to-manage presentation technique. Normally used in grocery stores, shelf displays are equally effective for other product categories too (Figs. 4, 5 and 6).

*Figure* 4 – Products
displayed on shelves.

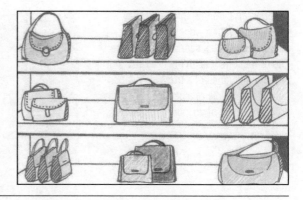

*Figure* 5 – A weight-bearing column that
turns into a shelf.

*Figure* 6 – A pyramid of books that turns
into a shelf.

## *Hanging displays*

Products can be hung on big hooks or hangers placed on rods inserted
into gondolas or wall units (Figs. 7, 8 and 9). Some clothing stores use this
technique, with garments strung up from floor to ceiling on clotheslines
or invisible supports of some kind. This gives customers an overall view of
the clothing while creating a sense of movement, and all without resorting
to mannequins.

*Figures* 7-8-9 – Hanging products using various techniques and supports.

 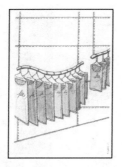 

*Figure* 10 – Hanging out the laundry or selling clothes?

## Hook displays

Small merchandise can be displayed on hooks slotted into gondolas or wall units. This presentation technique conveys a sense of order and precision, and facilitates cross-merchandising, proposing product adjacencies either in terms of category or function. Cross-merchandising, in turn, can generate add-on sales (Figs. 11 and 12).

*Figure* 11 – Small products are hung up on hooks slotted into gondolas.

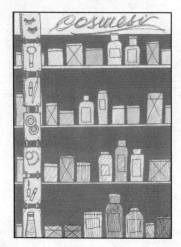

*Figure* 12 – For every book, a sweet!

*Table displays*

There are two distinct purposes for a table display:

- to welcome customers; and
- to sell products.

A table set up to *welcome customers* is placed close to the store entrance, to give people a moment to stop and prepare for the visit. (This is the "decompression" zone.) Then they can get their bearings with quick look around to see the layout of the store (Underhill, 1999). The store positioning will dictate whether to place either decorative accent pieces on the display table or a selection of products. From a simple piece of artwork or a single flower arrangement in a luxury boutique, to similar items interspersed with merchandise for a store with a middle to high positioning, to exclusively products, which are often promoted in other retail outlets (Rizzi and Milani, 2013) (Figs. 13 and 14).

*Selling tables*, which can be placed anywhere in the store, give customers the advantage of direct contact with the offering. People can pick up merchandise and look it over at their leisure. What's more, physical barriers – and more importantly psychological ones – are minimized if not eliminated completely (Figs. 15, 16, 17 and 18).

*Figure* 13 – Gio Moretti welcomes customers with lovely fresh flowers in a pastel-colored setting, creating the ideal backdrop for any fashion collection.

*Figure* 14 – In a Desigual store, a table marking the entrance and making the first impression of the Kids Department serves first and foremost to display merchandise.

*Figure* 15 – At Desigual display tables are scattered throughout the store to facilitate customer interaction with products.

*Figure* 16 – At Excelsior in Milan, tables serve as frames for contemporary art exhibits where the products are the subjects, and the customers are simple spectators.

*Figure* 17 – Lush's wonderfully colorful soap balls are iconic items that gives customers a multisensorial store experience, highlighting an offering free of physical or psychological barriers. The company motto echoes throughout the store with signs that assure customers: "Here you can touch everything except the staff!"

*Figure* 18 – At & Other stores, display tables aren't the only things that encourage customers to try products.

Table displays can be arranged by theme or by function, depending sole-ly on micro-marketing strategies and contingent factors, which are also linked to commercial considerations. What matters most is to "change it up", varying the presentation at regular intervals in terms of products and/ or display techniques.

### Folded merchandise

This display technique merely consists of folding and stacking soft mer-chandise or large cumbersome items on racks instead of shelves or tables (Figs. 19 and 20).

### Basket displays

Baskets and bins set in free-standing displays or placed along the path that customers follow through the store, overflowing with products thrown randomly in: the message this sends is "cheap". Stores that use this type of display aim to move large volumes of low-cost merchandise (Fig. 21). But sometimes baskets can even be used to accentuate a prestigious offering, without necessarily creating dissonance (Fig. 22).

*Figures* 19 and 20 – Stacks of folded items placed on racks or shelves

 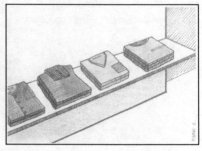

*Figure* 21 – Products displayed in baskets.

*Figure* 22 – At Eat's, in the Excelsior department store in Milan, baskets of fruit harmonize perfectly with the luxury atmosphere, striking a note of order in the midst of apparent chaos.

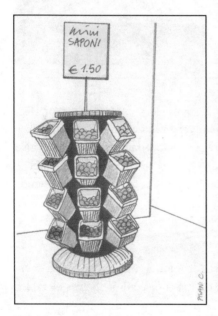 

## Mannequins or bust form displays

Lastly, bust forms and mannequins communicate the availability of the offering, and suggest how garments can be mixed and matched while conveying a specific theme (Fig. 23). When this communication is effective, it generally translates into a major boost in sales. In fact, these sales support tools are used more and more often to promote products that don't belong to the fashion system, such as electronics in Sony corner shops.

*Figure* 23 – Bust forms and mannequins for mixing and matching products to convey a display theme.

*Figure* 24 – At Nike Town in New York, life-sized mannequins standing in a line symbolize team spirit in soccer, promoting the idea and the product with high visual impact.

The backdrop has to flatter the garments on the mannequins, recreating just the right atmosphere, and changing with every "change of clothes" (Fig. 24).

Naturally, there are infinite options to choose from for store mannequins. The basic model is molded on the human body, which is then elaborated or stylized, taking on a vast array of shapes and materials: with or without a head; made of metal, plastic, fabric and so on (Fig. 25).

*Figure* 25 – Mannequins or products? American Girl dolls pose like mannequins in the children's clothing department.

There are three specific types of mannequins:

- tailors dummies (bust forms, made of papier-mâché, wood, fiberglass or resin, normally covered in fabric);
- realistic (in plastic or fiberglass); and
- stylized (in a wide range of materials).

On occasion, the mannequin itself becomes the distinctive mark of a brand. An example is the metallic model used by Jean-Paul Gaultier, which later became the symbol and logo for the designer's perfumes and advertising campaigns.

Inside the store, mannequins and bust forms can offer customers a complete vision of the stylistic offering. What's more, these sales supports can also serve as a sort of sign post to delineate various departments, marking out product lines as well as customer segments (Fig. 26).

*Figure* 26 – In the women's department at Topshop in London, mannequins arranged along a path mark the flow of traffic and introduce customers to the fashion collection.

*Figure* 27 – The variety of displays in this specialty food shop in Paris is particularly tantalizing, creating movement in the presentation of sauces, marmalades and jams.

In light of the advantages and limitations outlined above, ideally a combination of different displays should be used. While never neglecting the need to convey a certain uniformity in presenting merchandise, by adopting several different techniques, even in the same department, retailers can liven up the sales floor while keeping the customers' attention (Fig. 27).

### 2.3    Display dimensions

To minimize monotony in product displays and enhance legibility at the same time, stores can resort to techniques that exploit three-dimensionality, with products positioned at three different heights (Fig. 28):

1. foreground;
2. mid-level; and
3. backdrop.

### The foreground

The foreground is also called the "grab and go zone." This is the front part of a display area, closest to the customer flow, the equivalent of a window display located on the main pathway leading through the store. Generally

*Figure* 28 – Display height.

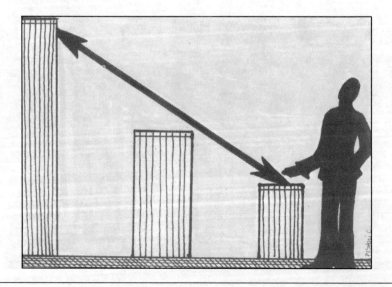

positioned from 70 to 100 centimeters (28 to 39 inches) from the floor, this space is dedicated for the most part to products that customers need to touch before they buy. In a big box, for example, the foreground of each department presents a current sampling of the merchandise on offer, highlighting the specific products customers will find there while reinforcing the overall store image (Fig. 29).

*Mid-level*

A mid-level display, from 100 to 140 centimeters (39 to 55 inches) high, lies between the foreground and the backdrop, and so has the advantages of both. In other words, it's the best place to display products, giving customers the impression of a complete and varied offering, one that's set out in a clear, functional fashion. While high-impact displays are used in the foreground, here fixtures are positioned at middle to upper levels, to guarantee display capacity without blocking visibility of the backdrop or nearby departments. Product presentation at mid-level is intentionally more casual, creating "orderly disorder" which prompts customers to reach out and touch the merchandise. The aim is to continually catch the customer's eye.

*Figure* 29 – The Jil Sander shop in shop opens with a foreground display of fashion accessories to accent the clothes collection and to draw customer attention to the higher display fixtures.

## The backdrop

The backdrop is set against the walls that delineate the department or the store. This area, the most visible from a distance, is where the higher display fixtures go (higher, but not so high that customers can't access them) (Fig. 30). The main goal for vertical displays here is to communicate, to show the store's offering, with items that can attract the attention of the customers who are farthest away. This display is the most methodical and meticulous. And by adding focal points, retailers can further magnify the function of the backdrop as a "pole of attraction," as is common practice in department stores and boutiques.

As a general rule, as we'll discuss further on, products should be positioned on the vertical from 40 to 170 centimeters (16 to 67 inches) from the floor. This is the zone that offers immediate visual and physical contact from an ergonomic standpoint, which means that anything placed higher or lower than this is hard to see and to reach. For small to medium-sized objects, such as jewelry and accessories, a more limited range in terms of display height applies, from a low point of 90 centimeters (3 feet) (corresponding to the top of a display table) to a maximum of 160 centimeters (5 feet 3 inches).

*Figure* 30 – The backdrop provides a setting for foreground and mid-level displays, completing the presentation of the offering.

Unfortunately, the rules on three-dimensional displays are often over-looked due to the need to optimize space. In these cases, however, re-tailers should carefully consider which products they place where. For instance, above 170 centimeters (5 feet 7 inches) is the best position for medium-to-large items that can attract attention from a distance. In oth-er cases, the limitation is purely physical: the three display dimensions require a minimum depth of 3 meters (9 feet); in a smaller sales area a two-dimensional display approach is the better choice. In addition to these three levels, there are also *free-standing displays* in the center of stores, which should be no higher than 150 centimeters (5 feet), so as to avoid blocking the overall view of the sales floor.

## 3    Space allocation

Retailers manage their stores like factories, striving to fully exploit factors of production, which in their case are linked to work and space. As for the latter, modern retail outlets, which are often located in suburban areas, have exploded in size. Yet they still aren't big enough to contend with the exponential expansion of product assortment. As a result, space has be-come a scarce and inflexible resource. This has fueled the growing trend of *space management*, which serves to maximize output where all products in a given assortment compete for space, in terms of quality and quantity.

In light of space management strategies, to fully understand the impact of in-store factors on visual attention and product evaluation we'll briefly turn once again to purchase planning. Let's take a closer look at three possible decision-making scenarios (Fig. 31):

1. *planned purchases by product family and SKU*, typified by high brand loyalty;
2. *planned purchases by product family and impulse purchases by SKU*, with a strong commodity connotation, for which the brand may or may not necessarily guarantee a final purchase; and
3. impulse purchases by product family and by SKU.

1. *Planned purchases by product family and specific SKU.* Here typically there is high price transparency and extremely narrow profit margins, which means that merchandise is not usually allocated high-quality space. Be-cause relative products are basically pre-sold and have little space elasticity, the quantity of space becomes critical both for producers and distributors.

In fact, if space doesn't suffice to serve demand, stockouts would be commonplace. For wholesalers that equates with lost sales, and for retailers, with a disservice for customers which could eventually erode their trust and ultimately their loyalty toward the store.

2. *Planned purchases by product family and impulse purchases by specific product.* This encompasses an extremely varied category. With brand name goods, customers won't choose what to buy until they're standing in front of the shelf; but whatever they end up choosing, they're willing to change often. So these items are sensitive to both the quality and the quantity of space. On closer consideration, quality becomes a precondition for quantity, since space elasticity increases as visibility grows and space quality improves. This is the very situation that triggers the most frequent conflicts between industry and distribution. For the former, sales are directly impacted when quantity of space and visibility are limited. The distributor, instead, will simply see customers turn to other products, without feeling like they've experienced any disservice.

3. *Impulse purchases by product family and by SKU.* Generally speaking, because these items generate solid profits they get visibility, as far as available space allows. However, what is more critical here is visibility for the entire product family, seeing that sales performance is sensitive to product exposure, which in turn is affected to a great extent by shelf positioning. What happens in this scenario is that buyers evaluate their options, scanning the shelf sequentially, from higher to lower quality, and they often end up choosing a brand before they've even seen the entire assortment. In these cases, the channel relationships tend to be collaborative as far as shelf management and, to an even greater extent, in developing category management initiatives that directly impact visual merchandising.

*Figure* 31 – Space allocation in terms of quality and quantity, based on planned vs unplanned purchases.

| Planned/unplanned purchases | Quantity of space | Quality of space |
|---|---|---|
| By product family and SKU | | |
| By product family | | |
| Impulse purchases | | |

Now we'll explore in-store factors that impact space, in terms of quality (vertical and horizontal displays) and quantity (number of facings).

## 4    Quality of space

When analyzing the quality of display space, we need to specifically consider vertical and horizontal dimensions. In doing so, what becomes clear is that this quality varies tremendously. In fact, sales sensitivity depends on product positioning: not only where the item is placed in terms of the shelf height from the floor, but also along the length of the gondola (in the middle or at either end), and finally the position of the gondola with respect to the in-store traffic flow.

As far as shelf height, there are four levels:

1. *Ground level* (from 20 to 60 cm off the floor) (8 to 24 in) refers to the lowest shelves. Since customers have to make an effort to reach down to this far, it offers the least accessibility and visibility. The ground level is often reserved for heavy, cumbersome items, for big multiple packages, for bins and baskets, and for products that customers can easily read vertically, that is, when looking down from above (like placemats).
2. *Hand level* (from 60 to 110 cm) (24 to 43 in) is an easy-access zone, which facilitates purchases. This space is best exploited for product adjacencies; impulse purchases; high-rotation, daily necessities; and articles with solid spontaneous demand, such as local and seasonal items.
3. *Eye level* (from 110 to 170 cm) (43 to 67 in), also called the "level of perception," is the most visible, so consumers focus most of their attention here. This is the optimal position for impulse purchases and products that generate high margins.
4. *Hat level* (above 170 cm) (above 67 in) yields variable sales results depending on the height of the shelf: the higher it is, the less accessible. This space is useful for products with packaging that customers can recognize from a distance. These items act like road signs, conveying information, and serving for presentation and communication of the product category. Hat level is also a good place for stocking products that are displayed on the shelves below, providing instant access to inventory.

Summing up, products are more likely to sell at hand level or eye level; in fact, customers only check lower and higher than this when they can't find what they're looking for. As a general rule, the better profit margins a product generates, the better the placement it should get on the shelf. But as we've already seen, tactical or operational needs may arise that might justify other choices. Examples are positioning overstocked products at eye level to move them more quickly, or placing new products here to encourage customers to try them out. Putting highly legible products in less favorable positions might make sense because they'll be subject to less negative fall-out anyway thanks to their natural visibility. This is also a way to draw the attention of customers to shelf levels that are normally overlooked. Lastly, accenting different color variations can liven up any product display.

Before setting down any hard and fast rules about displaying merchandise, the relational approach dictates that first, customer needs and behaviors must be analyzed, both of which can also depend on physical requirements. For example, let's take a clothing display. When presenting coordinates, each piece should be positioned at a different height so the overall view is consistent with customer expectations, giving a better idea of the total look. So suit coats always have to be above trousers, with footwear beneath that, following the logical "vertical" order of these items. Another point to remember is that when adult customers are standing in front of a display, they can't see merchandise below 30 to 40 centimeters (12 to 15 inches) from the floor, or goods positioned above 200 centimeters (6 feet 8 inches). These measurements change, obviously, when the customers in question are children (Fig. 32).

## 4.1   Vertical product presentation

There are two different ways to display merchandise:

1. from right to left (horizontally on one or more shelves); and
2. from top to bottom (vertically the entire height of the shelf).

The most practical and popular option that retailers use is vertical for product families and horizontal for brands. This allows for more discretion in product displays, as well as more variables to bring to the table in negotiations with industry (Fig. 33).

More specifically, this kind of product presentation gives customers a better view of the assortment. Normally people fix their gaze on a height

*Figure* 32 – A whole world of books scaled down to child size in the Kidz space in la Feltrinelli bookstore.

*Figure* 33 – Vertical display by product family and horizontal display by brand.

| Eye cream | Face cream | Body lotion |
|---|---|---|
| Brand X | Brand X | Brand X |
| **Eye cream** | **Face cream** | **Body lotion** |
| Brand Y | Brand Y | Brand Y |
| **Eye cream** | **Face cream** | **Body lotion** |
| Brand Z | Brand Z | Brand Z |

of around 150 centimeters (5 feet), looking right to left and back again, rather than up and down. At a glance, customers immediately note the different product families, take in most of the assortment and pinpoint what items interest them most (Fig. 34).

In other words, this method reinforces the traffic flow, makes for a tidier display, and helps customers compare their options. So there's no need to backtrack through the store to check out different product lines on offer. At the same time, the assortment is more legible, the display is more harmonious in terms of color coordination, and customers can immediately perceive the transition from one line to another. So, in a sense,

*Figure* 34 – Order, clarity, and legibility in a display, vertical by product category and horizontal by brand.

the departments in a store actually become a series of stores, giving the impression of order and clarity, while enhancing the value of each product category thanks to strategically placed adjacencies. All this makes it easier to use specially designed Point of Purchase materials (POP), and to organize items by price range and size. What's more, this display technique slows customers down as they move through the store, browsing among all the products and quite probably making add-on purchases. Another display option is to alternate lines by popularity, that is, high-demand and low-demand products.

There's one final advantage to the display tactic following the vertical for product families and horizontal for brands. In doing so, retailers can position the most profitable items at eye level, or at least balance out the sales generated from a single product family, rotating merchandise on different shelf levels to ensure more equality in product exposure while preserving consistency and disrupting monotony. In fact, rotating products on display is a sure-fire way to boost sales, even for items that are penalized on the less visible shelves.

## 4.2    *Horizontal product presentation*

Unlike vertical displays, with a horizontal presentation a different display level is assigned to each product family. This calls for a qualitative distinction between lines, which can be dealt with by putting lines associated with planned purchases at hand level, and impulse purchases at eye level (Fig. 35).

*Figure* 35 – Horizontal display by product family and vertical display by brand.

| Eye cream<br>Brand X | Eye cream<br>Brand Y | Eye cream<br>Brand Z |
|---|---|---|
| Face cream<br>Brand X | Face cream<br>Brand Y | Face cream<br>Brand Z |
| Body lotion<br>Brand X | Body lotion<br>Brand Y | Body lotion<br>Brand Z |

Although this isn't the most popular display technique, the horizontal presentation does offer certain advantages. First, there's no need for a high number of facings for customers to see products when they first step into an aisle; in other words, people don't need to be directly in front of the display. Furthermore, horizontal displays are the perfect solution for small-quantity items. And when using this technique, retailers can allocate the most valuable space to the product families that are more likely to be impulse purchases.

What's more, this technique lends itself well to seasonal sales, since it's easy to expand and contract the space dedicated to single product categories as need be. Lastly, this type of display works well both for the bottom shelf, which can hold bins and baskets of random products, and the top one, which is ideal for items that are easy to see.

### *Brand blocking*

Suppliers with broad brand portfolios can use a vertical display for all the brands in the same product category and a horizontal one for specific packaging/formats. This technique is called *brand blocking*, the ideal display solution by far. The only limitation is managing the quality of the vertical display.

Here are the key advantages of brand blocking:

- the color code of the brands serves to guide customers as they browse through the shelves;
- the brand is more visible, making it easier to spot a product for a planned purchase, while at the same time facilitating impulse purchases;
- the number of customer-product interactions increases;
- the quality of the horizontal space can be optimized by sequencing different brands according to profitability;
- new product launches boost sales of existing products;
- if one product runs out, consumers are less likely to buy a different brand;
- customers get a stronger sense of clarity and order;
- there is less direct comparison between competing products; and
- the communicative impact of the individual brand is reinforced.

But for all the pros of this model, there are cons as well. There are only a few exceptional scenarios in which retailers actually like brand blocking. One such case is when effective brand management has created a perfect symmetry between brand image and customer needs, so the brand becomes top priority in the purchasing process. Naturally this solution is only viable when the brand in question covers a wide range of products (Fig. 36).

*Figure* 36 – Brand blocking is well suited to beer, where the most recognized brands guide purchase and consumption.

Normally, it is more often the case that distributors diminish the impact of suppliers on the final customers, hindering brand exposure. The motivation in doing so is to underscore their own role as retailers in selecting and re-combining the industrial offering based on their customers' needs. In any case, just as critical as all these visual merchandising choices are decisions on space allocation. Here there is no single option that universally applies to all stores and all merchandise categories. Deciding how to allocate space is actually the outcome of a compromise between producers and retailers. For the final decision, a number of factors come into play: assortment and pricing policies, results in terms of profit margins and stock rotation, the characteristics of product categories, and consumer buying behavior. So space allocation is ultimately a tool for differentiating product offerings and building store identity.

Moving on from this, as we pointed out above, for retailers the optimal display is vertical for product family/line and horizontal for brand/product. But this solution can prove to be out of synch with how customers mentally organize their needs. In some cases, for instance, stores try to boost add-on purchases by frequently rotating product categories and brands on shelves. This forces customers to search out the products they planned on purchasing. Although it's true that some degree of change can spark interest and curiosity; going too far would mean running a huge risk. Customers could end up feeling disoriented and frustrated, and may even decide not to buy anything after all.

In other words, once again the key is striking a balance between short- and long-term goals. The first are all about maximizing the profitability of space, while the second are more concerned with earning customer loyalty by creating clear, legible displays that help simplify the purchase process.

### 4.3 Shoulder out, face forward and stacked product presentation

Continuing our discussion of display quality, at this point it's worthwhile taking a closer look at specific techniques that work for products such as books, music, and clothing. These are only a few of the departments where retailers can alternate displays between shoulder out and face forward.

Specifically, a shoulder out or sideways display is a way to align products by occupying less space while accenting assortment variety. An example here would be basic menswear such as classic suit coats, a purchase which is usually planned. A shoulders out product presentation is highly effective because the choices customers need to make revolve almost exclusively around colors and fabrics. In other words, aligning items side by side works best with a planned purchase of a known product, because it involves a more immediate decision-making process. In this case, there's no need to draw attention to the model; the priority is putting as many products as possible in the available space, with the display spotlighting functional product features. The side or shoulder out display is also a useful option during clearance sales or promotional events. Displaying products by function facilitates the choice of styles and sizes, and reinforces the typical message of massification.

Face forward or face out displays, instead, highlight the individual item, maximizing visibility and accentuating certain features. Here, what emerges more clearly than ever is the function of the display as a sort of personal shopper that customers can look to for ideas and inspiration, encouraging impulse purchases while drawing attention exclusively to certain merchandise. In some cases, we can go even further and converge customer focus on a single item by setting it apart, outside the context. But we need to emphasize once again that with the exception of certain specific products, it's always best to alternate the two different types of displays to create a more attractive and aesthetic presentation (Fig. 37).

*Figure* 37 – Different display techniques give movement to a sales area creating a balanced and aesthetically pleasing wall composition at Non Solo Sport.

Another tactic for making certain products stand out on a normal linear display is to pile them up in "stacks" that break up the linear, starting from the floor level. Products placed in piles on tables, instead, are called 'half stacks' Either one helps avoid monotony in the product presentation, intercepting the flow of customers by interrupting the linear movement of the shelves (Fig. 38).

An effective way to give the display a sense of movement while accenting a product or product family is to stagger items on shelves, or even stagger the shelves themselves (Fig. 39).

Regardless of the technique retailers opt to use, by highlighting the product (beyond the context of a sales promotion), they can effectively achieve a number of goals: sell excess stock, enhance the appeal of a product (especially but not exclusively during the launch), propose an adjacency, draw attention to a special offer, break up the monotony of the linear (Fig. 40).

## 5    Quantifying space and saturating the linear display

A number of studies have shown that if a product is given too much space on a store shelf, sales elasticity starts to fall. Specifically, as product exposure increases beyond the minimum visibility threshold (which varies depending on the volume of the product and the total linear allocated

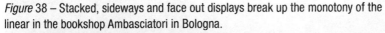

*Figure* 38 – Stacked, sideways and face out displays break up the monotony of the linear in the bookshop Ambasciatori in Bologna.

*Figure* 39 – In this Kiko store, cosmetics are placed in staggered rows, injecting energy into the rhythm of the display.

*Figure* 40 – A face out display combined with book profiles is a powerful validation for recommended reading in the Advice from the Authors section in Feltrinelli bookstores.

to the product family), turnover grows more than proportionally up to a maximum saturation point of the linear. But beyond this point, sales performance stays constant. In fact, elasticity of the linear display is measured by a *saturation curve*. Whatever the product, this curve is always asymptotic, and identifies the optimum linear, which will clearly fall between the minimum and maximum.

The first person to verify this curvilinear relationship between space and sales was Lee (1961), documenting the fact that customers are highly sensitive to the visual impact of a display. In fact, as display size grows, so does the propensity to buy. Naturally, many later studies that explored this relationship also revealed its limits. For an example, simply recall what we discussed in the first section on variations in visual attention.

That said, beyond a doubt the space/sales relationship still holds true. Taking a closer look, the *minimum linear* is the smallest amount of product needed to ensure that it is perceived and identified. Clearly, the perception and identification of a product, in other words product visibility, depend on its size and packaging, as well as its proximity to the customer. This minimum threshold can range from 20 centimeters (8 inches) in a non-food store to 45-50 centimeters (18 – 20 inches) in a supermarket.

At this point we should add that space elasticity also varies depending on how planned or unplanned a given purchase is. So impulse purchases and new products need a bigger linear minimum. What's more, above the lower limit of visibility, expanding the linear doesn't significantly increase planned purchases, but it does boost impulse purchases. In fact, the more space impulse items get, the more they sell. Beyond this, the minimum threshold also has to optimize replenishment and help mitigate the risk of stockouts. What this boils down to is making sure that the composition of the facing is determined by the sales volumes expected from one replenishment to the next. This minimizes mistakes in stock management and cuts maintenance costs. In any case, the linear minimum should correspond to a stock capacity of at least one entire box of product, to avoid having to send "partials" (half-empty boxes) back to the store room.

The *maximum linear* coincides with the saturation threshold. In other words, beyond this point, increasing display space for a product doesn't translate into a significant rise in sales, so there's no sense in overstocking. We calculate the maximum linear based on profit margins measured by the gross turnover (that is, taking into account the total investment of the store plus handling costs) compared to the total number of linear meters/feet.[1] To be specific, when the profit margin of a linear meter/foot of that product is lower than the profit margin for its relative product family, the product does not justify its handling costs, so it should take up less space on the linear. Viceversa, when the profitability of an individual product exceeds that of its product family, that is a signal to extend the linear to maximize overall turnover both for the family and the department.

Put another way, the ideal linear not only enhances product visibility, but also attracts customers' attention, sparking the desire to buy. At the same time, retailers are guaranteed higher profitability per unit of shelf space than the department average without lost sales, and they can maximize productivity while minimizing the risk of stockouts.

## 6    Shelf management for maximum performance: linears, ends and end caps

Regardless of the display technique in question, sequencing products along a shelf can enhance the visibility of individual product lines, placing the so-called loss leaders (the fastest moving items) in areas that funnel customers toward more profitable product lines. In particular, keeping traffic flow in mind, positioning of high- and low-rotation products can follow a *progressive* or *mixed family network* approach. Product positioning based on a *progressive network of families/lines* is a way to expose customers to products on a rotating basis. The idea is to sequence items from low to high rotation, with the highest at the end of the display (Fig. 41).

Another option is *mixed families/lines*. This involves placing high-rotation families/lines at the beginning of the pathway that customers follow; next come medium-rotation and then low-rotation items, ending once again with products with maximum rotation (Fig. 42).

---

[1] The word "linear" refers to the length of a horizontal display: the floor linear (FL) is the length of the shelf measured across the floor; the developed linear (DL) is the floor linear multiplied by the number of shelf levels. (A gondola measuring 1.33 meters/yards in length (FL = 1.33) with 5 shelves (DL= 5) has a DL of 6.65 meters /yards (1.33 x 5)).

*Figure* 41 – Product positioning with a progressive network of families/lines.

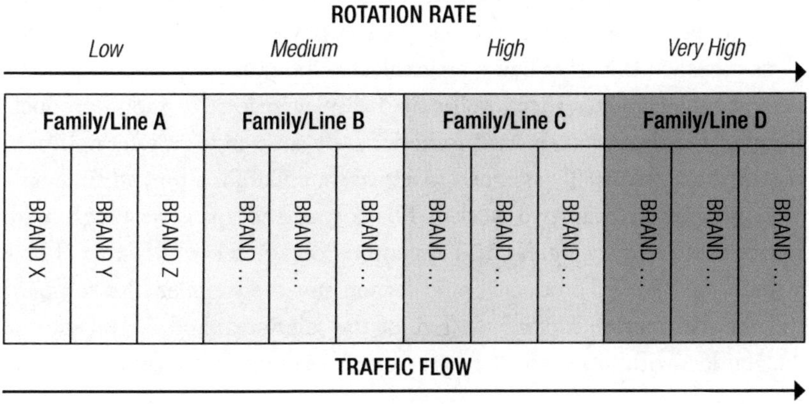

**ROTATION RATE**

| *Low* | *Medium* | *High* | *Very High* |
|---|---|---|---|

| Family/Line A | | | Family/Line B | | | Family/Line C | | | Family/Line D | | |
|---|---|---|---|---|---|---|---|---|---|---|---|
| BRAND X | BRAND Y | BRAND Z | BRAND ... | BRAND ... | BRAND ... | BRAND ... | BRAND ... | BRAND ... | BRAND ... | BRAND ... | BRAND ... |

**TRAFFIC FLOW**

*Figure* 42 – Product positioning using mixed families/lines.

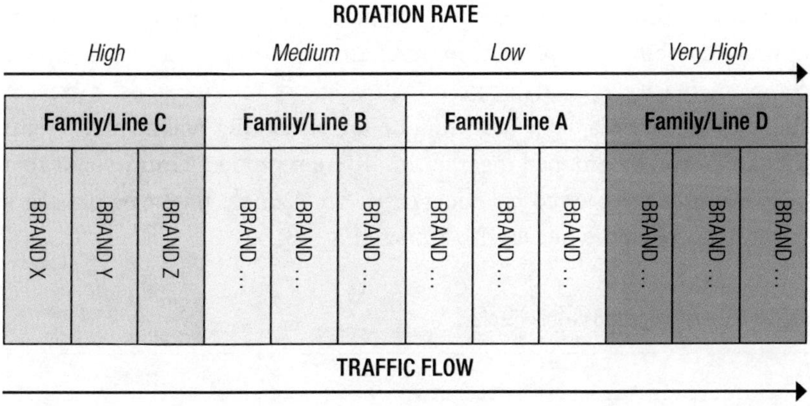

**ROTATION RATE**

| *High* | *Medium* | *Low* | *Very High* |
|---|---|---|---|

| Family/Line C | | | Family/Line B | | | Family/Line A | | | Family/Line D | | |
|---|---|---|---|---|---|---|---|---|---|---|---|
| BRAND X | BRAND Y | BRAND Z | BRAND ... | BRAND ... | BRAND ... | BRAND ... | BRAND ... | BRAND ... | BRAND ... | BRAND ... | BRAND ... |

**TRAFFIC FLOW**

Whatever the approach, keep in mind that customers' attention gradually dissipates as they walk down the aisle in the store. This means that the families/lines/brands that the retailer wants to push as impulse purchases need to be as near to the beginning of the aisle as possible.

By the same token, there are also some salient points to make about the ends (the first and last sections of a row of gondolas), and the endcaps (the display units that round off the gondola at either extremity). The ends of aisles normally offer limited visibility because they're partially hidden by the endcaps. So to exploit the first and last sections of shelf space to the fullest, the idea is to place products here that have a powerful communicative impact, items that can also serve to signpost various departments.

Endcaps, on the other hand, are dedicated to massifying product presentations, which makes them well-suited display spaces for mono-product/brand or multi-product/brand promotions. Because endcaps offer optimum visibility, they're usually assigned to a given supplier for a limited time only (usually no more than two weeks). The cost of endcaps is very high, with a price that can vary a great deal depending on a number of factors. These include the type of product, brand leadership, the supplier, the company and the distribution format, the size of the sales area, and the position of the gondola with respect to the store's entrance and exit, to name just a few.

## 7    Cross-mix displays

When there are one or more adjacencies in terms of product families/lines, they can be displayed in cross-shaped patterns. This prompts customers to make combination and add-on purchases. Depending on the degree of complementarity, retailers can opt for a single or multiple cross mixes. A single cross-mix display is a technique for presenting one or more items that are normally grouped together in different product families, but that have a high degree of complementarity. An example might be placing a family of jams in the linear with scones (Fig. 43).

*Figure* 43 – A single cross-mix display.

| Scones | Jams | Scones |
|--------|------|--------|
| Jams   | Jams | Jams   |
| Scones | Jams | Scones |
| Scones | Jams | Scones |

With multi-cross-mixes on a store shelf, several complementary product families are grouped together on the same linear, such as bread with jams and juices in the breakfast foods category (Fig. 44). By doing so, customers are exposed to myriad stimuli while they are moving down the aisle, where they find one or more products that are among their planned purchases.

*Figure* 44 – Multi-cross-mix display.

| Scones | Jams | Juices | Jams | Juices | Jams |
|--------|------|--------|------|--------|------|
| Jams | Jams | Jams | Scones | Scones | Scones |
| Scones | Jams | Juices | Jams | Juices | Jams |
| Scones | Jams | Juices | Jams | Juices | Jams |

## 8  Double displays

A double display reinforces a brand and/or product line by positioning the items in question not only with their product family, but also grouped with other product adjacencies which normally would have some consumption criteria in common. This is not a case of a temporary promotional display, but an actual product presentation which, depending on the products, might even be permanent (Fig. 45).

*Figure* 45 – Fashion accessories displayed alongside cosmetics invite customers to visit other departments at "& Other Stories", a multi-floor store in Milan.

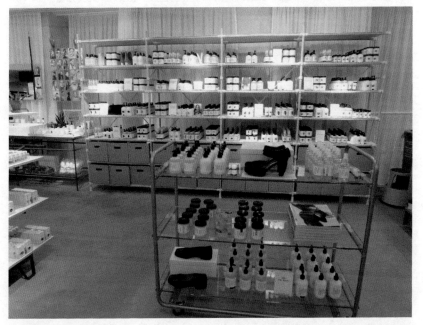

This doesn't necessarily involve cross-selling, a strategy that can also include positioning products outside their relative family. But like cross-selling, double-displaying an item in a complementary product family can encourage impulse purchases. Instead, a traditional display in the product family of reference is a more powerful prompter for planned purchases.

What often happens, in fact, is that customers who have no intention of buying a certain type of product do not even go into the relative department in the store. So by placing products in other areas of the store, there's a greater probability that customers will actually see them. This serves as a reminder once again how crucial product visibility is, which is inextricably linked to customer flow and ease of movement in the store itself.

The chief advantages of a double display are obvious: sales accelerate, missed sales drop, profit margins grow for the product family, displays become more dynamic and less boring, the image of the department and/or the entire store improves. But despite all this, the double display has some serious limitations too. First of all, a product's exposure can't be doubled in its own department. Moreover, displaying twice the amount of product calls for more stock. Another logistical concern is that double displays make replenishment more risky, so there's a chance that the store could run out of the product on the shelves (not necessarily due to stockouts in the warehouse). Lastly, displaying an item outside its own department means making way for it in another one. More often than one might think, though, that department managers more or less openly resist this "space invasion", making it impossible to take full advantage of new display initiatives.


## 9    Massified displays

A massified display is similar to a promotional display which, as we've seen, can achieve a variety of aims: spotlighting new products and/or brands, effectively underscoring convenient pricing and accentuating special offers. From a purely technical viewpoint, various display methods can work to this end, but the most effective are baskets, bins, and fixtures where large quantities of merchandise can be placed in piles (such as pallets and tables) to massify the product presentation (Fig. 46).

This kind of display can be a mono-promotion with large numbers of a single product, or a multi-promotion with various items jumbled together. Naturally this last solution works best to highlight deep-discounts. But it

*Figure* 46 – Mono-product pallets in a store aisle and on endcaps.

*Figure* 47 – An Easter promotion offers a striking and attractive visual impact with off-the-shelf displays set perpendicular to the cash desks at the Iper hypermarket in Vittuone, near Milan.

can prove potentially damaging for brand-name products, not to mention more fragile items (which could break).

Generally speaking, an effective massified display has to respect certain basic prerequisites:

- the in-store location must maximize visibility in a high traffic flow area, to attract customers (Fig. 47);
- potential impulse buyers can freely pick up the product, look it over and evaluate it, and easily read the packaging;
- clear, visible signage helps not only to communicate the position of the display for customers who are farther away, but also to convey the offer in a way that's immediate and intelligible;
- the display should be constantly cleaned and properly kept up; if it gets damaged it should be replaced right away; and
- the promotion should have a time limit so that customers don't lose interest.

The sales potential and the effectiveness of massification plummet if any of the following happen:

- the display isn't properly placed relative to the main traffic flow or to nearby displays;
- the display remains in place for more than two weeks, or more than two to three store visits for the average customer;
- there are unexpected stockouts, which as a rule lead to lost sales in the case of impulse purchases;
- signage isn't visible, or informative, or immediately understandable or simply isn't there;
- informational material is excessive, which makes the message redundant and overloads the presentation for no reason, diverting attention away from the product; and
- damaged or obsolete material isn't replaced.

These last points underscore the need to constantly monitor displays to analyze results in terms of sales, rotation rates, and average profit margins.


## 10    Empirical criteria for space allocation

Producers have long been engaged in a battle to ensure that their flagship products don't get penalized in stores; but the truth is, control over the

final retail price of their goods is often out of their hands. To prevent retailers from discriminating too much against brand name items with little
or no profit margins, producers have tried to build a common analytical
frame of reference for assessing the profitability of each individual item.
The aim here is to raise awareness among distributors of the need to develop product costing systems. This has given rise to a product profitability
approach that takes into account product rotation, off-invoice revenues (or
trade marketing revenues) and direct costs (in particular, the cost of space).
The idea is to come up with a more accurate estimate of the actual capacity
of every single item to generate profits for distributors.

In fact, the profitability of brand name products turns out to be better
than what the gross profit margin would indicate, invalidating some of the
reasons for penalizing these items in terms of space allocation. But calculating certain parameters such as elasticity is a complicated task, so gradually simpler empirical rules have evolved to determine space allocation.

When divvying up the linear among different products, retailers can pursue a variety of objectives. These include boosting turnover, increasing the
gross profit margins, or maximizing net profits from product sales. Added
to these are other aims more specific to sales space which differ depending on the time frame of reference. In particular, there are short-term goals
(such as selling out stocks quickly or prompting customers to try new products) and long-term ones (minimizing warehousing costs or accelerating
rotation rates). So different objectives, even if they are partially complementary, follow different criteria for space allocation. These either are based on
sales or gross profits, each of which can both be delineated further as we'll
see below.

## 10.1 *Breaking down the linear by sales*

With this method, the more sales volumes a product generates, the more
shelf space it gets. But there are as many variations of this system as there are
displays in stores. Next to random space allocation, this is the most common
shelf management approach because it's the easiest to put into practice.

This technique for space allocation can be based on one of two specifications:

1. in proportion to past sales; and
2. in proportion to market share.

## In proportion to past sales

This criterion takes into account the proportion of turnover a single product generates in relation to the total sales of its relative product family. The key advantage of this system lies in its simplicity, yet it does present some limitations. First, past sales, the basis of the calculation, can be impacted by several factors that are liable to change almost continually, for example, the linear previously allocated to the product, product promotions, the display's position within a store department, and the sales period used as a frame of reference.

To circumvent this problem, at least in part, the linear can be broken down proportionally to turnover, but corrected for the growth rate in sales. For instance, a product with a 10% share of its family's sales and an annual growth rate of 30%, compared with 20% for its family, will earn a linear equal to 10% x 30/20 = 15%. In this case, using a coefficient equal to the ratio of growth rates is a way to introduce a dynamic element to the equation.

Another limitation of this method derives from the fact that it is self-fulfilling. The linear is determined as a function of every product's quota of the store's or department's overall turnover which, in turn, depends on allocation of the linear. This means that a product may generate low sales volumes simply because it only gets minimal shelf space, and not for reasons linked to market trends.

In addition, this criterion does not take into account the linear that's already assigned to products. In other words, we implicitly assume that the products which already generate the biggest sales are the ones that should be given extra shelf space, even when these items may already be approaching their saturation point. Furthermore, if more display space is assigned to a product based proportionally on the increase in indices, there is less space for the next product on the shelf. Retailers often overlook this logical consequence, and run the risk of triggering negative chain reactions impacting the product category as a whole, which may reverberate onto the entire assortment. The last and most salient criticism is that sales turnover is not the main objective for a store. Instead, the top priority is maximizing profit and returns on capital investments.

## In proportion to market share

The principle here is similar to the once described above, the only exception being that in this case the calculation takes into account all the sales realized at a regional or national level. This is a net improvement over the simple sales criterion. In fact, an analysis of sales performance at a regional or national level is no longer limited to evaluating the specifics of consumption and sales potential among target users who shop at a single store, taking this as a true reflection of regional or national dynamics.

Though sales are still the benchmark, we abandon a dangerously misleading approach, especially if we base our reasoning on the assumption that one of the cornerstones of visual merchandising is micromarketing.

### 10.2   *Breaking down the linear based on gross profit margin*

As we've already pointed out, pragmatic methods based on past sales are most commonly used when allocating shelf space. These methods are simple yet preferable to the empiricism that is still prevalent in many retail contexts. But there is no denying that these systems are still linked to the goal of maximizing sales. Instead, criteria that utilize gross margins appear to be more in synch with the aim of maximizing profits.

In this case too, two distinct configurations are possible:

1. in proportion to the share of gross profit margins; and
2. based on a combination method.

*In proportion to the share of gross profit margin*

The point of this method is to estimate the average gross profit per unit of linear, and assign each item a share of shelf space proportional to its own gross profit. Once again, the primary advantage to this system for breaking down the linear stems from its simplicity and logic. The more profits an item generates, the more space it gets on the shelf, the more profitable the sale of that item becomes. This said, the same criticisms apply as for the method based on past sales.

First of all, the criterion uses the results of a relatively brief period, deriving from the dynamic of sales, purchase price and sales price: three factors that are not only extremely variable over the short term, but also highly interdependent. What's more, the assumption is that for products which generate higher margins, profits can be increased even more per unit of linear space, as can the overall margins of the entire department. But this neglects to consider sales elasticity in relation to sales space. An additional assumption is that regardless of the display space that a product already occupies, increasing this by a unit of linear will generate an identical increase in quantities sold and gross profits. But this scenario is extremely rare. Lastly, gross profit per unit of space is an inadequate parameter, because it doesn't factor in return on the capital invested in stock, or the cost of commercializing the product. These expense items could render net profits null or even negative.

In light of the fact that this method can't guarantee optimal use of space, over time several variants have emerged. One of these is the combined criterion that assesses sellability of the product (measured by rotation rate) along with its gross margin and the sales potential of the linear, which we'll discuss below.

*Based on a combination method*

The objective of this method is two-fold: to cut back on investments in stock, and at the same time to allow flexible and dynamic display management, with an eye to optimizing the profitability of the entire linear.

This technique is based on three criteria:

1. quantities above and beyond the minimum threshold of visibility have to be synchronized with the different rotation rates of individual products, measured in the optimal display period for each one;
2. the imbalances between gross margins and rotation rates can be compensated by various levels of sellability on the linear;
3. here's how to achieve maximum sellability:
   - Placing products with average rotation rates and average gross margins on *levels* of the linear with the maximum sellability, and at the same time put the slowest moving product at the *point* of maximum sellability on the linear.
   - Positioning products with lower levels of gross margins but high rotation rates on the vertical levels of the linear with low sellability.
   - Allocating space for products with higher gross margins but lower rotation rates on the vertical levels of the linear with average sellability.

An even more comprehensive approach would also take into consideration the interdependencies of demand, reflecting the nature of the assortment, which obviously is made up of myriad products. This contrasts with the method of analyzing the direct profitability of a product in terms of a single unit. The fact is, the display area of a store consists of a limited amount of space. So while it's true that retailers can boost sales by giving a product more space, that inevitably means taking away space from another item, which can cause a drop in sales. So considering profit margins alone means running a greater risk of cannibalization. To mitigate this risk, a joint analysis is needed of the interdependencies among various products. In an attempt to evaluate this 'cross elasticity' phenomenon, software has been developed that manages the linear by using algorithms to compare the interdependencies among products with their level of profitability. These factors are measured based on overall gross margins, net margins, or contribution per unit of space, which in turn can be gauged in linear, square or cubic units of measure.

Clearly, the chosen unit of measure influences the result when the industrial products in a given category vary as far as brand image. This in turn means that the position of a given brand in a store can vary noticeably as well. Based on the variables slotted into the program, the software determines not only the minimum and maximum linear to assign to each product, but also the number of units per product to display.

## 11   The planogram

Shelf management techniques serve to compare the costs of managing display space versus product performance. With the growing popularity of these techniques, specially designed software has been developed to create planograms. A planogram can identify and track a time series of parameters on shelf profitability, such as sales, profit margins, and rotation rates.

Having said this, it should be noted that until a few years ago, planograms were seen exclusively as visual models, and not tools for effective shelf management; in some cases this is still true today. Luckily, recent innovations in IT marketing systems and support have spurred the development of models for space management that are even more sophisticated and evolved. Now it's finally possible to respond to the actual decision-making processes that customers use.

Specifically, for distributors these models are quite useful for ascertaining the neutrality or effectiveness of display solutions, and for introducing visual merchandising in a more systematic way by actually addressing related activities in contractual conditions and in negotiations with industry. Thanks to these software programs, in fact, negotiations have taken a major leap forward, qualitatively speaking. These specialized systems formulate planograms that factor in and weigh out the interrelationships among all the relevant variables. The output of this process offers a technical framework for comparing different product presentations, a tool which can minimize any uncertainty as far as the effectiveness of space allocation for products. So producers and distributors can come to a consensus on the best display solutions, which may be quite different from what they originally had in mind.

Admittedly, the planogram can't provide neutral solutions that apply in every circumstance, because space allocation strategies are so complex they call for some form of simplification. This is done by making calculations based on parameters which are partial and discretionary, and defining a priori allocation criteria, in particular with respect to the quality of the display space. Yet a planogram does offer undeniable advantages: it's flexible and transparent with respect to how results are conditioned by the criteria and the variables that are used.

In detail, planograms make it possible to achieve a number of obvious benefits:

- bringing to light areas where space is over- or under-allocated;
- sizing how much maneuvering room is available when adding new products to the shelves;
- assessing how much leeway there is with respect to logistical restrictions, for example when stocking shelves; and
- curtailing situations in which space allocation is determined directly in the store based merely on subjective criteria.

Specifically, to properly allocate display space, these are the steps to follow:

- determine logistical restrictions in terms of minimum number of facings or standard stocking procedures;
- assign the quality of the display space, either manually or by following a specific routine;
- once shelf quality is assigned, designate quantity depending on the service level required for each product, which in turn depends on product rotation;
- allocate any excess space to current products and/or new entries (according to elasticity and profit margins);
- when there isn't enough space to serve all products adequately, adjust the number of items or the minimum number of facings, or modify shelf stocking procedures;
- track and compare yield on various shelf configuration options; and
- dress shelves, making manual adjustments and using POP materials to create an aesthetic display.

Optimizing display space allocation calls for a methodical assessment of the competitive context as well as the retailing strategies and policies of the store. Added to all this is experience, which would naturally prompt retailers to periodically reevaluate the display areas in every store with an eye to incrementally enhancing the productivity of the linear and the satisfaction of the customers. In this sense, space allocation programs shift the focal point of the discussion. Instead of how to assign shelf space to individual products, the central concern becomes which variables to use to optimize the model. The outcome is to raise the quality level of negotiations which can pave the way to reaching collaborative solutions.

At the same time, competition is intensifying and value for the customer is becoming top priority. These trends are prompting retailers to resort to more sophisticated control techniques as well as more careful and efficient display management. From this perspective, realizing planograms at retail headquarters and disseminating them throughout the retail network is an effective way to save time in implementing visual merchandising decisions, to limit errors when setting up in-store displays, and to verify and quickly rectify product presentations when need be. This is all the more relevant considering that producers and distributors get the chance to integrate their marketing activities.

On the other hand, competitive strategies are changing, as are the needs of customers. All this makes it even more critical to strike a balance between the goals of maximizing efficiency and productivity in space allocation and enhancing the level of customer service. Considerations which, as we will see later on, often lead to redefining space according to rationale which diverges to some degree from the configuration that a planogram would create.

## 12   Correctives for the linear display

Regardless of the criterion we use, it may be a good idea to introduce qualitative or quantitative correctives to improve the productivity of the linear and boost customer satisfaction. As often reiterated, space allocation systems for product displays such as planograms are tools that serve for shelf management. Yet more than that, they can substantiate the effect of the choices made upstream. These choices constitute temporary constraints that derive from both the internal procedures of distributors and factors that are controlled by industry.

From a quantitative standpoint, marketing criteria can be implemented that take into account product range expansion policies used by producers, along with the evolution of market share. For instance, as already discussed, in some cases it makes sense to position the same product/SKU in two or more different places in the display area, and not necessarily when the product is on special offer (Fig. 48).

Specifically, multiplying the number of facings is a useful tactic when retailers have the following objectives in mind:

- novelty, when launching a new product and/or proposing a new use for an already-existing product;
- seasonality, to boost the productivity of space allotted to products with a limited life cycle;
- add-on purchases, to propose adjacencies;
- marginality, to prompt impulse purchases; and
- substitution, to fill display space in case of stockouts.

There are certain spaces that are best-suited for double displays. First, when there are adjacencies, the same item can be displayed twice on the

*Figure* 48 – Placing apple corers near the apples is a way to prompt impulse purchases by customers who would never venture into the housewares department in the Iper Portello in Milan.

same linear. Instead, the end cap and the aisle may be the best solution for new products or seasonal items. Lastly, the cash wrap is particularly effective if the aim is to hit profit margin targets.

Continuing on the topic of quantity of space, it's also useful to add a purely physical criterion that serves to minimize replenishment costs. In this case the linear would be set up in such a way as to contain reabsorption and realize expected sales from one replenishment to the next, stocking one or more boxes of product at every replenishment. Obviously the limitation in using this approach is exclusively an economic one.

From a qualitative standpoint, other considerations are distribution choices in terms of aesthetic balance within the store department or section. This is the reason that product positioning often takes into account the best combinations of colors, shapes, and objects: customers feel a strong attraction to displays that are tidy and clean, with products that are placed in an attractive and enticing way on the shelves.

## 13 The shift toward micro visual merchandising

In light of these final observations, what becomes clear is that visual merchandising should take on a micro-marketing orientation. As we've already said, this is the only approach that enables retailers to implement solutions customized for individual stores, not only in light of competitors' retailing mix policies, but also the architectural features of the store itself, and the demographics of target customers.

What we need to remember, is that the most effective visual merchandising solutions are always the outcome of an astute and complex balance between the needs of supply and demand. As we know, the key goal in the store is to optimize profitability, driving the flow of customers in such a way as to expose them to as much of the display area as possible and to facilitate their decision-making processes. At the same time, customers need to be in the right frame of mind for making a purchase. Yet there are two additional priorities that can't be neglected: rationalizing the replenishment process and minimizing inventory gaps. These business needs tend to run counter to the needs of demand. In fact, customers would not only prefer a simpler, time-saving purchase process, but they also want to gather information and at the same time feel gratification on a psychological level.

We can conclude beyond a doubt that visual merchandising follows a short-term rationale. This is closely connected to the capacity to shape customers' purchasing behavior in order to maximize profits generated by the display area, prompting people to make impulse purchases and modifying the sales structure to favor items with higher profit margins. However, in the most successful cases there is also a long-term vision centered on qualifying the company image; respecting the mental organization of customers' needs; facilitating, energizing, and enhancing the buying experience and ultimately promoting loyalty. In other words, the most strategic approach to visual merchandising attempts to satisfy the need for information to propose solutions that accurately reflect the marketing orientation of the store, while creating added value for customers. All this contributes to the process of differentiating the store and creating a store identity.

It goes without saying, then, that the key is to strike a balance between short-term and long-term objectives: efficient and high-quality commercial service on one hand and customer loyalty on the other. Where exactly this point of equilibrium lies is highly contingent on the strategic positioning of the store and the marketing strategies that store management intends to pursue.

A micro visual merchandising approach calls for the joint effort of industry and distribution in ensuring the necessary information flow. At one end, distribution needs to furnish sales data that are cross-referenced by the sales space, the target customer profile, and the store location. At the other, suppliers have to run market research, and provide their distributors with updated information on customer profiles as well as the benefits people are looking for in the various product lines on offer. The end result that everyone should strive for is the creation of display models that are more centered on specific customer segments and tailored to particular local contexts.

## 14    What factors impact the choices that shoppers make in the "moment of truth"? *by Matteo Testori*

In this chapter, we've explored the most common practices for managing and allocating retail space in the store, focusing our attention on two key questions: How do customers behave when they're in front of a product? What influences them?

To delve more deeply into these topics, we studied a number of stores in Northern Europe over a 12-month period (from November 2015 to October 2016). During this time, in three food categories we analyzed the path customers take from the store entrance to the items in question; we segmented these customers by gender, age, and purchase behaviors using video analytics technologies. Specifically:

- *Face Detection Systems* – Sensors installed at store entrances and on shelves which count the number of customers who walk past, the number who look at the products, and how long they stop and focus on the items in question, based on gender and estimated age.
- *Shelf Detection Systems* – On-the-shelf sensors that measure interactions between customers and products: when items are touched, put back on the shelf, or purchased.

This set of input, associated with data provided by the retailer from scanners (cash desks), allowed us to get continual tracking in real time of shoppers, their behaviors, their shopping journey, purchase criteria, and the factors that impact their purchase decisions. Based on the empirical observations made in the store, we came up with a number of metrics which proved effective in understanding the salient phases in the purchase process (Testori, 2015):

- *Store traffic*: the number of customers who enter the store;
- *Aisle traffic*: the number of customers who enter a given aisle;
- *Shelf traffic*: the number of customers who come up to the shelf/product category under analysis;
- *Attraction*: the degree to which the category attracts people passing by;
- *Attention*: the percentage of available time (total time spent standing in front of the shelf) dedicated to observing the products;
- *Relevance*: the degree of interest of the customer in the category/product;
- *Sale index*: the number of purchases per 100 potential buyers, i.e. among the customers who looked at the products;
- *Proximity*: the percentage of customers passing by who approach the shelf and actually touch it;
- *Interactions*: the percentage of interactions (i.e. customers touch, put back, or purchase the item) out of the total store traffic;
- *Positive interactions*: the percentage of interactions that culminate with a purchase.

Applying the technologies and analytics described above, first we examined a single product initially positioned on the second shelf (from the bottom) and subsequently on the fifth shelf. We then looked at the same (recently launched) product in two different categories, similar as far as use function but very different in the eyes of customers. We started by measuring the traffic flow. On average 2,300 customers entered each store per day. Around 4% of them approached the product categories. Here are our findings for the two products in our study:

*Table* 1 – Comparison of the two categories

|                          | Category A | Category B |
|--------------------------|------------|------------|
| Average Attraction       | 77 %       | 80 %       |
| Males                    | 56 %       | 57 %       |
| Females                  | 44 %       | 43 %       |
| Sale Index (category)    | 15 %       | 31 %       |

Category B showed more than double the preference or effectiveness (sale index) as compared to Category A. This means that more customers accessed the products in the category, more were attracted (attraction index), and above all more made purchases (sale index). The sale index is a metric that establishes a relationship between the customer and the product at a store level. In other words, 100 customers observe a product, which generates a certain number of sales (clearly, this datum needs to be interpreted alongside the number of multiple purchases). So we can conclude that Category B attracted more customers, and once they were in front of the shelf, they made more purchases.

In Category A, after eight weeks the product in question was moved from the second shelf (from the bottom) to the fifth, to assess the effect of the change in position. Here is what we found:

*Table* 2 – Shelf Effectiveness

|                                    | Second shelf | Fifth shelf |
|------------------------------------|--------------|-------------|
| Proximity                          | 0.2 %        | 0.53 %      |
| Interactions                       | 0.22 %       | 0.73 %      |
| Positive interactions              | 65 %         | 75 %        |
| Average number of items (per week) | 0.7          | 1.8         |
| Market share                       | 1.5 %        | 5.36 %      |

The advantage of the position is clear: more customers approached the product (proximity), the number of interactions rose (i.e. how many times customers touched and potentially purchased the product) as did sales (+80%). Positive interactions (which translate into purchases) increased. This effect may be due to greater product visibility, as it's easier to see on the fifth shelf compared to the second shelf. Once customers touched the item, in most cases they ended up buying it.

Now let's look at product performance in the two different categories. From November 2015 to February 2016, the product was tested on the shelves of both categories. From February to May the product was only present in Category A.

Remember that in early January 2016, the product in Category A was moved from the second to the fifth shelf. Also, the product in question was a recent launch, so customers had yet to acquire awareness. In fact, when we placed the Category A item on the second shelf at the beginning of our study, we didn't get relevant results. We need to consider that during the period in question the total number of items sold of Category B was 107% more than Category A, with a 20% higher customer presence. The price was identical for the two categories, there were no promotional initiatives for either one, and the number of facings was the same in each case (2). All this means that we have to interpret the data we collected in light of the general dynamics of the categories.

*Table* 3 – Positioning in the different categories

|  | Category A | Category B | Only Category A |
|---|---|---|---|
| Market share | 1.8 % | 6.1 % | 11.6 % |
| Attraction | 72 % | 81 % | 79 % |
| Attention | 31 % | 37 % | 34 % |
| Relevance | 1.32 | 2.21 | 1.72 |
| Sale Index | 0.3 % | 2.9 % | 2.1 % |
| Multiple purchases | 0 | 3.9 % | 2.9 % |

So we can conclude that:

1. Product performance and the relationship between product and customer are influenced by shelf position.

2. Category B performs better than Category A (Table 1), registering more attraction and more sales. In practice, this means that customers prefer Category B; they look for relative products, which are best-sellers.
3. Placing product categories that are related but that have dissimilar use functions gives rise to a divergent perception of the product and different sales results, at least in the initial phase.
4. Category B sold 107% more than Category A; sales of the product we studied were markedly stronger when it was positioned in B (Table 3). The spillover effect of the category onto the product seems higher than the impact of moving the item to a different shelf level (Category A – Table 2). This also proves true in relative terms: in Category A, after changing shelf level, the product earns a market share of 5.36%, while in B this figure is 6.1%.
5. The market share when the product is positioned in Category A alone is 11.6% (Table 3). This effect is contingent on the position of the shelf (fifth level). Also, once awareness is established, customers look for the product, even in a category with lower performance (A).
6. After an initial phase that lasted around six months, the importance of the brand and the chance to try the product are factors that prompt customers to actively seek out the item, regardless of which category it's placed in.

So to sum up, the case quantitatively describes the effect of spatial modifications (changing the shelf level) and perceptive ones (changing the category). Our empirical evidence confirms the influence of spatial factors and visual attention to the product. A key element that emerges from our findings is the relationship between customer, product and position.

When the product position moves vertically, or when the item is located in a different category, our study corroborates previous ones (Raghubir and Valenzuela, 2006, 2008; Antonietti and Balconi, 2009; Fiocca and Testori, 2017) with regard to access and "accessibility" of the product, in other words, the chance that customers have to consider it and make it a selection (and potentially a purchase). Our study opens new possibilities in determining how products are displayed, no longer basing this solely on long-standing, consolidated criteria (space quotas relative to market share, turnover rates, value per linear space, or margins). Instead, synthetic indicators can be used (e.g. sale index) that combine aspects pertaining to competition (market share), system (sales volumes and overall profitability of the category), structure (the need to minimize stock outs), with the relationship between potential purchaser (the observer) and purchase, defining the offering on the shelf in relation to customer flows, focus, and preferences.

## 15  A sense of space: the Lush case[2]

Founded in the south of England in 1994, Lush makes beauty products sold in over 900 shops worldwide. The company's tenth biggest market is Italy, with 36 locations and turnover totaling 20 million euros in 2016. The cornerstones of Lush's green approach are the organic materials used in its products (fresh fruits and vegetables), the eco-friendly packaging, and its battle against animal testing. What Lush stands for is clear and unequivocal: fresh handmade cosmetics. This slogan encompasses the two key values that underpin the competitive advantage of this firm:

- Fresh: In keeping with the central tenet of the Lush philosophy, 100% of all products are vegetarian (and 70% vegan). To guarantee freshness, Lush goods have a maximum shelf life of five months.
- Handmade: Inspired by traditional artisan experience, and rejecting industrial production, the company has set up actual "kitchens" where employees make Lush products by hand. In fact, each individual item is labeled with the name of the "master compounder" who created it.

This positioning strategy is conveyed by *A Lush Life*, the company credo, displayed at the entrance and/or in the windows of all the stores (Fig. 49).

The ethical principles that are Lush's constant touchstones have led the company to set up an Ethical Buying Team, specialized in sourcing ingredients. Another ethical initiative is the Lush Prize, rewarding scientists who conduct cruelty-free research.

---

[2] The content of this case is an excerpt from "Il senso dello spazio. Dialogo sensoriale tra cliente e negozio. Il caso Lush" (A Sense of Space. The Sensorial Dialogue between Customer and Shop. The Lush Case), by Chiara Brancadoro, presented in 2016 as a Master's thesis for her degree in Marketing at Università Bocconi.

*Figure* 49 – A Lush Life.

---

## We believe...

**We believe** in making effective products from fresh, organic* fruit and vegetables, the finest essential oils and safe synthetics.

**We invent** our own products and fragrances. We make them fresh by hand using little or no preservative or packaging, using only vegetarian ingredients, and tell you when they were made.

**We believe** in buying ingredients only from companies that do not commission tests on animals and in testing our products on humans.

**We believe** in happy people making happy soap, putting our faces on our products and making our mums proud.

**We believe** in long candlelit baths, sharing showers, massage, filling the world with perfume and in the right to make mistakes, lose everything and start again.

**We believe** that all people should enjoy freedom of movement across the world.

**We believe** our products are good value, that we should make a profit and that the customer is always right.

\* We also believe words like fresh and organic have honest meaning beyond marketing.

---

*Source*: https://uk.lush.com/article/lush-life

The company is also developing responsible packaging, which means that 40% of Lush products are "naked," and the remainder are wrapped in recycled and recyclable packaging. As for the product offering, no animal ingredients are utilized; instead, Lush items are made of fresh fruits and vegetables, with little or no preservatives.

The company's product portfolio is very broad, with leading lines encompassing skin care, hair care, fragrances, makeup, gift sets, bath and shower. Beyond the vast selection, Lush products are also considered highly innovative. The most famous creations include bath bombs, massage oils, and solid shampoos. Originality also comes in clever product names, such as "Sexy Peel" and "Grease Lightening." The product formats – a cross between foods and cosmetics – are also unique, carefully copying edible items like sweets and cheeses. Lush founder Mark Constantine uses the word "delicatessen" to describe the company's approach to creating goods that stimulate our taste buds, with clearly visible bits of vegetables, spices and whatever fresh fruit is in season. Other marks of distinction are the vibrant colors, intense scents emanating from essential oils, and specific tactile qualities of certain products. Examples are shampoos with sea salt or shower soaps with the consistency of gelatin.

All these merchandising decisions are perfectly aligned, moving in a single direction toward a shared aim: enticing the customer by fully exploiting the polysensory communication of Lush products. Taste, touch, sight and smell act synergistically to capture the attention of every person who comes into the store. It's certainly no coincidence that more often than not this is a woman aged 16 to 50 who falls in a middle to high socioeconomic bracket, who cares about the ingredients and the quality of her skin care products and cosmetics, who often gets involved in environmental and ethical issues, and in general who enjoys an active, healthy lifestyle.

## 15.1  *The new Lush format in Milan, Via Torino*

With a markedly British approach, the design choices permeating all the sales areas make ample use of wood, and warm, recyclable materials to create spaces reminiscent of more traditional shops selling fruit, vegetables, and cheese. The aim is to further accentuate one of the basic principles of the Lush philosophy: freshness. Although the goal of Lush has always been to leverage design to emphasize freshness, the approach has evolved over time.

When Lush was first breaking into the Italian market, all efforts were focused on creating brand awareness by opening more and more small stores all over the country. During this introductory phase, the concept was quite economical, consisting of simple modules, quick and easy to design, using for instance pine for store furnishings and ceramic plates for product displays. Once brand awareness was consolidated, the company embarked on the current development phase with a change of strategic course: instead of expansion, corporate objectives now revolved around shoring up quality and customer service.

In terms of processing, planning and selecting materials, Lush is taking steps toward sustainability, and incurring added costs in order to offer greater comfort, in particular with an eye to creating a pleasing aesthetic. In light of this change in direction, many stores are being revamped by expanding or relocating in higher impact, higher income areas, from a commercial standpoint.

This is also the case of the Via Torino store, in the heart of Milan's retail center. The grand opening in 2014 followed the closing of a Lush location in the Sarca Shopping Center. The store is housed in quite an old building (nineteenth/twentieth century) on the corner of Via Torino and Via San Maurilio, and covers 190 square meters (2,000 square feet) of floor space on three levels. The first floor is dedicated to sales. The second offers a party room where events can be organized for customers; the staff room and toilets are also on this floor. The basement is used as a storeroom. A wooden staircase connects the three floors, as does a dumbwaiter.

## 15.2   Exterior design

The first distinctive element of the store's exterior is the sign, displayed from multiple angles to ensure that every opportunity is exploited to mark the location of the store. Above the doorway, positioned at the intersection of the two roads, we find the main sign, classic Lush, which reads: LUSH – FRESH HANDMADE COSMETICS, in white lettering on a black background (Fig. 50)

In both streets, protruding out from the wall are two more smaller signs on level with the second floor; these give the store greater visibility from farther away. When people come closer, they notice the windows, three on the main road and one on Via San Maurilio. One of the windows on

*Figure* 50 – The traditional sign that connotes the chain, making the store stand out along the sidewalk (courtesy of Lush).

Via Torino is covered with a wooden panel to protect products from direct sunlight, which would cause them to deteriorate. At the same time, this panel provides an internal wall that can be used for displays, while the external side is used to present the logo once again, reinforcing the message: Lush is here. The window in Via San Maurilio is also closed, but in this case because it corresponds to the internal staircase leading to the upper floor. The remaining windows are open, allowing people to see inside.

The arrangement of the sales space is changed up every two to four weeks if a promotional campaign is running; for an ethical campaign instead this timeframe is compressed to one week. There are several themes with regard to planning displays: scheduled events, ethical campaigns, new product launches, and seasonal and promotional sales. As previously mentioned, products are arranged to look like fresh fruits in a grocery store, both in the windows and on the shelves inside. The key words for achieving this aesthetic effect are abundance, color, and freshness.

To reinforce this positioning, plants and flowers are interspersed among Lush products. In some cases back-lit panels are also set up with images of the current campaign or the store logo. The accent on planning and arranging the window displays explains the decision to measure their effectiveness, beyond purely collecting commercial data. In fact, the store manager makes a monthly assessment of customers' reactions to different sorts of window displays.

The store entrance was designed to be level with the sidewalk, with large glass doors formed of four panels. The two central panels are always wide open, which allows for easy access and underscores the openness of the store. The two laterals remain stationary, leaving space on both sides of the entrance that can be used like smaller windows for additional visual communication.

Often a wooden cube is placed just outside the store entrance with a Lush catalogue sitting on top to create an obstacle to traffic flow. To capture the attention of passersby and encourage them to stop, sales personnel stand at the door and offer product demonstrations using a humorous and theatrical approach, prompting potential visitors to try the items on offer.

## 15.3  *Interior design*

As we know, normally the decompression zone (the passageway from the outside to the inside of the store) plays a crucial role for potential customers from a psychological perspective, because this area is where they decide whether or not to continue their store visit.

In the Via Torino store, this area provides a positive response to customers' needs, helping them get a sense of the space in the store and allowing them to size up the offering quickly and effortlessly. In this zone they find shower products and soaps. On one hand these items are highly representative of the Lush offering, and on the other they don't require any consultation with store personnel, as do more complex product lines such as face and hair. This means visitors feel free to interact with the product assortment in their own way and at their own pace. In the middle of the decompression zone there's a focus table. Thanks to the frontal position with respect to the entrance, this can be considered an additional display space with the same impact as a window.

Generally speaking, the design of this Milanese Lush store follows the guidelines set by the British creative team to guarantee the Lush standard. However, there are some adaptations to the local context in the form of details which help the store harmonize with its surroundings (Fig. 51).

One of the most prominent and distinctive design elements of the shop is the lighting system, with spotlights that create an effect very closely resembling sunlight, ensuring a warm, welcoming and natural atmosphere. Complementing these spotlights are circular pendant lights hanging from the ceiling. As for the store walls, the creative team opted to go with black,

*Figure* 51 – The interior design generates an environment in which nothing is left to chance: from the lighting to the walls covered with eye-catching messages, to the materials used for store furnishings (courtesy of Lush).

green, and certain shades of gray. Specifically, black with a touch of green creates a more relaxing store atmosphere. The walls are also decorated with short phrases welcoming customers or describing product categories, written in Lush font.

The décor consists of furnishings and shelving made of recycled wood, while store personnel wear white or black clothes covered with black aprons. Last but not least, in keeping with a polysensory approach, visitors can smell the classic Lush perfume that comes from a mix of essential oils found in Lush products. As for background music, there are no hard-and-fast rules as to genre; what's important is an upbeat atmosphere that stimulates the senses.

## 15.4  *The display arrangement*

The layout of the sales area on the ground floor is based on a free flow model which allows customers to move around the store as they please. Beyond the decompression zone, the retail space is structured in the same way as the entrance, with shelving along the walls and a refrigeration unit for fresh products in the center. At the rear of the store there are two cash desks, and a scale for cutting solid soaps sold by the pound. As in all Lush stores, in Via Torino we find recycled wood for furnishings and shelves, along with second-hand designer accents (lamps and stools). The display structures are built out of scaffolding, a first-time design choice for Lush which aligns with the modern character of the street where the shop is located. The resulting style suggests a slightly more industrial soul, as reflected in these materials typically found in construction sites.

To facilitate the shopping experience for customers, there are wooden baskets throughout the store they can use for their purchases; taps, water basins and paper towels make it easy for them to sample products; trash cans collect waste paper, and stools mean they can make themselves at home while they try out the items on offer. Areas reserved for store personnel are found on the upper floor.

## 15.5  *The product layout*

Currently the rule for product groupings follows along the lines of product affinity, divvying up the offering by category. But this was not always the case. In fact, the Milanese store once set the stage for experimentation.

The aim of the original display criterion was to promote the sale of complementary goods, clustering together items from different subcategories (for example shampoos and conditioners with hair masks) to push cross selling and encourage customers to purchase kits. But this approach gave rise to displays that were not always clear or easy to read. As a result, a more linear display was subsequently adopted, with clear differentiation between categories and sub-categories (also facilitating silent selling). The new approach not only boosted sales, but also engendered a better aesthetic impact in terms of order and "usability". In fact, the rule of thumb that stores follow today in planning the product layout is: let customers use the products.

When customers enter the store the first items they come across are from the shower line, while the area dedicated to skin care and body care is more reserved and comfortable, furnished with stools for more comprehensive and intimate consultations.

Instead for the bath line, where product demonstrations are more theatrical and social, displays are placed in areas that are much more warm and intimate, where the accent is on atmosphere. In fact, on the topic of positioning product displays, if on one hand the company sets down certain guidelines, on the other store designers are given some leeway to personalize their projects. So, one adaptation of the British standard springs from both cultural and strategic choices. To be specific, the bath category in England is one of the top sellers, since most British prefer a bath to a shower. But the opposite is true in Italy, where the best selling lines are skin and hair care. As a result, in the Milanese store bath products are positioned in the back of the store next to the cash desks, while the skin and hair lines are placed nearer to the center of the store.

There is a three-fold motivation for the decision to position the bath line, a somewhat "underdeveloped" category. Since bath bombs lie in the lower price range, they're leveraged as possible add-ons at the cash desk. Second, to make wait times more enjoyable, store personnel can offer group product demonstrations. And third, new customers are introduced to the Lush universe starting with these loss leaders, so positioning them at the cash desks means obliging interested buyers to pass through the entire sales area.

As with the bath bombs, other products in the lower price range are displayed on the counter next to the cash desks to prompt customers to make add-on purchases. These items also include pocket-sized products such as tooth powders or lip balms, or best-sellers or new launches. Note that all these items are always double displays, which means they're available both at the register and on the store shelves (Fig. 52).

*Figure* 52 – Even the cash desk respects the trademark characteristics of Lush design, displaying not only packaging materials, but also offering inspiration for purchases (courtesy of Lush).

Departing from the general rule of grouping together similar products, men's skincare has a separate display. This makes it easier for male customers to read the assortment, seeing as they are less accustomed to the world of cosmetics than women.

### 15.6   *The display*

As for the display, the aim is to highlight eye-catching color contrasts. With packaged items, the criterion used in the store is to divide various formats building on the vertical, always giving priority to bigger sizes. Wherever possible, for instance with naked products, pyramid arrangements are used to give displays movement and avoid monotony. Along these lines, cubes and shelf risers made of wood also serve to "shake up" the display and spotlight the best-sellers in each store (Fig. 53).

*Figure* 53 – Pyramid displays, crates and cubes, and wooden risers add dynamism to the displays and help accentuate specific items (courtesy of Lush).

Last of all, to intensify the aesthetic effect of freshness, abundance, color and genuineness, decorative accents such as plants and flowers are placed alongside the products.

## 15.7 *Design and visual merchandising, together in eternal evolution*

Over time, sell-out analysis together with traffic flow monitoring by store managers and staff have brought to light the need to expand the sales space. This has prompted a remodel of the store, opening up the second floor to sales (no longer reserving it as a party room), and increasing the number of cash desks from two to four.

As with design, visual merchandising has undergone various transformations in recent years. The most recent input comes on the heels of the opening of the Oxford Street store in London. Here the creative team has made a number of changes, providing new material to Italian merchandisers who in turn have disseminated this information by compiling new guidelines for store design.

Specifically, here are some of the key innovations:

- For the bath bomb displays, ceramic plates are replaced by recycled wooden containers, placed at different angles to create the effect of movement.
- Testers are no longer set on small stainless steel plates, but on tiles of lava rock or stone, natural materials that harmonize with the Lush identity.
- Decorative accents such as glass jars contain the ingredients found in the products (coffee beans or almonds, for example); these are placed at intervals between the displays to convey the message that all Lush ingredients are fresh, genuine, and sustainable.

Naturally, even with these most recent changes the company has not come to the end of the design process for its retail space. Indeed this process is destined to evolve continually, following – and in many instances anticipating – the market, to reinforce Lush's competitive advantage.

# 7 Point of Purchase communication

## 1 Moving toward integrated communication

Industry is increasingly escalating investments in brand marketing, with an eye to shoring up company and product identity through communication activities in the Point of Purchase (POP). By definition, POP communication encompasses all activities involved in planning and handling support material used for displaying and selling products. This material is provided by producers with the aim of securing an in-store space that is desirable, recognizable, and exclusive for the product and/or brand they want to spotlight (Zaghi, 2013).

As we have underscored several times throughout this book, the intention to purchase does not always translate into an actual purchase. This is due to situational factors, such as when competing brands are offered at discount prices and/or presented on attractive displays, or when stockouts occur. Beyond this, the retail setting may also influence customers' choices, facilitating the search for information and giving rise to new needs.

Taking a closer look at this last point, we can refer to a 2011 study run by Symphony IRI on the behaviors of European consumers. The findings showed that out of the 18% of customers who planned to make a purchase on special offer before entering the store, 39% said that a sign indicating the promotion helped them find the product on the shelf. What's more, in 48% of the cases, appropriate in-store communication can make all the difference: to be exact, 28% decided which brand to buy once they were in the store, and 20% purchased a product category with no prior planning at all.

Further confirmation comes from research conducted by CERMES – Università Bocconi investigating where consumers source information about new products. As we can see in Table 1, shelf displays are the preferred channel (78.1%), followed by flyers (72.1%) with special displays trailing close behind (65.5%). Traditional advertising media clearly has far less impact.

*Table* 1 – Where consumers source information on new products (% consumers): 2010

| Information Channels | Yes | No | Total |
|---|---|---|---|
| Television ads | 55.2 | 44.8 | 100.00 |
| Magazine and newspaper ads | 45.7 | 54.3 | 100.00 |
| Radio ads | 27.9 | 72.1 | 100.00 |
| Internet | 19.8 | 80.2 | 100.00 |
| Word of Mouth | 69.0 | 31.0 | 100.00 |
| Shelf displays | 78.1 | 21.9 | 100.00 |
| In-store taste-testing/product testing | 44.5 | 55.5 | 100.00 |
| Special in-store displays | 65.5 | 34.5 | 100.00 |
| In-store samples | 47.7 | 52.3 | 100.00 |
| Flyers | 72.1 | 27.9 | 100.00 |

*Source*: CERMES – Università Bocconi

It is hardly surprising then that the attitude of distribution toward in-store communication is becoming more and more flexible and favorable. Naturally, POP communication works to greatest effect when it exploits existing synergies to achieve a perfect alignment with all the investments made in various media in the same timeframe. In other words, integrated communication of the brand and the product portfolio is the approach to follow.

Studies show that the joint action of advertising and POP communication skyrockets sales by over 100% compared with investments in out-of-store communication alone. Likewise, when combined, the dual levers of POP communication and price cuts are far more impactful than when one or the other is used singly. In addition, when customers are scanning products in the store, powerful stimuli come from visual clues, the first being the packaging (Law *et al.*, 2012). In light of all this, what becomes apparent is the need to ensure not only that a given product is actually available on the shelf, but also that it is clearly visible and easy to find in the store. This can be guaranteed by using visual materials that serve not only to promote the product, but also to enhance the overall appeal of the store.

Having said this, POP material should never overwhelm the product offering. After all, it's not a work of art! Instead, it must be consistent with the positioning of the brand and functional as far as putting the product on display. In other words, managing the brand image in the store is the *sine qua non* for competing on the market, and is essential to preserving the intrinsic value of the brand itself. Based on this premise, companies that outperform their competitors in optimizing the perception of their brand will succeed in boosting sales and encouraging repeat purchases, as well as satisfying the expectations of their clientele.

## 2    Tools and objectives

Since the start of the new millenium, POP material has evolved from simple shelf stoppers to draw attention to special offers, to the sophisticated communication tool it has become today.

In addition to window displays, off-the-shelf displays, checkout counter racks and stands, POP communication now encompasses totems, ads on shopping carts, coupon dispensers, brochures, videos, and interactive kiosks. Put another way, POP communication is no longer only about advertising. Store image, store design, shelf customization, and even product packaging are integral components, along with the scents we smell and music we hear in the store. So POP communication actually encompasses all the aspects of the store and the sales environment that can send messages to customers regarding the values of the brand, the quality and price of the products, and the composition of the product assortment, regardless of the source of these messages, be it producers or distributors.

As we have just seen, more and more often POP communication represents a moment of synergy in which the impact of commercial and marketing investments combine to realize extremely integrated objectives. These include: enhancing the visibility of the product/brand to attract customers' attention, spurring them to detour from their pre-set path; encouraging and facilitating customer interaction with the product; reminding customers of out-of-store communication; informing them of the functional qualities of the product; triggering impulse purchases; reinforcing price positioning; ensuring effective coordination with other promotions and displays; prompting add-on purchases of complementary products; and shoring up brand image.

## 3 Focus

As with all of industry's visual merchandising activity, we can identity three distinct approaches that aim to maximize POP communication:

1. productivity of the space;
2. communication of the product; and
3. value of the brand.

1. *Focus on productivity of the space*: Today, as retailers and manufacturers are well aware, it's no longer enough to put products on shelves. To be more specific, in retail settings where product assortment saturates the available space to the point of overflowing, what counts most is visibility. In other words, focusing customers' attention on the product on the shelf is one of the keys to success, measured in terms of sales and market share. From this standpoint, POP communication can be seen as a way to sharpen this focus, which also serves to maximize the yield of display space to attain objectives such as:

- boosting product turnover rate;
- raising average profit margins;
- improving production efficiency by optimizing financial results; and
- lowering the cost of managing and maintaining stock.

2. *Focus on communication of the product*: Putting products in the right place at the right time, with the help of effective visual merchandising, can be both a source of higher sales and revenues, as well as better brand recognition. This explains the growing interest in designing and implementing POP communication with the following aims:

- to accentuate the distinctive features of the offering;
- to compel customers to try the product;

- to promote new product launches on the market; and
- to reinforce promotions, reducing the risk that customers ignore them.

3. *Focus on the value of the brand.* If we think of the store as a setting/where brand loyalty can be reinforced, POP communication can also play a leading role in marketing activities:

- making retail settings more attractive and pleasant; and
- enhancing the offering by providing information on relative products and services.


## 4    Design

The process of designing and managing POP communication follows a set sequence of stages, each marked by distinct but ideally constant interaction with the channel, from conception to assembly, setup and maintenance. In terms of design, all POP communication can be classified based on certain parameters:

1. physical-technical characteristics;
2. duration; and
3. functional features.

### 4.1    *Physical-technical characteristics*

POP materials can be differentiated according to the physical-technical, characteristics of the display unit:

1. *fixed and/or semi-fixed*, including displays (on countertops, walls, floors, etc.) totems, countertop racks and stands (Figs. 1, 2 and 3); and
2. *movable*: signs, posters, stoppers, stickers, bins, and banners (Figs. 4 and 5).

### 4.2    *Duration*

POP material can be designed as permanent, semi-permanent, temporary, or promotional. How long it's meant to last depends on the product category, the use and the expiration date, as well as the product features of the items in question (Figs. 6a and 6b).

*Figure* 1 – Oakley's fixed counter display, set in front of a movable panel, reinforces recall of the communication campaign.

*Figure* 2 – A semi-fixed structure placed against the wall marks the shelf location of one of the most famous board games in the world.

*Figure* 3 – Casa Modena promotes its products by framing them in a stand-alone floor display that calls to mind the nature of artisan goods.

*Figure* 4 – An Acqua Lurisia poster using irony and clever wordplay to draw attention to its products.

*Figure* 5 – Welcoming all hypermarket customers with movable communication in the form of entrance sleeves placed on the entrance gates, Mulino Bianco creates a powerful reminder of its products on offer inside.

*Figures* 6a and 6b – Wall displays dedicated to each brand and personalized by design, materials, and displays, differentiate between the various worlds of value offered by Salmoiraghi & Viganò in Piazza San Babila, Milan.

Regardless of the intended duration, overall investments are on the rise, so manufacturers want displays that last, not only from a design standpoint, but also with regard to the quality of materials. This second aspect is gradually becoming a central one, because a critical ingredient in a successful communication campaign is keeping POP material in good condition. Along the same lines, permanent structures also need to be refreshed periodically, at the very least with updated graphics.

### 4.3    *Functional features*

We can classify POP communication as:

1. *push* tools, created to present and promote products, such as on- and off-the-shelf displays (Figs. 7 and 8); or
2. *pull* tools, designed to convey information and/or messages, with the aim of sparking customers' curiosity; examples are stoppers and posters (positioned in store windows, on shelves or on the sales floor) (Figs. 9 and 10).

*Figure 7* – This display wall by Bialetti catches the eye thanks to its colors, size, structure, and position in a multibrand housewares store.

*Figure* 8 – Heineken showcase invites customers walking through the aisle to take a detour into the world of this brand.

*Figure* 9 – Pull graphics and brochures effectively delineate the space dedicated to Stihl and Viking.

*Figure* 10 – An arresting Ray-Ban window with pull graphics and videos inspired by the brand's current advertising campaign.

The decision to opt for push or pull material has a major impact on choices pertaining to: display size, quantity of product, space earmarked for communication and brand visibility, position in the store. With regard to this last point, pull materials must enjoy the highest possible visibility, which means a position where customer traffic is the most intense, such as the entrance, the perimeter of the sales area, or on the end caps (Fig. 11).


## 5    Assembly, installation and maintenance

Before discussing this stage, an essential one for ensuring the best possible results from any POP communication program, we need to remember that over half of all POP material doesn't make it to the store. In fact, most doesn't even leave the producer's warehouse. It's abandoned, forgotten, in the trunk of the sale rep's car or in the retailer's storeroom. According to recent European studies, around 80% of all such material is never used, for one reason or another.

So it comes as no surprise that within the context of vertical channel relationships, the most critical steps are assembly, installation and maintenance of POP materials. The fact is that 80% of all materials are not prop-

*Figure* 11 – A large, roomy display space at the Windows showcase, perfectly positioned in the center aisle of a Unieuro store.

erly assembled, and most are not even tested in actual stores. This problem is even more serious when we consider the fact that, along with precision and care, we need speed and efficiency when installing dedicated promotional areas and/or assembling sales support structures specially designed for specific stores. Yet many innovative approaches to managing POP programs fail because no one is clearly tasked with stocking and upkeep of the displays, or the person who is given this responsibility does not do the job well. In these cases, cooperation can quickly turn into recrimination.

In light of this, the supplier should carefully consider alternative methods for implementing POP materials, and choose the best fit for the specificities of the distribution channel in question. In particular, there are three possibilities in terms of who should be in charge of delivering, assembling and installing POP materials:

1. store personnel (visual merchandisers or sales staff);
2. external agencies; or
3. the distributors themselves.

To determine the best option, we need to do a comparative analysis of costs, degree of control, and the relative impact that investments in POP communication have in reinforcing the overall product marketing strategy. Clearly, the bigger the investments, the more crucial direct control becomes. This is also due to the fact that very often store personnel lack not only the motivation, but more importantly the ability to properly handle POP materials. But even when suppliers opt for direct management, they must always be very sensitive to the needs of both retailers and their customers. In fact, normally POP materials are installed when the store is open for business. That means careful attention and expertise are essential during this process to avoid obstructing customers as they move through the store and to keep clutter to a minimum.

The supplier, on the other hand, expects the store to streamline the bureaucratic procedures linked to authorizations/certifications needed to grant access to visual merchandisers who will assemble and install the POP materials. From this standpoint, using an agency may prove more effective. In fact, with a number of commissions in hand, an agency can easily achieve significant economies of scale. This in turn means that agency personnel not only will be sure to visit the store more often, but they'll also establish closer ties with the sales staff.

There are three methods for setting up and displaying POP communication, each involving a different degree of complexity as far as implementation and organization:

1. on the product;
2. on the shelf; and
3. off the shelf (stand-alone POP).

### 5.1   *POP on the product*

In this case, POP materials such as stickers and stoppers are applied directly to the surface of the product. This easy-to-manage method works for most mass-market goods, even small to medium-sized items, and is particularly effective not only in highlighting the product on the shelf, but also in drawing attention to special offers and new product launches.

The chief advantage lies in the fact that this technique is limited in scope and linked to the product alone. In other words, no additional sales space is used up, beyond what the parties involved already agreed to and what would normally be allocated to the items in question. However, this is the very aspect that can prove to be counterproductive if the product assortment is overcrowded. Intense competition among brands and products could nullify the creative and attractive plus of POP materials applied directly to the product when this effect is overshadowed by competitors' marketing initiatives with higher impact.

### 5.2    POP on the shelf

POP materials placed on hooks or bars installed in gondolas are particularly effective in capturing the attention of customers with communicative and informative structures that extend out into aisles or beyond and/or above shelves. This technique involves materials such as crowners, wobblers, talkers, roll-ons, banners, and standees of all shapes and sizes (Figs. 12 and 13).

Generally speaking, the effect is eye-catching, especially when using attractive images and warm, vibrant colors. What's more, a stronger accent can be placed on attention-grabbing new product features, ones that relate to entire product categories or several product families, for example. At the same time, a greater sense of order and clarity is created in the store aisles.

This vast expressive capacity, along with exceptional potential for attracting customers thanks to enhanced intrinsic visibility, represent the primary advantages of POP materials on the shelf. On the other hand, there is more visual and physical clutter in the aisle, which in some cases may limit the use of this technique.

### 5.3    POP off the shelf (stand-alone displays)

Some POP materials can be set up in a store without any physical supports connecting them to shelves; examples are corner points, displays, stands, totems, and A-stand posters. Without a doubt, these off-the-shelf POP tools are becoming more and more popular thanks to their impressive communicative impact, spotlighting certain products with respect to others, enhancing not only visibility but accessibility. Naturally, these POP materials are excellent tools for boosting promotional sales and impulse purchases in general. Beyond this, benefits can also be seen in relation to sales trends, limiting the risk of overstocking which could disrupt the linear display. Although all types of stand-alone POP materials are worth mentioning, below we will take a closer look two types that have particularly distinctive features: totems and brand showcases.

*Figure* 12 – Shelf stoppers and standees provide a clear, instant accent on the vertical brand displays in the toy department of a hypermarket.

*Figure* 13 – Heineken captures high visibility in the aisle and on the shelves thanks to an elaborate combination of mobile material positioned vertically and horizontally.

## Totems

With the exception of A-stand posters, totems represent the minimum possible space that brand communication can occupy as an isolated unit. As such, a totem must stand out, conveying a decisive image that sets it apart from the rest of the display area, highlighting the unique features of the brand in question. The physical characteristics of totems are linked to their communicative function. Since space is limited, this type of display extends vertically to achieve maximum visibility, reflecting the brand identity through materials and colors (Fig. 14).

*Figure* 14 – This Stihl totem serves as a display and info point thanks to clearly visible graphics and product descriptions.

A totem can't surround customers completely as it doesn't occupy a three-dimensional space. But to compensate for this, a powerful ergonomic component can be introduced which allows people not only to physically interact with the products on display, but also with the totem itself, especially if it's equipped with digital signage.

The display structure of a totem must be designed in light of the myriad functions it serves: from presenting products to communicating product specifications and innovative components (when applicable), to include service accessories such as holders for stocking flyers and brochures. In some cases, totems make use of multimedia tools that provide further informational support on production methods, as well as product features and/or uses. Once again, an analysis of buyer behavior should provide a guideline for decisions on design and display options.

Obviously, when designing a totem display, the product must play a central role, offering a moment of contact with customers. Touching the product, picking it up and handling it: the possibility of product engagement is a powerful attraction. By drawing people in this way, they'll be more apt to evaluate the item in question in terms of product categories and/or technical-functional features.

Like all materials that guarantee extra customer exposure, totems can generate impressive results not so much due to their unique design (although obviously this helps), but more importantly thanks to their position with respect to in-store traffic flow. Naturally, staking out these high-traffic zones for placing off-the-shelf displays is no simple feat. Brands are constantly vying to fill these spaces, which, being limited are all the more valuable. In fact, many producers are willing to go so far as to rent these areas. In some markets, this cost can be calculated as a contribution to visual merchandising, and is one of the items renegotiated on an annual basis. In other circumstances, allocation of this space may depend on the quality of the project, or the negotiating skills of the people providing the POP materials. Many stores have compiled a portfolio of suppliers they work with on a regular basis to design permanent and temporary off-the-shelf displays. Of course, the companies in question have to invest more time and money in design, materials, and research, but the extra effort is definitely worth it.

*Brand showcases*

At the opposite end of the spectrum we find brand showcases. These display areas undoubtedly represent the largest space that an individual brand can occupy in a multibrand store, with the exception of shop in shops, which are actually autonomous retail outlets with dedicated personnel and separate cash desks. Originally found mainly in large department stores (Fig. 15), brand showcases gradually appeared in hypermarkets and big box non-food stores, where they tend to be temporary structures.

Regardless of the duration, the design of a brand showcase is determined primarily by the need to present the brand as a well-defined identity, independent of the surrounding retail area. As far as the position in the store, these display areas can have a central layout, or be set in a corner,

*Figure* 15 – The prestigious Bulgari showcase on the ground floor of La Rinascente in Milan stands out elegantly from the surrounding space.

occupying two- or three-dimensional space; a linear configuration is also an option. (Fig. 16).

A fundamental rule in creating these displays is that they must be modular, consisting of a series of shapes and forms that can be reassembled to make various structures and product presentations. This is the only type of design that allows visual merchandisers to create a perfect fit with respect to the retail setting and the available space, while preserving intact the expressive language of the brand.

The current trend is to develop projects that occupy a limited amount of space on the sales floor, to respond to the needs of distribution. Normally temporary brand showcases are built on a dais to give customers the impression that they are entering into an autonomous space (Fig. 17).

Using a false ceiling is a way to make a brand showcase appear to be even more of a separate space. To convey the identity of the brand, specific materials and finishings are combined with distinctive lighting that sets the display area apart from the surrounding environment. In fact, in three-dimensional displays, space is often delineated by movable panels, which serve to accentuate the break with the surrounding area, recreating an actual miniature store.

*Figure* 16 – The elegant Oakley corner display stylishly highlights the design and the colors of eyewear in the Salmoiraghi & Viganò store in Piazza San Babila, Milan.

*Figure* 17 – Pink is the color of the world of Barbie, just like the carpet in this charming child-sized Barbie doll house.

Regardless of the final size, when designing a brand showcase, the objectives to achieve are:

- to be noticed, that is, tall enough for people to see even from far away;
- to attract attention, creating a pathway that leads to the area in question, if possible;
- to offer hospitality with a welcoming, orderly space where customers can feel comfortable;
- to communicate, organizing space so as to convey the values and institutional communication of the brand without creating conflict with the other messages in the store;
- to evoke emotion in customers, acting on their affective system to elicit pleasure and spur them to make add-on purchases;
- to stimulate customers, serving as an effective sales support tool; and
- to offer advice, creating an area that exerts a powerful pull on customers, where they can be guided in choosing the product that best meets their needs.

Leaving aside the brand showcase which, with its unique features, makes it impossible to compare with the other off-the-shelf options either in terms of design and management, as a rule, suppliers prefer POP materials that retailers can install on their own. The reason for this preference is that the technique in question entails a far less complex relationship with the retailer. The biggest benefits are that assembly requires less personnel, and setup is simple and quick. However, POP materials in general constitute a sensitive topic in the context of channel relationships because they extend beyond the traditional display areas, and occupy space that could be allocated for other activities or other brands. This, not to mention that they create obstacles for the normal flow of traffic in the store.

In fact, it's more critical than ever to ascertain the actual installation, activation, as well as the proper management and maintenance of these displays. Yet all this involves tasks that are definitely not top priority for the store manager. So ideally the producer should assign its own personnel to deal with POP materials in stores, or hire an agency to do so. But when neither option is possible, at the very least two basic conditions need to be met. First, the materials designed for and supplied to the store should be simple to assemble, and second a visual book should be included that serves as an easy-to-use, step-by-step guide for the store personnel when building and implementing the displays.

## 6 International POP communication

In international firms, POP communication projects are developed at Group headquarters and then disseminated throughout the network. Branch stores, in turn, are frequently expected to take these international projects and interpret them in a way that reflects the national context. Normally, the effectiveness of this entire germination process depends a great deal on how the global project is adapted at a local level. Here marketing research can lend a hand, analyzing relative markets to ascertain the possible restrictions that may be put in place by various distributors.

Clearly, the more modular and flexible the program, the more room for maneuvering there is on the original project, which can be modified to fit the specificities of the distribution channel in the local context. What can happen is that in some countries, such as the UK, up to 24 different displays might be created in response to stores that leverage differentiation as their competitive strategy. Elsewhere, as in Germany, where distributors use more similar competitive configurations, two displays may be more than enough.

In order to maximize the results of an international campaign in diverse local contexts, a set of basic conditions must be met. Taken together, these factors enable companies to implement an approach which is differentiated, but still in line with a shared investment project. These conditions are listed below.

* adopting a micromarketing approach, supported by research on local markets;
* upholding a consistent goal across all markets, while being open to working together to made small modifications to satisfy specific requests;
* establishing and maintaining close ties with local distributors to fully comprehend their needs and guarantee the highest possible visibility for in-store POP materials;
* creating materials with simple designs and graphics: the golden rule is "less is more" reflecting the fastest and most effective approach for international campaigns; and
* planning costs and logistics flows to assess the possibility of centralizing production of materials for rapid delivery to various local markets.

In other words, on one hand, consistency with brand identity is the central, shared goal. But on the other, different strategies, competitive configurations and cultural approaches necessitate maximum flexibility and efficiency for the people who have to interpret POP communication to formulate a version that works for their individual markets. The success of international initiatives, if possible even more so than national projects, is almost exclusively linked to issues related merely to management and logistics; the creative aspect often proves to be the simplest part of the process.

## 7    Channel relationships

As we'll discuss in detail in the next chapter, channel interaction relative to design, implementation and control of POP communication is still a highly critical issue today. In fact, growing investments by industry are equally matched by a rising interest in these programs by distribution. At the same time, retailers are becoming more and more selective, and starting to place restrictions not only on the POP communication they'll accept, but also how relative materials are designed. An example that would not likely win approval, for example, is an off-the-shelf display that blocked the view of the shelves situated behind it.

To be more specific, collaboration on in-store communication activities is shaped by the type of relationship that develops between the two parties in the distribution channel. The basis of this relationship centers on one of these three components:

1. contracts;
2. competition; or
3. strategy.

1. When relationships are forged mainly through *contracts and negotiations*, the top priority of the two parties is purely an exchange of products for payment. As a result, their efforts focus on leveraging their relative bargaining power to maximize short-term results. To this end, POP materials must serve as clearly visible promotional tools that can be combined with elements of the store's design, without invading the sales space excessively and/or hindering the natural flow of visitors.

In these cases, the company that supplies POP materials has be particularly adroit in designing them so as to satisfy the myriad needs of distribution. In doing so, retailers are more likely to be willing to install these materials in the store and to use personnel to optimize the process, when necessary.

2. *Competitive relationships*, instead, develop when producers fear possible "invasions" into their territory by distributors, and vice versa. Here the prevalent mindset is certainly not reciprocal integration or mutual collaboration; cooperation is not an option, as far as the two parties are concerned. Each one builds up its defenses to protect its own positions, providing fertile ground for conflicts in an environment rife with heated disagreements on abilities and areas of competence. Distribution sees POP communication for the most part as an ineffectual activity, one that is at best unnecessary, at worst actually an attempt by industry to overstep its boundaries. Often, in fact, this merchandising tool is the pretext for engaging in fruitless disputes, ultimately forcing customers to go without the innovative solutions that support the purchase process, and to miss the chance to gather more information on the products on offer. It goes without saying that the fallout on the two channel players results in no small amount of damage.

3. *Strategic relationships* emerge when industry and distribution recognize the mutual advantage of collaborating on their respective activities. The orientation of these relationships is medium to long-term, and the foundation is the recognition that there are reciprocal benefits to be had from shared strategic management. This approach allows both parties to face the market and the competition by putting in play their competencies and resources, to realize the only solution that can achieve the best possible medium to long-term results.

Throughout the entire distribution channel, free and open collaboration emerges. In this context, POP communication is seen a real opportunity, not only to reach sales targets, but also to achieve goals relating to conveying and reinforcing brand and store identity. From this perspective of cooperation, when industry adopts a sell-out approach, this leads to the development of trade marketing actions that funnel investments into visual merchandising activities, with the aim of shoring up the connection with the channel. The purpose of producers here is clearly to succeed in securing an advantageous position for their products in the store, and to find more room for collaboration. This, also within the context of POP communication, can be exploited to build a systemic offering capable of maximizing the value created for the final consumer.

With reference to this point, a study by Symphony IRI carried out in 2011 surveyed distributors to find out their opinions on POP material: compared to an overall average score of 3.4 out of 5, effectiveness in increasing sales recorded the highest mark (3.8). In fact, the more evolved distributors, those more likely to establish a collaborative relationship, are pushing more and more to maximize not only the effectiveness but also the efficiency of all the material designed and managed by industry. As far as channel relationships, the two parties are aware of the many areas of overlap in strategic activities, marketing and interface initiatives, all of which lead back once again to the numerous advantages that POP communication offers. But despite this realization, there is still much room for improvement in channel relationships.

Yet, over 38% of the material delivered to the store is never used. In fact, a study published in the February 2006 issue of InStore magazine shows that this situation appears to depend on the following: too much material (15%), too little space (11%), inappropriate material for the store (7%), wrong size (7%), no time (3%).

Delving into detail, distributors have a long list of complaints about suppliers of POP materials and how they do their job.

- Industry shouldn't force its initiatives on all retailers, regardless of the positioning of their stores. The whole process would be far more efficient and effective if it were coordinated. In other words, POP materials should be more consistent with the various kinds of initiatives that distributors develop based on their own assortment policies in relation to their segmentation and positioning strategies.
- All too often, organizational and managerial limitations of POP material suppliers are passed down the line, and fall to distribution to contend with.
- The people who are more directly involved in designing POP communication should spend more time "in the field". If they rarely ever leave their office, they can't get a clear idea of the potential that they can exploit from dealing with spaces and materials in different ways.
- Long-term planning with distributors would eliminate many of the issues that arise when carrying out initiatives, and would ensure an

appropriate response to the frequent and varied requests they make. While retailers are reasonably open to "light" POP communication in the store (such as shelf talkers, hanging signs, informational flyers, brochures and posters), as far as product displays and other off-the-counter initiatives, they are far more cautious, carefully evaluating and scheduling all these activities.

- Distribution wants more integrated promotional and communication plans and more coordinated scheduling; ideally, industry would provide an infrastructure that the store can resort to when need be to handle POP material.
- The entire process would be facilitated if industry took an open attitude toward feedback from the sales staff in the store; the store manager should also be more involved in designing materials, through a continual process of co-optation.
- The use of prototypes to test out in certain stores would lower the risk of errors in design, and at the same time make it possible to accurately assess benefits.
- If display dimensions and communication formats were respected more often, problems with obstructions to in-store traffic flow would be less common.
- When POP materials are easier to assemble and display, fewer mistakes are made, in particular when these activities are handled by individual stores.
- By clustering distribution formats, ad hoc materials can be designed to meet the distinctive characteristics of each target, size, and retailing mix.
- Flexible structures, and materials that are durable and easily adaptable to changing environmental conditions would reduce waste and inefficiencies and guarantee greater effectiveness throughout the entire process of designing and managing POP communication.

Industry, for its part, also complains of various points of friction with distribution that complicate the process to no small degree. Clearly, these points correspond to the limits indicated by retailers, listed above, simply seen from a different perspective.

- Every distributor has its own rules; greater standardization would reduce costs and errors.
- Often distribution does not embrace a collaborative mindset.
- Several inefficiencies in the system are linked to ineffective communication: the first contact between the brand and the store comes at a

central level with the buyer, who obviously is not in a position to be able to support the process of managing POP material in the store.

- Though retailers may initially be open to accepting new POP materials, they do not always follow through in the store.
- The decision making process is often very slow.
- There is a very high risk that POP material is removed before it should be to make room for activities proposed by other competitors.
- The sales staff in the store does not pay much attention when competitors encroach on shelf space. This often leads to an all-out war to grab the best space and use the most POP material.

Delving into more detail, according to a study conducted by the author on industry's brand investments in the store (Zaghi, 2013), there are a number of reasons that explain the major inefficiencies that emerge in the management of POP communication: the material does not reach the store; material is delivered later than scheduled; material does not correspond to what the distributor agreed to; material is not used; material is assembled incorrectly; damaged material is not replaced.

Summing up, it's clear that more interaction and transparency between the two channel players could resolve any number of open issues. Working together to improve the results of product categories, differentiating POP programs at a store level to guarantee customized interventions, collaborating to consolidate what works and to improve the rest, building trust among the parties involved: these are only a few of the bricks to use for building the foundation for a true partnership in planning and managing all in-store communication activities.

## 8    Digital POP: the Canon case[1]

Canon 4-me is an interactive kiosk introduced in 2013 and installed in stores belonging to the network of Canon Professional Partners (CPP). This group of specialized retailers have the exclusive on distributing certain Canon products and offering special promotions. As a result, these

---

[1] Thanks to Elisa Contarini for providing the content of this case, based on her 2016 Master's thesis in Marketing from Università Bocconi, entitled "Digital Visual Merchandising in ottica di omnicanalità: il caso del chiosco interattivo Canon" [Digital Visual Merchandising through an Omnichannel Lens: the case of Canon's interactive kiosk].

stores are points of reference for professional photographers looking for expert advice from sales personnel. It was with this in mind that the kiosk was originally conceived, to serve as a support tool for sales staff who could then provide detailed, up-to-date information to customers. But very quickly Canon realized the value that the kiosk represented for the customers themselves. Thanks to its myriad functions and potentialities, the kiosk has turned into an irreplaceable touchpoint that can enrich the purchase experience for the modern, omnichannel consumer.

In light of this transformation, the aims of the interactive kiosk have become far more challenging. First it must attract visitors, offer instantaneous interaction, and provide relevant information on products and services, to create and sustain customer engagement. After acting on the aspects of awareness and acquisition, the kiosk works on the in-store experience to increment purchases by old and new customers alike. But the common denominator remains the same: to bring online services into the physical store, to establish a continuum between these two dimensions, which many customers already perceive as contiguous.

Since the primary function of this tool is linked to providing information, it can be classified as a "high information dissemination kiosk". Although it can't process commercial transactions, it does provide a substantial amount of precise, technical data which are updated regularly. The kiosk also generates tangible outputs that evidence how it's utilized, that is, not by people who are simply curious, but by customers who are seriously contemplating a purchase.

In terms of the four dimensions of an interactive kiosk, Canon's covers three: informing, interacting, and engaging.

## 8.1 *Technical specifications*

The Canon kiosk has a 32-inch, high definition touchscreen. With a keyboard and speakers, users can input letters and numbers and listen to audio tracks. The kiosk is also linked to a printer.

Retail space permitting, the kiosk consists of a structure that rests on the ground with a small stand on top holding the keyboard and a front-facing screen. This type of interactive station aesthetically aligns with the brand, with its smooth no-frills construction and corporate colors: red, white and black (Fig. 18). If space is limited, the totem rests on a sales counter or hangs from a wall on extendable/retractable braces.

*Figure* 18 – Canon's interactive kiosk, installed near the area dedicated to the brand (courtesy of Canon).

The decision as to where to position the kiosk is up to the store manager, who takes into account both commercial considerations as well as the store layout. Naturally, the best option is to position the kiosk where it is clearly visible, but often the store structure dictates the final decision, because the kiosk needs to be wired to the IT system to ensure a stable connection.

The start screen displays a white box with red lettering which reads "enter", allowing users to access the other sections. While the customer navigates these sections one by one, a toolbar appears in the upper portion of the screen with links to all the other accessible pages, for easy orientation. After clicking on a specific section, on the left hand side of the screen the user sees all the available options. The graphic interface was designed to be clear and simple for every kind of customer, from novices to professionals. The screen saver shows videos and photographs alternating with periodic promotional presentations.

*Figure* 19 – The screen shows the digital datasheet with images of the product, its key features and benefits (courtesy of Canon).

As for the configuration, there are five sections: products, tutorials, services, technology, and promotions.

### Products

This section is actually a digital catalogue of the entire Canon portfolio, divided into product families. For each model, a digital datasheet provides images and lists all the main features and benefits of the product (Fig. 19). The customer can print and/or email this datasheet. There are also photos and videos realized with the product by other customers. This guarantees a significant component of User Generated Content that allows customers to see output that doesn't come exclusively from the company, but from their peers. Each part of every page can be enlarged to fill the entire 32-inch HD screen.

### Technology

Beginning with a product segment, users can choose a specific technology and see which products offer it. This function is based on inverse reasoning: rather than picking a product, customers pick a product feature. Professional photographers find this option extremely helpful when they're looking for a specific benefit that provides a certain performance, rather than a particular product. Naturally, product features can be combined, and the system generates options based on whatever requests users input.

After selecting the product type, the two figures below show how the specific features appear, so customers can discover which item best fits their needs (Figs. 20a and 20b).

Another very useful function allows users to find the components and accessories that Canon offers for each specific model. By inputting the name of the camera they own, they can generate a list of all the compatible accessories. Considering the high number of items in the assortment, it would be impossible for salespeople to know every single possible product combination, so this function helps them to better assist customers, but also lets customers help themselves.

*Tutorials*

This section contains videos that illustrate product uses, functionalities and features. There are also clips of official product presentations that

*Figure* 20 – On the screen the product is presented from various angles, to clearly show all its unique features (courtesy of Canon).

customers can stream with exclusive access. For example, some stores organize events for screening videos of new product launches. This is a way to make customers more active and engaged in market innovations.

*Services*

In this area we find registration forms for product guarantees, firmware, and the Academy. First, customers can register the product they've just purchased to get an extended warranty, which lasts longer than items purchased through other channels, including online (which often offers no post-sales protection). What's more, for the products they already own, customers can download firmware. These are updates that facilitate the interface between software and hardware components of relative photographic equipment. Firmware can also correct possible errors, introduce new functionalities, and enhance product performance. Lastly, the Academy is dedicated to photographers (and teachers) who are affiliated with the Canon network, listing their biographies, presenting their major work, and inviting customers to sign up for the courses these professionals offer throughout the year.

*Promotions*

This section is the most active one in terms of direct communication between the brand and the store. All the ongoing sales are uploaded here, and customers as well as store personnel can consult these pages directly.

As useful as the kiosk is, both for customers and sales staff, the potential of this tool is not fully exploited. Content could be more varied, and generated from different sources, but currently it's uploaded and totally controlled by the company. Instead, creating a cloud dimension could allow for communication and information sharing at the same time, perhaps including opinions on products, reviews, comments, photographs, and questions for the experts.

## 8.2   *The project designer*

To realize the kiosk project and the related software, Canon opted to commission Thron S.p.A., an Italian company specialized in developing Enterprise Software. The system they came up with is based on Digital Asset

Management (DAM), which handles all save, file, memory, and retrieval functions for digital assets. These encompass digital photos, animated clips, videos and music, in other words, the main content components of the interactive kiosk.

Thron focuses on enabling its customer companies to manage all their digital content, often by means of an ad hoc cloud platform which maintains constant connectivity and has the ability to verify the reactions of end users in real time. One of the cornerstones of this type of activity is omnichannel dissemination. All the customer company's assets are centralized in order to facilitate the development of an integrated online/offline strategy. This is achieved via customized platforms that link all existing content available on various channels, making it simultaneously accessible to meet the needs of each individual user.

Canon Italia was seeking to create a system capable of offering quick and easy exchange of information, not only numerical data but photos, videos, technical data and promotions as well. This is why the interactive kiosk was configured with a touchscreen, a tool that makes it possible to access different kinds of content easily and intuitively. Installing content intelligence systems also allows the company to constantly monitor activities, directly verifying customers' reactions. Currently Canon pays Thron an annual fee for handling system maintenance. In calculating the total cost, obviously this fee is added to the expense of the initial investment, which was entirely covered by Canon.

## 8.3   Installing the interactive kiosks

In launching this project, Canon offered the kiosks to a small number of stores, a "starting lineup" in a sense. From this initial group, thirty retailers decided to accept the proposal. To choose the potential participants, multiple variables were taken into account, not all of which were dictated by economic motivations. (Store size and a modern store atmosphere are two examples.)

As a result, some top performers were not considered; these included some small stores with cramped floor space and/or stores run by retailers with little inclination to exploit multimedia support tools. Specifically, the agreement with Canon Italia required the participating locations to pay for the touchscreen monitors, while the company provided the display structure, the computer and the software.

Naturally, as we've seen, by introducing a high-tech tool, Canon hopes to enhance not only the purchase experience for its customers but also the sales experience for its retailers. By doing so, from a trade marketing perspective and following a sell-out approach, future benefits will have positive repercussions on the reputation of the store and the brand.

# 8 Visual merchandising in channel relationships

## 1 Visual merchandising by industry in multibrand distribution

Planning and managing visual merchandising is a process in which industry can play a critical role. In particular, with more advanced modern distribution, producers need to develop related activities to guarantee that their brands and products get the proper quantity and quality of space, ensuring visibility and accessibility. But that's not all. As we've already pointed out many times, visual communication has a powerful impact on sales. Recognizing this reality, companies are striving more and more to achieve bigger and better exposure with an eye to seducing potential buyers, ultimately to become the object of their desire.

This brings us to the foundation of visual merchandising in industry, which is based on two spheres. The first pertains to the organization of space, within the framework of an orientation toward productivity. The second has greater expressive impact, with a focus on enriching objects on an emotional level. This is achieved through a continual dialectic between the informational and suggestive functions of messages, synergistically anchored in an orientation toward communication of the product and the value of the brand.

To sum up, investments in visual merchandising activities enable producers to attain myriad objectives, all of which are associated with three distinctive strategic orientations (Zaghi, 2013):

1. productivity of the space;
2. communication of the product; and
3. value of the brand.

1. Productivity of the space represents the technical-formal approach to visual merchandising. The main aims here are:
   - to boost the number of facings;
   - to maximize the productivity of the linear;
   - to promote different product lines;
   - to optimize management of product shelf life;
   - to grow cross-selling activity;
   - to monitor product rotation;
   - to verify the positions of loss leaders;
   - to trigger impulse purchases;
   - to cut down on stockouts;
   - to defend display space;
   - to enhance visibility of market share;
   - to compress competitors' market share;
   - to facilitate up-selling; and
   - to increase sales for the entire product category.

2. Product communication, instead, is based on the underlying aim of customer-product interaction, in order to achieve a series of objectives:
   - to attract customers' attention;
   - to augment brand visibility;
   - to enhance product legibility;
   - to spotlight promotions;
   - to facilitate interaction with the products;
   - to inform more efficiently;
   - to spark curiosity;
   - to analyze buyer behavior;
   - to guide visitors through the entire store;
   - to stand out from the competition;
   - to educate customers on new categories and technologies; and
   - to differentiate between various store identities.

3. Lastly, brand value is the orientation that begins with product communication objectives and leads to investing more in the store itself, with an eye to shoring up brand identity by realizing the following goals:
   - to underscore the symbolic dimension of the brand;
   - to reinforce the magnitude of the brand;
   - to consolidate brand equity;

- to support new product launches;
- to enhance the purchase experience; and
- to differentiate product and service offerings.

In other words, on one hand we have an orientation which places the productivity of space at the center, based exclusively on a commercial rationale. On the other, communication with regard to the product and the brand value are founded on a marketing approach, leveraging the values that lie at the very heart of visual merchandising.

Let's consider the four levers that combine to determine the use of sales space, namely design, layout, display and allocation of space to each item in the offering. These factors are becoming less essential to positioning/value and communication, and more critical in terms of maximizing productivity. As a rule, when dealing with visual merchandising (and in-store communication in general), the various objectives that producers strive for do not fall within the scope of a single orientation. But we can usually draw a clear distinction between companies that focus mainly on maximizing the productivity of retail space, following a more efficiency-based approach to visual merchandising, and others that see the store through a more value-based lens, channeling investments into communicating and consolidating brand identity.

## 1.1   *The technical-formal core of visual merchandising*

As for the more technical component of managing the linear and off-the-shelf displays, visual merchandising by producers should pursue a comprehensive combination of objectives (Zaghi, 2013). First of all, visual communication and activation activities are ways to gain a deeper understanding of the distributor's value chain: from inserting the items in the product assortment to managing logistics and information flows. This knowledge can span all formats and distribution channels, providing useful input for optimizing the effectiveness of ad hoc in-store actions.

On one hand, producers can predict the best product assortments and display techniques for maximizing results in terms of turnover and profitability of the sales space. All this while keeping in mind the variety of distribution formats, retail spaces, store identities, locations/positioning, and areas of attraction. On the other, producers can estimate product profitability for distributors, weighing the prominence of various factors on a case-by-case basis, such as sales price, purchase price, discounts, quantity of goods sold, stock, rotation, promotions, year-end refunds, deferred payments and special cooperation agreements (when applicable).

The outcome is more seamless control over the assortment as established at company headquarters or the main office. Control is another activity that is becoming increasingly complex due to the gradual disappearance of centralized management. This situation has not only diminished contact between producers and direct interlocutors (such as the department heads in stores), it has also augmented the bargaining power of distribution. In this sense, visual merchandising by industry guarantees more efficient physical product handling thanks to data analysis on in-store commercialization. Specifics to consider are the presence of a given product, the price, the linear and the stock, in order to verify that the items in the assortment are offered on sale to customers as agreed.

Responsibility for monitoring stores can be assigned to specific roles, which take different names (customer category, field account, in-store representative, Point-of-Sale (POS) manager, store manager, sales merchandiser, sell-out specialist, store account, trade supporter, visual merchandiser, etc.). Much effort has also been made to introduce innovative IT systems that provide better support for these activities in the field, improving efficiency and reducing margins of error at the same time. Visual merchandising also allows producers to verify the true potential of the store by carefully studying how to allocate space to individual items. This involves testing the sales potential and profitability for each type of store (on the basis of square meters, location, etc.). In this way, for stores that perform below par, display guidelines can be implemented that have proven more effective elsewhere.

It is also possible to adapt the sales force structure to the distribution structure, to enhance productivity and ensure that each decision-making level of the distributor is matched with a counterpart to interface with in the sales force. This person must be well informed, competent, well respected and responsible for activities such as: determining the functions of regional managers, sales reps or merchandisers; planning and scheduling store visits; tasking specific activities; identifying cases in which physical management of the store is inefficient, so as to implement interventions that will solve these issues; designing score cards for observing and assessing in-store activities, and so forth.

Added to this is the growing need for companies to transform what they expect of their sales force, from performing exclusively sales-oriented tasks to offering advice and recommendations. This in turn leads to the introduction of new methods for negotiation based on communication investments in the store (where possible).

As far as negotiations between producers and distributors, tools should be adopted that are clear, objective, thoroughly documented, updated, constantly tested, and capable of offering the distributor a demonstrable advantage. Such tools include: reports on in-store visits, a handbook for sales staff, templates for the linear, models for product presentation, the visual book, software for in-store planning, profitability studies and income projections.

Naturally, all this cannot, and more importantly, would not be possible in the future without conducting studies that reveal and track customers' purchase processes in terms of their actions, behaviors, and perceptions. Under examination is everything from how they use store space to how they behave when they come to the entrance of the department or when they see the displays; from their purchase motivations to any uncertainty they may have in reading the visual messages for classifying and displaying products; from their reactions to promotions and prices to their attitudes toward packaging, and the power of attraction of other items.

## 1.2 *The value-based core of visual merchandising*

Our discussion up to this point simply reiterates the importance of the technical-formal framework that characterizes in-store communication. However, it would be a gross oversimplification to equate visual merchandising by industry with a policy for enhancing the visibility of merchandise or monitoring the retailing mix used by distributors, especially in today's world.

A notion that has come to the fore is brand equity, which explains why companies are gradually moving toward a new conception of marketing which is referred to as "aesthetic" and "experiential". The aim here is to make customers feel physical and emotional sensations as they experience the product or the brand.

It is true that these emotions can also be elicited by products and through traditional communication levers, but innovative connotations of retail space can play an incisive role in sparking sensations. Creating a theatrical, aesthetic, multisensory experience which generates emotional engagement: this represents the new universe of consumption, the new market, and the new consumer. In this reality, retail spaces become magnetics, imbued with a high symbolic value, with the scope of delighting customers, not simply entertaining them. It is often said that the postmodern era has brought about a profound transformation of customer needs and demands: they no longer simply want to purchase a product and acquire its use value; instead they desire global experiences that captivate the senses, the heart and the mind.

This evolution of the store is a phenomenon we can read beginning with the changes underway in consumer priorities. The store is no longer a simple container; instead it has become place where customers have experiences, where they are attracted and enthralled by the use of techniques, atmospheres, and contexts that can engage them in an experience that appeals to all the senses. A place where visual merchandising takes center stage.

In other words, the store once and for all is taking on a new strategic centrality, becoming the channel that allows the company to establish an actual interactive relationship with consumers. In the store, all the physical and symbolic features of brand identity are represented in a tangible way. Above all, the store provides its customers with a brand experience that is multisensory and emotionally engaging (Borghini and Zaghi, 2007a). Naturally, along with this transformation of the store – from a machine for selling products to a tool for communicating and enhancing brand identity too – comes the need to redefine the structure and managerial approach.

Today the primary objective is to transmit messages to customers and elicit in them physical and emotional sensations that align with brand values, while accentuating the educational and hedonic aspects of shopping. This activity has become a decisive one in the development of behavioral decision-making models for consumers, who are constantly on the lookout for appealing experiences that are worth repeating.

As we have clearly shown, a store visit can satisfy functional needs, offering utilitarian value linked to the purchase of products. But hedonic needs can also come into play, making the store a generator of emotional gratification. This kind of satisfaction is only marginally associated with the benefits deriving from actually making a purchase (or even deciding not to). On the other hand, again we should emphasize that the rapid proliferation of the number and variety of products launched on the market leads to a manifest risk that the commercial offering will stagnate. In other words, if there is little to differentiate various product assortments, they all begin to look the same.

Put another way, today every single proposal must stand out from the surrounding context (normally from the other items on the shelf), or face the certain danger of becoming invisible. This necessitates a sharp focus on the product's intrinsic features (its commercial properties), to link them to motivations that are innately associated with symbolic, cultural, and psychological aspects. All this calls for a development strategy that isn't based on a product per se, but instead encompasses the entire world of meanings connoted with it. Goods must be anchored to symbolic systems that are clearly recognizable and have a powerful evocative impact. Product features must be interpreted in such a way that is logically consistent and emotionally seductive; relative value content must emerge intuitively, unequivocally and instantaneously.

Summing up, then, we can consider the store a communication tool, or better still, a privileged point of contact between the worlds of production and consumption. In adopting this perspective, what becomes undeniably clear is that visual merchandising plays a critical role in orienting the brand company, and slots into the commercial transaction as the main channel of direct communication between the product assortment and the product purchaser.

All this is leading companies to consolidate investments in enhancing brand equity, framing products in perceptive settings (and not only visual ones) which are clearly perceivable, legible, understandable and provocative. This is the only way that the product, or better still the product's intrinsic features, can access deeper interior worlds, eradicating the risk of banalization, an all the more serious danger in times of consumer crisis (Zaghi, 2013).

## 2 The organization of visual merchandising by industry

The more salient question today does not center on the relevance for industry of visual merchandising, which is now unanimously considered the fifth lever in the marketing mix. This status has emerged mainly thanks to the capacity of visual merchandising to finalize marketing activities in operative terms in the store itself, contributing to consolidating the value of the brand. What warrants reflection are the relative methods that industry uses to plan and manage this process. Very often the different levers of visual merchandising are designed and implemented by various company departments which, beyond a lack of coordination, also overlap at times in allocating resources to take on related activities.

The separation between product marketing and trade marketing often proves to be a source of serious inefficiencies, based on a set of distinct relationships between the brand and its end users. On one hand, consumers are the targets of communication and promotional activities undertaken by marketing; on the other, distributors are seen as intermediaries in this relationship. In fact, their role is becoming more interactive with the consumer. This contrasts with the position of the brand company, which uses trade marketing to control, and if possible reduce, this interference.

Looking more closely, however, industry and distribution provide a combination offering of goods and services directed at consumers who are clients first, and then buyers. This means that the same person encompasses three diverse profiles and behaviors, which come together in various ways in the store. This is where these different aspects amalgamate with the consumption experiences that form the personal baggage of the customer, the ultimate target of this composite offering.

Visual merchandising must be perfectly aligned and wholly consistent with brand strategies. It follows, then, that the work of the visual merchandiser is multidisciplinary, with the potential to provide high added value. This is precisely the reason why many companies are gradually hiring on qualified professionals who provide qualitative support to the traditional sales force. Case in point, today we find a wide range of approaches to organizing and managing visual merchandising activity, carried out by a specialized network or an external agency, in cooperation with or in place of the sales force (Zaghi, 2013). The competencies of the sales force, or a network of visual merchandisers, or a third party organization can vary tremendously as far as the ability to display products, to carry out negotiations, and to manage and monitor the store. Regardless of the visual marketing solution that a company may adopt, the critical success factor of any communication in the commercial context is the capacity to standardize it from the highest level down.

The following sections present three organizational models, and provide overviews of the strengths and weaknesses of each, with an eye to improving the efficiency and effectiveness of the entire process, regardless of the chosen orientation toward visual merchandising.

## 2.1 *Visual merchandising by the sales force*

Seeing that sell-in activity can no longer guarantee the full exploitation of sales potential, the company should get its sales staff directly involved, at least in the preliminary stages since they provide customer service, beyond simply making sales. The sales staff takes over responsibility for monitoring the store, in order to glean information on general sales trends and to become more familiar with their clientele. (Otherwise this kind of analysis would only take place at company headquarters during negotiations.)

However, in this case, visual merchandising is nothing more than a residual activity with respect to sales in the strict sense. In fact, when visual merchandising is done mechanically, with no specialized training, from a qualitative standpoint relative efforts focus solely on the store windows, permanent and temporary display fixtures, and POP material (but only in specific situations covered by agreements with distribution). Industry personnel do not get any special training, and the structure of their visits is a fairly accurate reflection of traditional sales activity. In fact, converting these people into true visual merchandisers would be no easy task.

When dealing with displays, the approach of the industry-merchandiser is simply meticulous observation, supported at best with specific sales information on their products, which serves only to enhance visibility and sellability. The tasks these professionals perform, albeit relevant, are limited to the following: replenishing products, analyzing the retail space assigned to each item, tracking stockouts, controlling the freshness of perishables, verifying that POP materials are set up in the store and in good condition, preparing and organizing promotional activities, monitoring the implementation of all investments for activation and communication, as determined at headquarters, sharing information on new products and technologies, as well as data on sales trends and purchase behaviors. Despite our initial premise, today the sell-in mindset still predominates, which means that visual merchandising activity almost entirely revolves around soliciting new sales orders.

In conclusion, this organizational model presents certain critical elements that make it very weak indeed. First, the sales force lacks the proper training and sophistication to transfer the company's marketing policies to the store. The risk here is that they attempt to do so using methods that the distributor does not – and actually cannot – share. Second, when the sales force does get involved, their activities tend to be limited exclusively to collecting and monitoring data. The reason for this is the progressive propensity of distribution to take back some degree of control over their stores, including performing visual merchandising activities to establish the desired market positioning. The natural outcome is that the point where contact and dialogue takes place moves upward to higher levels in the company hierarchy, creating greater distance from the local market.

What's more, the actual impact on the store is hard for the heads of sales or trade marketing to ascertain. In these cases, as we've already seen, it is almost impossible to root out the real reasons behind poor sales performance, when it occurs. But beyond this, the very lack of objective data also dramatically hinders the sharing of information assets in the channel. This input is precisely what would provide the foundation for joint, systemic action by industry and distribution. Working together, these two players could potentially maximize the efficiency and effectiveness of the entire distribution process, while improving customer service and ultimately enhancing overall satisfaction.

Summing up, this organizational model places producers in a very tenuous position in their relationship with stores, and an even weaker one with control structures that they depend on at the level of distribution centers and company headquarters. In the evolution of modern distribution, it is highly likely that this configuration will become even more counterproductive with regard to bargaining power as well as the actual effectiveness of in-store initiatives. For these reasons, in time this model will become more and more marginal.

## 2.2 *Visual merchandising by a network of specialized professionals*

In light of the limitations of the efforts of the sales staff, more and more companies are turning to networks of visual merchandisers. These professionals work synergistically with retailers, acting as consultants and offering assistance in store management. In this case, the visual merchandiser unites competency in the managerial approaches and operational processes of visual merchandising with extensive product experience and a thorough understanding of purchase behavior in the target customer segment. This professional is capable of supporting the store by sharing knowledge of development strategies, positioning, and the associated marketing policies of the company. All this guarantees an effective and efficient exchange of information. The list of activities tasked to the visual merchandiser is long, and has become consolidated over time:

- setting up permanent display spaces and promotional areas;
- verifying proper maintenance of display solutions; specifically, replacing or reconditioning any damaged or worn out POP materials;
- checking the expiration dates on perishable items, ensuring a fresh image also by disposing of items past sell-by date;
- ascertaining the qualitative and quantitative positioning of products, also with respect to the competition;
- filling any free space in the store with additional displays;
- soliciting reorders;
- monitoring stock;
- controlling standard pricing;
- anticipating future activities, reminding department heads of upcoming initiatives, helping them with product orders and planning extra spaces, when possible; and
- organizing proposals regarding possible improvements, evaluating the store's problems and opportunities.

Many of these activities actually coincide with what the sales force already does. What differentiates the work of visual merchandisers is their proactive approach, together with their specific competencies. First and foremost, they must be aware of corporate and market priorities, to ensure that the "must-haves" in the offering are never missing, and to give these items prime positions in store displays, also in relation to market share. Visual merchandisers must also be well aware of product prices in the surrounding area, understanding product positioning and pricing strategy; identifying the companies that are price setters on the local market and what orientation they implement; instantly intuiting and acting on the more dangerous price breaks that put profit margins in jeopardy.

Visual merchandisers also need to be able to adapt to the people they are interacting with, to more clearly assess the following: the possibility and/or willingness to intervene; the degree of sophistication and cultural/professional level; the need and/or interest in coming up with a consistent approach. Knowing how to optimize energy and time is also part of the job description. This means on one hand leaving aside the stores where there is no apparent opportunity for growth, and on the other shoring up efforts in situations where there is a real chance to achieve the expected results. Creative use of POP material is another key aptitude, deciding whether or not to personalize displays and linears, exploiting the materials on hand to come up with new twists on the company's recommendations. Last of all, visual merchandisers should constantly work to consolidate and maintain their relationships with the department heads to find the best possible solutions for the local store.

From an organizational viewpoint, internal networks of visual merchandisers are set up by territory, to ensure a deep knowledge of the specific characteristics of the local markets and competitive arenas. This is especially pertinent with respect to current demand among the stores' target customers and retailing activities of competitors. As we've already underscored, this knowledge is invaluable as it allows stores to preempt moves by competitors. In some cases partnership agreements also facilitate these actions.

Despite the undeniable source of competitive advantage deriving from professional specialization, a dedicated network of visual merchandisers presents certain limitations that cannot be overlooked. To begin with is the sharp spike in commercial cost deriving from a dual structure. In addition, efficient and effective internal coordination tends to be quite complicated. The only way to achieve this is by perfectly synchronizing communication flows between the sales and visual merchandising networks. Particularly crucial is timely information on specific initiatives regarding certain distributor-customers or marketing activities. But this objective is not easy to realize, considering the need to put mechanisms in place that provide a quick connection with customer care units, for example, relating to issues regarding investment proposals.

This approach also calls for a radical cultural transformation in the sales force, who must learn to work jointly with visual merchandisers to design and implement selling activities in an atmosphere of mutual trust and complicity, which is not always easy to create. Often, at least in the preliminary stages (and even after that, unfortunately), the sales staff does not see the network of visual merchandisers in a positive light, suspecting them of being some sort of inspectors sent to monitor work performance. So it is up to the company to make sure that a proactive relationship based on open dialogue is established among all the parties involved, to improve the overall productivity of everyone's efforts.

Another operational limitation may arise when distribution centers have total control over the entire network. The point here is often to eliminate the personal relationship between the department heads and the visual merchandisers, since the latter could potentially interfere with the implementation of initiatives planned at the store level. Added to this is

the fact that often visual merchandisers do not possess the same professional skillsets. This means that some have a limited capacity to analyze
the context and to plan initiatives accordingly; the same is true with regard
to their people skills.

### 2.3   Visual merchandising by a negotiating group with the support of an external agency

Another organization model for visual merchandising by industry exists
in which relative activity is more and more often addressed during the
negotiation stage, in terms of consultation and collaboration by top company executives in distribution. Instead, promoters/visual merchandisers
are tasked with inspecting the stores. Companies that adopt this type of
configuration are normally more inclined to outsource certain functions
of the process to specialized agencies, hired and coordinated by a visual
merchandising consultant. This person supervises all related activity and
ensures that the agreements made at the central level are respected during
implementation at the store level.

Outsourcing visual merchandising activities would appear to be the
most efficient approach, but often it is not the most effective. With a few
rare exceptions, companies turn to specialized agencies when visual merchandising activities are not frequent enough to warrant a specially dedicated office. In fact, currently agencies are not a very common solution,
even if the reason is not so much the frequency of visual merchandising
activities as the fact that these very agencies still lack the competencies
required for the activities they are hired to carry out (Zaghi, 2013).

In this regard, agencies should theoretically be able to handle the entire
visual merchandising process, following these steps:

- coming up with the creative idea;
- developing themes;
- drawing up graphics;
- designing POP material;
- producing POP material;
- devising and developing gadgets;
- setting up POP material in the store;
- monitoring and maintaining POP material in the store;
- interfacing with distribution at a central level;
- interfacing with distribution in the store; and

• interfacing with other actors in the channel (printing companies, logistics companies etc.).

Normally, an agency is mainly tasked with the preliminary stages of the design and development process for POP communication: from coming up with the creative idea and producing the material, to devising and developing gadgets. Usually the companies that hire an agency prefer to have at least a few references, or more if the latter is delegated with the later stages in the process as well. This might include in-store setup of POP material, control and upkeep, and handing interactions with the distribution partner. In rare circumstances, the agency deals with all visual merchandising activities, encompassing the actual organization of in-store promotions, beginning with selecting and managing promoters.

If the company takes direct action in the store, this is seen as a necessary substitute to fill the gaps in management and operations, and as a response to similar measures taken by competing companies. In the future, similar direct intervention may be limited to control and assessment alone. In this way, visual merchandising would become, for all intents and purposes, a specialized function, a component of the negotiating group, along with Sales, Marketing, and Logistics, ready to interface with the distribution partner. But the question that remains to be answered is who will take on the on-site initiatives?

There are several advantages to having an external network that handles in-store activities. First of all, this solution is less expensive, both in relative and absolute terms, because it limits or entirely eliminates the costs associated with training, travel, and coordination. A network like this one can be used on a case-by-case basis, and is staffed by experts who leverage the know-how they acquired through experience in the field. Finally, the flexibility of this option makes it the only viable alternative for small companies.

Yet the disadvantages are equally clear, the first being the loss of control over contact with the customer/buyer. This contact instead would be delegated to people with no knowledge of the company, the brand, or the products they handle. As a result, visual merchandiser/agents are no longer dedicated to the specific company, but instead they handle its products as part of an entire portfolio, while pursuing their own objectives, which do not necessarily coincide with those of the companies they represent.

For all these reasons, this model is not often utilized by mass market companies, which prefer to set up an internal network of visual merchandisers, in particular when these experts work regularly in the store. The only activity that is entirely outsourced is shelf stocking (especially in big box stores), because this activity is solely operational and entirely without added value, and naturally also due to the associated cost.

Summing up, then, we can conclude that there is no such thing as the ideal organizational model to determine how visual merchandising is organized. In general terms, the choice depends on the competitive context. The greater the bargaining power and the more attractive the products, the more likely a company will resort to a negotiating group. Naturally, the less planning that goes into the purchase of a given product, the more critical an in-store presence and consequently the control over product management. This is due to the fact that, as we know, for impulse purchases, the quality of the space and its proper allocation for each product is particularly critical.

## 3   The organization of visual merchandising by distribution

The value of communication activities and display space management undertaken by industry is undeniable. However, modern distribution more and more often is under pressure to overhaul the methods it uses for in-store visual merchandising, when retail networks extend throughout the entire territory in question.

On one hand, the idea is to minimize the danger that the activities designed and activated by suppliers gradually erode distribution's control over this network, watering down the store identity with initiatives that are often uncoordinated and/or inconsistent with the positioning of the distribution chain. On the other is the danger of the so-called "marmalade effect" triggered by the growing overlap in activities undertaken by competing companies offering the same product families. This effect can typically be seen when there is an overload of communicational and informational messages.

Added to these considerations is an asymmetric view of in-store marketing policies. Indeed, industry focuses on managing display space and POP communication, while distribution wants to ensure that all the levers used for visual merchandising are consistent, with a view to a shared plan that reinforces the differentiation strategies supporting store identity. In actual fact, these two distinct positions are not necessarily incompatible, as long as the in-store interventions by industry are consistent with the choices of distribution. Naturally, the organizational methods that distribution implements in visual merchandising can take on diverse configurations, which are outlined below.

### 3.1 *Visual merchandising as a decentralized function*

When the design and management of visual merchandising are decentralized, consultations on layout options take place at the central office. The supplier interfaces with middle level management at the distribution center, if not with the stores themselves. This is more common when stores are run by members of purchasing groups or voluntary collectives which enjoy extensive entrepreneurial autonomy. The lack of centralized coordination exposes distribution to greater pressure from industry; this may also take the form of payments for merchandising to develop visibility and activation initiatives in the store.

But by the same token, this system is a very flexible one that can offer quick and incisive responses to moves by local competitors. This approach also makes it possible to adapt activities to the home market, such as incorporating proposals that touch on themes that connect with the host community and integrating them more effectively in display solutions. This model is also well suited to distribution scenarios that base competitive advantage on rapid response time to stimuli from the local market and from the competition.

### 3.2 *Visual merchandising both centralized and decentralized*

With this approach we typically find product assortment policies managed at company headquarters. This allows for modifications of layouts and displays in the store, as well as initiatives pertaining to assigning space to individual items implementing solutions that guarantee a certain margin of flexibility. The central office sets down the planogram or the arrangement of the displays, dictating where stores should place common products, and leaving some space earmarked for local items. In this case, the role of industry centers on consultation, in collaboration with headquarters, for all the activities which must be discussed and decided on upstream before being activated downstream.

## 3.3   *Visual merchandising as a centralized function*

In this model, visual merchandising is totally centralized and controlled at company headquarters, allowing distribution to achieve greater integration with the investments in institutional communication. This thanks to the possibility to coordinate themes and messages with visual merchandising activities. (An example would be taking imagines from the current communication campaign and featuring them in store displays.)

However, the lack of maneuvering room at a local level impacts the relationship with industry, and naturally reshapes the relative spheres of action as well. This is only natural, considering that industry can only play the role of "inspector", verifying the actual implementation of the initiatives determined upstream with headquarters. The central office becomes an interface that plans all the possible visual merchandising activities with suppliers, filtering and evaluating all their proposals and then transforming them autonomously into services offered in stores. This cancels out the direct intervention of their visual merchandisers.

In this context, industry maintains the role of consultant on issues relating to market dynamics for various product families and lines, proposing possible innovations in displays and product groupings, also in light of customer purchase behaviors.

## 4   Integration: a complicated task

Visual merchandising is undergoing a period of profound renewal, marked by a closer integration with the functions of Marketing, Sales, and Logistics. The forms of vertical collaboration that are emerging are shifting focus toward joint research and experimentation, following a new approach that responds to the rationale of micro-marketing.

On one hand, distributors are dedicating their efforts to a global process of redefining development areas, reconfiguring competitive levers in a context where price is no longer a competitive advantage that can be sustained over the long term. On the other hand, subsequent to concentration processes, industry is more and more intent on coming up with strategies for brand extensions that find the space to clearly and uniquely emerge only in the store. This occurs within the framework of an integrated communication project that taps into invaluable synergies thanks to visual merchandising.

New areas for potential collaboration are surfacing which necessitate turning attention from the product to the category and the department. This continuum can be secured only if roles, responsibilities, and internal procedures are redefined in the process of planning and managing visual merchandising following the rationale of integrated communication at a channel level.

In any case, there are many obstacles in channel relationships. The most significant of these are:

- reluctance to share data and information;
- operational challenges in monitoring the results of initiatives that hinder transparency and ascertaining the link between investments and objectives;
- divergent ways of understanding and interpreting visual merchandising activities, by industry as opposed to distribution;
- the signaling function of brand products and the associated use of space as a discretionary factor to guide purchase decisions by distribution;
- frequent downgrades in terms of quantity and quality of display space allocated to brand products;
- segmentation or clusterization that is superseded by the speed of organizational change; and
- little or no interdepartmental coordination by either channel player.

To sum up, the road to optimizing visual merchandising activities in channel relationships still looks long, and rough in some places. But what is reassuring is the pervasive awareness of the critical role of joint management of the process of in-store communication.

# 9 Evaluating the effectiveness of store design activity from an experiential perspective

## 1 The customer-product-space relationship

The store is a primarily a place where an interaction happens – a sale – which we can define as a relationship between supply and demand that results in an exchange regulated by some sort of contract. However, this isn't the only form of interaction we find here. People go into stores, meet other people, are subject to multisensory perceptive stimuli, and respond with gestural patterns that directly involve a totality of movements; they have the sensation of coming closer or moving farther away from the object they desire.

Drawing on models proposed by the postmodern theory of marketing, throughout this book we've reiterated the importance of adopting an experiential approach. In doing so, the focus should center on the main behaviors that customers display when making a purchase, as well as the cognitive processes they activate. Naturally this calls for redefining the methods we use for analyzing and understanding that very behavior. Normally, when a study on this topic aims to assess managerial implications, findings are interpreted from a strictly managerial viewpoint. In this case, the focal point is merely the aspects of behavior that take on particular significance for the company, but that are not necessarily priority for the customer.

The experiential theme, in contrast, places the perspective of customers back at the center of attention. As fundamental elements of analysis, buyers have to speak freely, without inhibitions, and express all the emotions they're feeling, both positive and negative. Now researchers concentrate on the quality of the information that emerges, since each indication, sensation, and observation is valid and interesting.

Yet we must admit that the interaction between the customer and the store is based on assumptions that are not always clear. For one reason, customers live their purchase experience by mediating it with their personal experience. For another, the store often misses the mark as far as sending clear, consistent signals; instead the message is often muddled and hard to understand.

On this topic, to grasp the role of design in influencing customer behavior, we've already underscored the need to identify the processes that customers use to assign meaning to the store, according to the tenets of environmental psychology and anthropology. We've also called attention to that fact that in order for an environment to exist, someone has to occupy it physically, or evoke it mentally. The reason for this is that any environment can only be "built" through sense-making, which means it takes on a wholly subjective value for the person who lives it and interprets it.

From *space*, expressing the physical dimension, to *place*, meaning "consumed" and experienced space: this is a transition that happens when space is definitively occupied by the individual. At this point the first managerial implication arises: designing a store necessitates interaction between the designer and the customer from the very outset of the creative process. It's true that the designer sets up the structure and organizes retail spaces in terms of layout. But it's the customer who interprets and experiences these spaces in an entirely personal way, adapting positively or negatively to them.

Specifically, the possibility to measure the path toward the gradual occupation of spaces is contingent on the intensity of the interaction and the level of utilization over time. We can quantify the first through emotion-based tests with tools such as biofeedback, which allows researchers to assess the emotional involvement of the customer in the purchase activity. As for the latter, we can identify three levels of analysis: experienced space, perceived space, and imagined space.

1.1   *Experienced space and the gestures customers use when interacting with the product*

Experienced space takes into account the real use of a given physical space in terms of movements, actions, and behaviors. The aim here is to evaluate the impact of the actual store design on customer behavior. The aspects of note in this stage are the pathways customers use when exploring the store (the flows and sequences of the visit to various sections of the store), the time they spend in the store and how long they remain in the different areas, the time they spend and the reactions they have to waiting at the cash register or the customer service desk, as well as the interaction with products while they contemplate their selections. Another key point is to analyze how customers use the structures and instruments available in the store. Examples might include interactive kiosks, dressing rooms, mirrors, labs, and even play areas for children and any additional services that stores may offer to customers.

A final observation covers when, how, and how far customers go to look for places where they can take a break, or have a bite to eat, or find information, also taking into account how much they interact with sales personnel and how they do so. Considering the distance between the customer and the product on one hand, and the degree of sensorial complexity in customer perception on the other, we can identify four possible abstract scenarios:

1. *The overview* (distant and monosensory): the customer moves around, observing without approaching or touching any products.
2. *The touch* (distant and multisensory): the customer continually sees, touches, and evaluates products, without having any planned purchase in mind.
3. *Immersion* (proximate and multisensory): the customer rummages through the products, holds them up, turns them over and inside out, trying out items, spending a long time weighing all the alternatives.
4. *The analytical eye* (proximate and monosensory): the customer evaluates and estimates, compares prices, checks the labels for product information.

Techniques for analyzing these behaviors are based on direct observation: photos, videos, observation through participation and any other ethnographic methodology that consists in analyzing on-site, taking notes and describing what happens.

## 1.2   Perceived space and perceptive stimuli

*Perceived space* relates to the experiential dimension, encompassing all the multisensory, synesthetic, and emotional perceptions that customers get while using a given space. In other words, here we need to evaluate their opinion on the project and how well it aligns with their expectations, to understand the image and perceptions of store design as well as the impressions of the quality of the space. Some pertinent questions: Is the store décor pleasing to the eye? Are the furnishings functional? Is the design homey and familiar? Or are there disturbing elements of the environment that make people feel uncomfortable?

To comprehend the aspects related to perceived space, direct observation of customers in the store isn't enough. So direct interaction is the only possible approach, which takes the form of qualitative/quantitative interviews to come up with a subjective, introspective analysis. But it's no simple thing for customers to express their impressions about the space they perceive. This explains why it can be useful to collect opinions and perceptions by asking them to compare and contrast the store with other stores or perhaps with completely different places, real or imaginary, from the past or from the present.

## 1.3  *Imagined space*

*Imagined space* refers to the dimension that customers conjure up in their minds to compare previous experience or find confirmation with reassuring mental representations they use to imagine spaces that may even be utopian or symbolic. At times this dimension shapes how the experience unfolds in the store far more materially than what customers actually encounter. As a result, analyzing imagined spaced can be very constructive in assessing how close the store format in question comes to matching the characteristics of customers' "ideal" or favorite or benchmark store. In this sense, the rich minutiae of their imaginings can represent fruitful input for designing spaces. Methods of analysis here incorporate elicitation and introspection techniques based on the use of metaphors and symbolic representations that can reconstruct highly detailed images of the ideal place.

## 2    Observational analysis: the Aspesi case *by Giusi Scandroglio*

For years now our 'consumers' have been officially recognized as "shoppers", in other words, "potential buyers" – those mythical creatures who shop to buy. One definition of the verb *consume*, according the Oxford English Dictionary, is "to use up." So it can be said that today consumers no longer exist, except in the context of food, and even here they don't necessarily finish or use up what they buy.

Today we're all potential buyers, and we make purchases when prompted to do so by a variety of different kinds of stimuli. We don't buy based on our needs, but on our desires. We go out thinking we'll buy a pair of shoes and we come home with a shirt instead. In the consumer's mind, the 100, 200 or 300 euro are meant to be spent, and the shop that's better at luring in the passing shopper is the one that will cash in on that money.

So the rationale of impulse purchases have been upended even for food products typically grouped into this category, such as tempting sweet snacks for instant gratification. But today a gratification purchase may even be a can of sardines in an aesthetically attractive, triangle shape: *"Look at this pretty package, I think I'll put it in my cart"*. Any good, item or garment can be substituted by any other kind of product. This is why it's crucial to understand shoppers not only in terms of target and habits, but also with regard to behaviors and reactions to stimuli that they encounter on their shopping journey. These stimuli nowadays are richer and richer, coming from the web as well.

To analyze behaviors we study the journey that shoppers take, and this journey might be shopping in a real supermarket, visiting a museum, buying electronics on the Internet, or browsing around a designer clothing store, perhaps after checking out the online site.

The physical store still plays an essential role, rising to the digital challenge and offering an experience that activates all the senses and engages people in a unique and exclusive way. Observing the behaviors of shoppers who go into a store allows us to analyze and evaluate their reactions to everything and everyone around them (*including other shoppers*). Observational analysis, now recognized as an actual research methodology, is conducted by a professional technical organization and can be divided into various stages:

- technical preparation of the track that the observer (or tracker) has to follow;
- specific training for trackers, who have to be selected among the people brought in for the observation (it's an aptitude in a very real sense);
- consolidated experience in data processing; and
- interpretation of results, which must go hand in hand with experience in the retail world, where intangibles play a vital role. Quantitative findings must be integrated with qualitative notes that extend and encompass the meaning of the brand and of the shopping experience that

the store concept is seeking to convey. More and more often, observers are people with skills that range from ethnography to semiotics.

As far as the quantitative data that can be gleaned from an observational study in a "model store," here is a series of questions that the research can answer:

- Are the windows attractive? Which target do they attract?
- How many people enter the store after looking at the windows?
- How is the store used? Which zones are hot? Which ones are cold?
- How are the different types of displays used and by whom? Are there any practical or functional problems? Are there problems with the positions of the displays?
- How do people interact with the products? Do they simply look at them, or do they touch them too?
- What are the focal points?
- How much time do shoppers spend in the store? In the individual departments?
- Last but not least what's the purchase conversion rate?

The aim of all of this is to identify strengths and weaknesses, which then allows retailers to implement practical and operational interventions to make the store more productive, aligning with the goals of the company and the needs of the clientele.

## 2.1    *The Aspesi flagship store in Via Montenapoleone*

The Aspesi flagship in Via Montenapoleone in Milan is arguably a retail anomaly in the landscape of clothing boutiques in the city's "Fashion Quadrangle." Aspesi conveys elegance, simplicity and authenticity to passersby on the most eminent shopping street in Italy (and beyond). The unique Aspesi style has remained unchanged over time, as unique as the garment displayed in the window, symbolizing a distinctive nature, careful regard for and attention to detail framed in an undeniably trendy way.

Aspesi offers nearly 700 square meters (7,500 square feet) to visit, to look at, to drink in, to experience. This vast space extends from Via Montenapoleone to Via Bigli, and unfolds along an articulated, captivating pathway allowing customers to enjoy spending time and interactions with the staff. The store is a discovery: gradually we see clothing and accessories that lead us to the heart of the store: the women's department. This area is actually a living room, or better still an open space, where we start to recognize and fully experience the spirit of the brand. Another aisle leads to the men's department where style and rigor complete the decor. Here there is also a secondary door, which very few people use to enter the store, and almost no one uses to exit. After the store visit, customers take pleasure in following this corridor, and finally exiting again in Via Montenapoleone.

## 2.2 Analysis of the flagship store

The two general goals of the study are:

- to analyze the behavior of store visitors; and
- to study their interactions with all the components of the store, including the structure, garments, elements of the decor, personnel, fitting rooms, and so forth.

We directly observed the behaviors of over one hundred shoppers, from the moment they set foot in the store until they left again. We also observed hundreds and hundreds of passersby in front of the store to study the windows. We carried out our fieldwork with a team consisting of a psychologist and a sociologist with a specialization in semiotics. The study ran for four days (two weekdays, one Saturday and one Sunday) in the month of October 2017.

## 2.3 Entrance and windows

The windows, the first representation of the brand, serve to attract, explain, and draw people in. The entrance, as we've always maintained, is not only an access door; it's also a window in every sense of the word. In fact, the entrance can be considered the most important window. If passersby look into the store through the entrance and see something that attracts their attention, there are no barriers in front of them. They simply need to take one small step and they're inside the store.

The windows at Aspesi always aspire to be original.

During our fieldwork, the only real store window displayed garments, or better still, a single garment. This piece wasn't even on a hanger or a mannequin; instead it was elegantly positioned on an inclined plane inside a simple stylish frame. This open window drew the gaze inside the store, allowing people to see much of the interior. With these windows Aspesi doesn't speak at a distance, or even to passersby walking on the other side of the street. The store opted for sobriety even in this respect: *I'll reveal myself to people who come near.*

Unlike all the competitors in the area, Aspesi doesn't use the upper part of the window, or lights that attract people from a distance. The main entrance isn't at the center of the store, instead visitors enter through a side door located on Via Manzoni. No one opens this door, because everyone is free to enter; Aspesi is open to everyone. Understanding the store from the entrance is not easy, because the architectural structure is highly articulated. As a result, Aspesi plays with a gigantic slanted mirror positioned in front of the entrance. This mirror reflects a combined image of the clothing in the store and the shoppers entering it (Fig. 1).

What emerges from our behavioral analysis of passersby is that people show similar interest in Aspesi store windows as they do for the other clothing shops. In other words, nearly half of all passersby "take a look." But this lasts only a few seconds, so there is very little time to attract, seduce, and prompt people to go into the store. But nearly 10% of passersby actually do enter this flagship. This is a positive result for Aspesi, thanks also to the high degree of customer loyalty.

*Figure* 1 – Aspesi: façade on Via Montenapoleone in Milan.

*Figure* 2 – Aspesi: map of the flagship store.

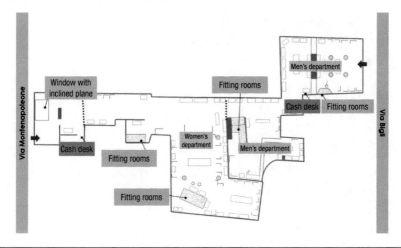

## 2.4 The structure of the store

As mentioned before, this flagship has extensive floor space and a very particular structure. The map in Figure 2 shows the men's and women's departments, the location of the fitting rooms and the cash desks.

As the map shows, the two departments have more or less identical weight. The target of store visitors in three-fourths of the cases is women aged 40 to 50. The high number of loyal customers reflects their confidence in the store and in the sales staff. Interesting to note is the presence of 15% of parents with their children (for the most part, mothers with children): the story continues.

## 2.5 The decompression zone

As numerous studies have revealed in a vast range of commercial contexts all over the world, once shoppers enter the store, they need space to adjust their pace and their gaze to the new environment. This acclimatization area is called the decompression zone, and plays an essential role in enabling visitors to get their bearings and understand the organizational rationale of the store.

In the Aspesi flagship store there is no true decompression zone, due to the architectural structure of the building. So shoppers are welcomed with

*Figures* 3 and 4 – Aspesi: the decompression zone.

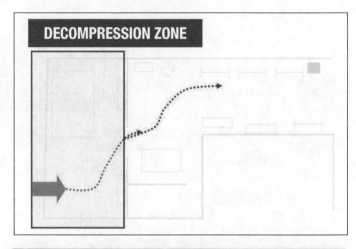

mirrors overlaying their reflections with the clothing on display; there are also large black and white photographs that showcase women's and men's clothing. This is where the shopping journey begins, wending along a curvilinear path of exploration that accompanies visitors from the moment in which the shop opens up onto a large living room, the women's department (Figs. 3 and 4).

These notes obviously are relevant to new visitors. Habitual customers are already intimately familiar with the store, so they have no need to understand; they are simply impressed and amazed by the first garments they see.

Figure 5 – Aspesi: the flow of visitors.

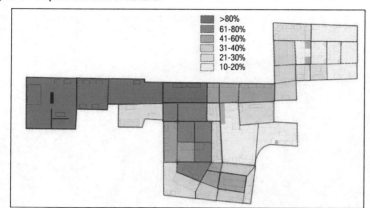

| | |
|---|---|
| ■ | >80% |
| ■ | 61-80% |
| ▨ | 41-60% |
| ▨ | 31-40% |
| ▨ | 21-30% |
| ☐ | 10-20% |

## 2.6    How customers use the flagship store

As illustrated in the map below (Fig. 5), the highest density is concentrated in the women's section, confirming the essence of this core target.

The men's department occupies an excessive amount of space relative to the actual number of visitors in this area. For this reason Aspesi seems to be focusing on investments to augment male clientele.

Customers spend a great deal of time in this flagship store. In fact, the average store visit ranks Aspesi at seven minutes more than the average for clothing stores, with older women who shop on weekdays holding the record for length of stay. Men on average spend half the time in the store as compared to women, another reason to shore up the male target. Table1 shows that a solid 20% of customers visit the entire store, although the women's department alone exceeds 50%.

This further confirms the need to intervene to increase the use of the men's department.

Table 1 – Aspesi: breakdown of the use of space.

| The use of space | % |
|---|---|
| Only the area near the entrance | 3.7 |
| The entire store | 21.6 |
| Only women's department | 52.3 |
| Only men's department | 22.4 |

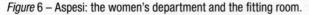

*Figure* 6 – Aspesi: the women's department and the fitting room.

A wonderful container (Fig. 6) repainted and converted into a fitting room with access from the rear, guarantees privacy for clients and creates a sense of engagement. This is a perfect place for the Aspesi staff to provide all their assistance and care, as they do so well.

Over two-thirds of the people who enter the flagship receive assistance, even though they have ample opportunity to navigate the store on their own.

## 2.7    *Interaction and purchase*

The purchase conversion rate in the Aspesi flagship is higher than mono-brand clothing stores, which leads us to conclude that the store achieving impressive results. For example, compared to women, the average man interacts with products far less. He requires visual support when deciding on combinations of garments, styles, and colors. This confirms the need for organizing the offering in terms of individual categories, but also by proposing outfits to increase cross selling.

Still today women make purchases for their men, organizing their wardrobes and in some cases putting together the outfit they might wear on a given day. Women, instead, the queens of shopping, love to look, touch, and try on items, and they can easily maneuver their way through even extensive offerings. The matrix below crosses two primary indicators:

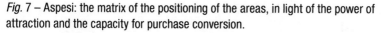

*Fig.* 7 – Aspesi: the matrix of the positioning of the areas, in light of the power of attraction and the capacity for purchase conversion.

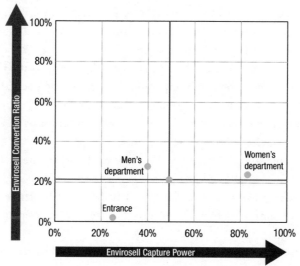

Envirosell Capture Power,[1] that is, the percentage of product interaction, and Envirosell Conversion Ratio,[2] referring to the purchase conversion.

The data show that the men's area, albeit showing lower product interactions, has an excellent conversion ratio. The women's area also generates an exceptional conversion rate, but with an extremely high degree of interactions.

### 2.8    *Conclusions*

The flagship store in Via Montenapoleone, while constantly maintaining its characteristic originality, conveys a consolidated brand that tells a story of passion, integrity, and attention to detail that turns into care for and attention to the customer. We could even say: *I am what I am, not what I seem.* Starting with the yellow dress in the window, boldly presented all alone with the expressive and evocative power of style, elegant sobriety and character. This single garment expresses uniqueness, standing out from the other brands on Via Montenapoleone, densely

---

[1] Indicator of the capacity of a given element to capture the attention of passersby.
[2] Indicator of the capacity to convert people who show interest in a given object into buyers.

populated with various kinds of merchandise and display styles, fixtures, and materials.

At all times, the environment is "The House of Aspesi": meticulous decor, elegant displays, refined design, with traces of vintage as reminders of the true authentic history of the store. Garments are displayed in an understated manner: they don't call out to us, they draw us in. The brand is consistently and immediately apparent, even in the approach of the sales staff who welcome visitors in a polite and friendly manner, courtesy with sincerity. There's no attempt to seduce, but rather a genuine and respectful willingness to assist. This is the atmosphere that permeates the store. The intangible component is magnificently rendered despite the fact that the store has a very complicated structure from an architectural standpoint.

There are innumerable obstacles that the store must contended with, so it is these very obstacles that are leveraged to create a pathway of meaning and discovery.

Lastly, there are a few aspects of the store that could be reinforced.

- The upper section of the windows could be exploited to make them visible from the sidewalk opposite the store; Aspesi would surely come up with a way to invent surprising solutions in terms of window displays.
- The decompression zone could also speak to men, considering the amount of sales space dedicated to men, but also young people.
- The internal organization of the store is functional, and even if there were "imperfections" they would fit in well with the free and authentic style of the brand.
- The clothing is always presented on fixtures that are simple, too; they don't call out to customers, but draw them in.
- The store personnel welcome customers with quiet courtesy that is genuine and respectful, with no intention to seduce them. This relational approach aligns perfectly with brand values in the context of respect that forms the foundations of Aspesi.

## 3  Conducting in-store qualitative research using mobile technology: the Kikke by Kasanova case, *by Giusi Scandroglio*

Now more than ever before, mobile technology is a part of our daily lives, and that includes our in-store experiences. In supermarkets, we see buyers snapping photos of products, asking someone on the other side of the web:

"Is this what you wanted?" Or girls going into shoe shops, trying on a dozen pairs, then recording videos and asking their friends what they think, using social networks and their mobile phones. Big box stores specialized in consumer electronics invite their customers to interact with the product assortment, utilizing their latest-generation smartphones.

To study these new purchase behaviors, a new tool is available for in-store qualitative research called WhazShop. This innovative analytical technique was invented by QT, a company specialized in market research in the retail arena. WhazShop leverages the potentialities of mobile technology, making it possible to amass impressions and comments in real time from potential customers while they're actually interacting in stores. To test this inventive methodological approach, the housewares retailer Kasanova agreed to let us use their new concept store Kikke, located in the shopping gallery in the Naples Central Station. The aim was to collect customer opinions and operational indications on this type of store.

Participants in the study, customers who spontaneously entered the Kikke store, were in constant contact with QT's retail experts via chat.

The research objective was to gather evidence on the following four thematic areas:

- Capture: what draws people into the store from the outside and what grabs their attention once they're inside;
- Experience: perceptive and emotional aspects, and evaluations on the personal in-store experience; what attracts or repels people as they move through the store;
- Shopability: what helps (or hinders) people in getting their bearings, navigating the store, identifying products, and having an enjoyable store experience; and
- Conversion: factors that lead to (or prevent) a purchase.

### 3.1  Capture: Kikke, a Kasanova store in an innovative designer context

Thanks to its location, Kikke by Kasanova intercepts a sizeable flow of potential customers, in particular commuters. Positioned in a rather dark part of the shopping gallery, the store itself is brightly illuminated, creating a stark contrast with the predominantly black color of the surroundings (Fig. 8).

Figure 8 – Kikke by Kasanova: the façade (courtesy of Kasanova).

Through a process of simplification and cognitive assimilation, shoppers activate a prior model of the store that they are already familiar with. In fact, from the outside, customers expect a smaller version of a Kasanova shop, with its signature bazaar-like setting, where they can find a complete offering of houseware items. A bit of everything, but exclusively accessories for the home:

> "I'd say that I want to go in [the store] because I know Kasanova and I think it's kind of the typical shop that you find in shopping malls."

## 3.2   Experience: a small space full of surprises

The moment customers step inside, they are caught up in the pleasant and carefree atmosphere of the store. It's only 90 square meters (1,000 square feet), but people spend as much as half an hour there. During their visit, they text their positive feedback, along with photos of all the things that catch their eye (Fig. 9).

As far as atmosphere, spaces are described as tight, but the emotional engagement and the interest sparked by the store make this spatial limitation a minor concern. What's more, the respondents noted the background music, commenting that it was upbeat and fun, the sort of soundtrack that

*Figure* 9 – Excerpts from chats with participating customers (courtesy of Kasanova).

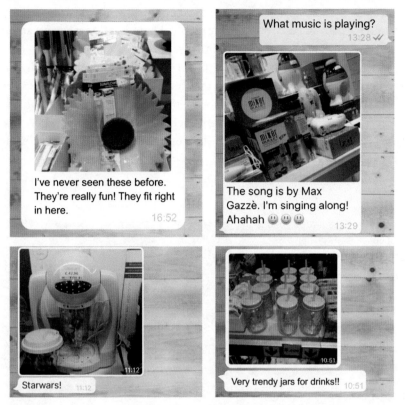

suits the atmosphere and the "feel" customers get. Feedback on sales staff is also positive, thanks to their willingness to help but without ever being pushy; this also seems to contribute to creating a relaxing atmosphere that customers can enjoy.

People are free to move around throughout the store, and this is another reason that they agree to interface with QT (sometimes even making spelling mistakes while they text). They feel absorbed in the assortment, and always find a certain something that piques their curiosity.

What emerges from this is the idea of a place with special offers for the home, and a place for the "unexpected," as emphasized in comments such as:

"I didn't expect ..."
"I never thought of ..."

The shopping experience starts to feel like a treasure hunt, and the treasure map that customers follow is staked out by the products themselves, creating a path to discovery and surprise. There's nothing boring about this store; in fact, before they even leave, people already want to come back again to see what new items they'll find. Kikke seems to represent the perfect cross between wonder and function. And it's all in the spirit of easy-to-use enjoyment. Although the atmosphere permeating the space is cheerful and fun, there are more serious areas too, where the store tries to educate its clientele by continually proposing intelligent new solutions. (Figs. 10 and 11)

*Figure* 10 – Kasanova as a store that educates its customers. (courtesy of Kasanova)

*Figure* 11 – Example of a "serious" area. (courtesy of Kasanova)

So more serious product proposals are welcome, as long as they're intelligent and up to speed with the latest trends. With this in mind, certain more elegant items, such as china for a wedding registry, could point shoppers in the direction of other Kasanova stores. But the message must always be fresh, modern and intelligent.

The store is entertaining, in part thanks to in-store communication made up of signs and videos that explain how the most innovative products work. Interviewees noted all this and reacted with very positive feedback. These solutions respond to the need to provide richer information, not by boring shoppers with long-winded product descriptions but delighting them with a few words and the immediacy of images. (Fig. 12)

*Figure* 12 – Comments on effective and attractive in-store communication (courtesy of Kasanova).

### 3.3   *Shopability: the product is always in charge*

Despite the wide range of products and the limited space, people can navigate the store very easily. Even if they don't manage to scope out the entire assortment (because it's truly vast), interviewees said they wanted to come back again to take a closer look. The display strategy is clear.

Written signs and arrows help customers find their way around and decode the areas dedicated to various consumption occasions and "conviviality": the barbeque zone, the cocktail area, pizza, cakes and cookies. All these are moments that bring expectations of joy and let shoppers anticipate the happiness they'll share with family and friends (Fig. 13).

Customers don't seem to experience Kikke as a destination, which explains why their expectations are of a store that's a place to be discovered, one that's not too rational or revealed. It's as if they want to be guided by the inspirations presented by the products, as customers gradually interact with them. In this sense, the process of reading the assortment appears to take place in two steps:

1. initially spotting the product and stopping;
2. looking up and noticing the information in writing and the arrows.

*Figure* 13 – Example of an area dedicated to conviviality in the food section (courtesy of Kasanova).

*Figure* 14 – The process of reading the assortment (courtesy of Kasanova).

After that, customers realize that the store is mapped out with precise indications that communicate the type of product and give relevant explanations (Fig. 14). Then they let themselves be guided by this map of sorts, facilitating the navigation of the store and making the journey more pleasant.

If screens and written signs are positioned right above the products, customers notice and find them useful. The other signs (Fig. 15) are sometimes placed higher, and serve a more "corporate" purpose; customer perception of these is more superficial. These communications strike

*Figure* 15 – An ironic poster ("Is something wrong?") (courtesy of Kasanova).

a very ironic tone, harmonizing with the store atmosphere. In the future, regular customers might find it amusing to read these signs; in fact, when they were pointed out to respondents, they smiled and appreciated the humor. Irony may gradually contribute to constructing the meaning of the place.

### 3.4    *Conversion: little impulse purchases*

Kikke is a store that inspires impulse purchases. It's personal gratification in the truest sense: in fact, the first desire shoppers have is for self-gratification through a small purchase. To encourage that impulse is the price, which is low – or even better, discounted. In finalizing the purchase, Kikke has accomplished its mission and earned its name. By way of explanation for non-Italian speakers, *Kikke* is a homophone for the word *chicche*, meaning treats, gems, juicy tidbits. In fact, at Kikke shoppers can always find a tempting tidbit, something frivolous and useful at the same time, a treat that they can take home like a prize for themselves, or a souvenir of a delightful shopping experience (Fig. 16).

*Figure* 16 – A useful little "chicca" (courtesy of Kasanova).

Despite Kikke's shared DNA with the other Kasanova stores, as a "place for special offers for the home and for the unexpected," Kikke shows less "destination intensity." Instead it's more closely associated with impulse purchases. But even the desire to discover curious new products can make the store visit a sort of destination: "The reason I go there is because I want to be amazed!"

# Glossary

**Accent light:** spotlight on an entire display or an individual product.

**Adjacency:** horizontal and vertical product presentation following a logical order based on different criteria, for example: product family, customer profile, use, brand, or origin. This prompts complementary and/or add-on purchases.

**Adjacent colors:** the combination of a primary color with the two colors on either side of it on the color wheel.

**Ambient light:** normal lighting in the sales space.

**Ambient media:** graphic, video and audio communication tools designed for use in stores.

**Anatomical display:** garments hung one above the other as they would be worn (for example, shirts above trousers) to create a complete look.

**ATM topper:** screen incorporated in the ATM (cash machine) totem which provides information and shows advertising.

**Barrier:** fixture used to redirect the flow of visitors.

**Biofeedback:** non-verbal methodology using brain wave analysis that reveals emotions triggered by specific stimuli coming from external impulses (such as looking at a display).

**Bracket:** a type of metal support that comes in various lengths and curves used to anchor and display products on wire racks.

**Brand blocking:** vertical display by brand, ideal for a broad portfolio of products.

**Bundling:** grouping several items together in lots, which become sales units.

**Captive audience network:** potential targets of messages sent from a digital signage network, such as store visitors.

**Central free-standing fixture:** display positioned in the middle of a retail space, away from the walls, which customers can access from all sides.

**Chevroning:** positioning displays at a 45° angle to facilitate the flow of visitors.

**Chromatic analogy:** combination of two or more colors that are side-by-side on the color wheel.

**Chromatic harmony:** balance and symmetry in colors; two or more colors are harmonious if, when visually combined, they produce a neutral gray.

**Coefficient of occupied space:** the ratio of the linear units of display x 100 over square units of sales area.

**Color tryptic:** the combination of three colors that are at the same distance on the color wheel.

**Color wheel:** based on three primary colors (yellow, red, blue); when mixed together in certain combinations secondary colors are created (for instance, orange comes from the combination of yellow and red); mixing a primary color with a secondary color yields a tertiary color.

**Combined function:** grouping products together that have combined top-and-bottom use characteristics, i.e. sweater/trousers or shirt/jacket.

**Complementary colors:** the combination of two colors that lie opposite one another on the color wheel. The complementary color of a primary is obtained by mixing the remaining two primary colors; the visual "sum" gives a neutral gray, or an "average" that comes from combining the same percentage of white (50%) and black (50%).

**Concourse display:** used to promote brands, products, and/or contests.

**Coordinated display:** themes and collections grouped together to create a coherent look; appropriate for textiles/fashion and home decor (for instance, a bed with a robe, a duvet, a decorative throw pillow, a rug, a painting).

**Coordinated function:** grouping products together to create a complete, coherent proposal.

**Corner:** a small sales space earmarked for a specific brand, furnished with its own fixtures and displays.

**Cross-selling:** sales technique using cross-mix displays that leverage customer interest in an item which may lead to the purchase of another product or brand; generally realized by displaying complementary products in adjacent displays; also useful in designing promotional areas or setting up point displays.

**Crowner:** element with high communication impact, normally positioned on top of displays or in the upper section of gondolas, generally showing the logo, institutional image and/or a reference to the claim of the brand being advertised.

**Developed linear:** length of the linear multiplied by the number of shelves.

**Digital in-store merchandising:** digital signage application for electronic communication that serves to focus attention on products and promotional activities, and to enhance the brand.

**Directional sound/sound shower:** technique that makes it possible to limit the transmission of sound, music, announcements, etc. to a restricted areas.

**Display density:** quantity of products, as well as the number and storage capacity of display fixtures.

**Display layout:** rational organization of retail space, including the choice and arrangement of display fixtures to direct the flow of customers through the store.

**Display point:** positioned next to in-store pathways in front of each merchandising grouping, this display communicates and signals the presence of products to passersby without blocking traffic flow.

**Display rhythm:** quantity of items permanently displayed per linear meter/foot.

**Display scheme:** idea and general concept for a visual merchandising intervention.

**Double complementary colors:** the combination of four colors, two primaries matched with the complementary color of each.

**Dumping:** display technique presenting a jumble of large quantities of small items in baskets, on displays or scattered around the store.

**Dwell time:** the time that the customer spends in the store; for market researchers, this is the source of all information, to include audiovisual input, on customer behavior in terms of actions, interactions with products and display structures, and observation of the surrounding space.

**Elasticity of the linear:** sensitivity of sales performance to variations in the linear.

**End cap:** the first and/or last section of a gondola, with shelving running perpendicular to the length of the gondola.

**Experienced space:** the actual use of a given physical space/store in terms of movements, actions, and behaviors.

**Eye-tracking:** a technique used to detect and record the micro-impulses of the human eye as it observes an image on a surface. The aim is to analyze the mechanisms of visual perception, recording the direction of the gaze through infrared technology to ascertain where a person's attention is focused and how long this focus is trained on a specific point. More advanced applications are used in combination with biofeedback to understand the emotions triggered by the visuals in question.

**Facing:** unit of product on the shelf displayed facing front, in other words, visible to the consumer; depending on the size of the packaging, the number of facings determines the quantity of linear space dedicated to each individual item.

**Floor linear:** linear measured along the floor, regardless of the number of shelves.

**Floor screen:** an image projected onto the floor which can interact with people as they walk over it using games with special effects.

**Floor stand:** display fixture placed on the floor used when referring specifically to off-the-shelf items.

**Focal point:** point of attraction that captures the attention of customers thanks to its placement, where traffic flows intersect or in another strategic position with respect to customer circulation and sightline.

**Folding:** a display technique that involves folding and stacking items, and setting them on tables; applicable for soft or hard-to-handle goods.

**Frontal fixture:** structure that displays garments facing forward, toward the customer.

**Function:** grouping products together that have similar use characteristics and/or that serve the same function: e.g. skirt function, sweater function.

**Gondola:** long freestanding display unit with multiple shelves on all four sides; may be equipped with a built-in lighting system.

**Hanging:** a display technique involving placing products on large hooks, on bars installed in gondolas, or on wall structures.

**High perimeter wall:** upper wall area that defines the layout of a sector or department; also usable for displaying and storing products.

**Imagined space:** the dimension that customers picture in their minds to compare past experiences or to find confirmation with reassuring mental representations, perhaps even envisioning utopian scenes or symbolic spaces.

**Interactive display unit:** IT platform that shows images, interacting with the observer.

**Interactive window:** uses digital signage to interact with passersby.

**Inventory turnover ratio:** measures the relationship between sales and inventory, that is, the number of times products are sold and replaced in a one-year period.

**Linear:** horizontal extension of product presentation, equivalent to the space available for displaying merchandise.

**Loss leader:** product sold with no profit margin or below cost.

**Maximum linear:** the threshold of saturation; above this point any quantitative increase in product display will not result in a significant increase in sales, but rather will create unproductive overstock.

**Micro-seasonality:** sales spikes seen by a set of products at certain times of the year corresponding to specific events depending, for example, on the weather, festivities or special occasions; the idea is to manage products that have opposite seasonality in such a way that high sales on one item compensate for low sales on the item next to it during a given period of time.

**Minimum linear:** the smallest quantity of a given product needed to guarantee that the observer will perceive and identify it.

**Module:** basic element of modular, interchangeable display structures.

**Monochrome:** combination of black and white.

**Optical balance:** the aesthetic balance of the product in the display (in the store window or the store itself), attained when the "optical weight" is evenly distributed.

**Overstock:** excess amount of product in stock with respect to planned level.

**Panel:** sample of consumers or stores which serve to establish sales statistics.

**Pegboard:** perforated panel positioned vertically on the endcap of a shelving unit or gondola; items can be hung on movable hooks anchored to said panel.

**Pegging:** display technique used for small items that can be hung on hooks inserted in gondolas or wall systems.

**Perceived space:** the experiential dimension encompassing all perceptions – multisensory, synesthetic, and emotional – that customers experience when using space.

**Permanent:** refers to an item included in a product assortment year-round which does not experience significant seasonal fluctuations.

**Personal digital shopping assistant:** screen installed on a shopping cart that displays information and advertising messages which can be activated at the entrance to various areas/departments by specially designed transmitters that call attention to specific brands or promotions.

**Point-of-Purchase (POP) material:** support material used for displaying and selling products, furnished by producers with the aim of securing an in-store space that is desirable, recognizable and exclusive for the product and/or brand they want to spotlight.

**Point of rest:** visual area within a display space that doesn't capture the attention of the observer, either because no products are on display or the assortment and/or prices aren't attractive.

**Prepping:** preparing products for display.

**Presentation display:** the permanent model used to present and distinguish the entire product assortment of a store, illustrating the essence and unique characteristics of the offering.

**Product affinity:** criteria used to determine which products to position where in a retail space.

**Product layout:** how items are grouped together by product family, potentially triggering product associations for purchases.

**Product scheduling:** commercial planning process involving defining values/prices, quantities and time-to-market for merchandise, in other words when products will reach the shelves, on a monthly basis for each department based on purchases and sales trends.

**Rack-jobber:** person responsible for managing shelf displays in the context of a rack-jobbing agreement.

**Rack-jobbing:** distribution system used when a producer rents or buys shelves in a store, and then hires a rack-jobber to manage them.

**Rail strip:** strip running along the front of the shelves in a gondola displaying prices.

**Re-merchandising:** re-grouping products following new criteria with regard to original parameters, with the aim of continuing the commercial season depending on the sales trends and inventory, for instance, during sales promotions.

**Sales area:** floor space dedicated to selling, including the cash desks at the door.

**Sales complex:** configuration of available retail space to maximize permeability and minimize hard-to-reach areas.

**Saturation:** in terms of elasticity of the linear, the point at which increasing the linear no longer impacts sales performance.

**Scanning:** electronic reading of product labels at checkout.

**Self-checkout:** self-serve terminals placed at store exits allowing customers to scan, bag, and pay for their purchases without assistance.

**Self-scanning:** product codes are scanned by customers while they shop using fixed or mobile scanners available in the store.

**Setup display:** the initial display model that the store proposes when opening for business, based on strategic decisions regarding segmentation and positioning.

**Share of wallet:** the portion of money spent in a given store by the same customer, in relation to the total amount spent for the same products.

**Shelving:** display technique consisting of placing merchandise on shelves slotted into display structures or wall systems.

**Shop in shop:** space in a multibrand store dedicated to a single brand, fitted out with its own separate fixtures and displays and managed independently.

**SKU (stock keeping unit):** individual item that differs in only one respect compared to products in the same product range.

**Slatwall panel:** a fixture consisting of horizontal slats forming a display surface, ideal for items with high turnover thanks to easy reassortment, and used with accessories such as slot-in brackets, tubes, and shelves.

**Space allocation:** method for optimizing the yield on a linear display, based in part on the elasticity of individual items in the display.

**Stack:** vertical display slotted into the linear that reproduces the effect of an end cap.

**Stand:** clothing rack that can be single, multiple, or circular; free-standing, T-shaped with access on two sides, or formed of four arms; a stand can also be anchored to a wall; a multiple stand is useful for displaying large quantities of merchandise, or the same garment in a range of sizes, or coordinated items.

**Still life:** display with no mannequins or bust forms, for products primarily positioned on a wall or countertop.

**Stockout:** the entire quantity of a given product is sold out; out of stock.

**Stopper:** small flag extending out from the linear display to mark the location of a product/brand and/or promotion in a specific section.

**Store check:** tracking of a series of variables relating to a set of products/brands in the store, such as availability, display and price.

**Supports:** fixtures used to enhance an installation based on the theme and compositional scheme.

**Theme:** referring to a display, the theme must be presented in a coherent manner, that is, following a set compositional scheme, in one or more windows, inside or outside the store.

**Touch screen:** a high-tech screen sensitive to even the lightest touch, equipped with software that generates codified response sequences.

**Turnover:** number of times that inventory is sold and replaced, or "turns over", in one year.

**Video wall:** large led panel set up on the external walls of buildings, to replace or integrate traditional outdoor billboards.

**Walk-through screen:** a nonmaterial barrier, usually created with vapor or mist, which people can pass through.

**Wall fixture:** display system used on a retail wall.

**Whispering window:** audio messages are sent from this window at low volume audible only to people in the immediate proximity, so as to avoid disturbing others farther away.

**Window calendar:** schedule for installations covering a fairly long timeframe ranging from 6 to 18 months.

**Zone of attraction:** area in the store with the highest concentration of customer traffic flow.

# Authors

**Karin Zaghi** is an Associate Professor of Practice at SDA Bocconi School of Management and a Professor of Marketing at Bocconi University. At SDA Bocconi she coordinates courses in Trade Marketing, and Atmosphere and Visual Merchandising. Her fields of interest center on retail management and the client-product-space relationship, in particular visual merchandising and experiential shopping. After her first book, *Atmosfera e visual merchandising: ambienti, relazioni ed esperienze* [Atmosphere and Visual Merchandising: environments, relationships, and experiences], in 2013 Professor Zaghi published *Visual merchandising e relazioni di canale: valore, comunicazione, produttività* [Visual Merchandising and Channel Relationships: value, communication, productivity], and in 2014, *Visual Merchandising: Orientamenti e paradigmi della communicazione del punto vendita* [Visual Merchandising: orientations and paradigms in communication of the store]. Author of a vast number of academic and managerial publications, she writes editorials for various journals specialized in Marketing, Store Management and Visual Merchandising. Professor Zaghi also acts as a professional consultant, sharing her expertise with a broad range of prominent retailers.

**Giusi Scandroglio**, who has a degree in Psychology, is founder of the marketing research company QT which partners with Envirosell, specialized in analyzing in-store customer behavior. QT and Envirosell together form a Retail Division that has been collaborating with leading retailers and big distribution for over a decade.

**Matteo Testori** has a BA/MA in Business and Economics, and complemented his studies with courses at Harvard Business School. He has held managerial positions in Marketing and Sales at Mondadori, American Greetings Corp, Coca-Cola Company, Bols Group and Campari. At Università Cattolica in Milan, he is the professor in charge of brand management and communication for the Master in Marketing, and he has authored papers and articles on marketing, brand management, and communication.

# References

A.A.V.V. (1995), "I colori della vita", *Atti del convegno internazionale Torino 27-28 agosto 1995 promosso da Fiat*, Editrice La Stampa, Turin, Italy.

Addis M. (2005), *L'esperienza di consumo. Analisi e prospettive di marketing*, Pearson, Milan, Italy.

Addis M., Holbrook B. (2001), "On the Conceptual Link between Mass Customisation and Experiential Consumption: An Explosion of Subjectivity", *Journal of Consumer Behavior*, vol. 1 (1): 50-56.

Addis M, Podestà S. (2003), "Il postmodernismo: alla ricerca dell'introvabile", *Finanza, Marketing & Produzione*, anno XXI, vol. 1: 5-41.

Alba J.W., Hutchinson J.W., Lynch Jr. J. G. (1991), "Memory and Decision Making", *Handbook of Consumer Behavior*: 1-49.

Altman I., Low S.M. (Eds.) (1992), *Place Attachment*, Plenum Press, New York, NY, USA.

Alagöz S.B., Ekici N. (2011), "Impulse Purchasing as a Purchasing Behavior and Research on Karaman", *International Research Journal of Finance and Economics*, vol. 1: 172-80.

Alserver J. (2005), "Showing Products in a Better Light", *Business 2.0*, vol. 6 (8): 62.

A. Antonietti, M. Balconi (2009) (Eds.): *Scegliere Comprare*, Springer Verlag, Milan, Italy.

Areni C. S., Kim D. (1993), "The Influence of Background Music on Shopping Behavior: Classical versus Top-Forty Music in a Wine Store", *Advances in Consumer Research*, vol. 20: 336-340.

Areni C.S., Kim, D (1994), "The Influence of In-Store Lighting on Consumers' Examination of Merchandise in a Wine Store", *International Journal of Research in Marketing*, vol. 11 (2): 117-125.

Arnheim R. (1962), *Arte e percezione visiva*, Campi del sapere Feltrinelli, Milan, Italy.

Arnold M. J., Reynolds K.E. (2003), "Hedonic Shopping Motivations", *Journal of Retailing*, vol. 79 (2): 77-95.

Arnold M. J., Reynolds K. E. (2012), "Approach and Avoidance Motivation: Investigation Hedonic Consumption in a Retail Setting", *Journal of Retailing*, vol. 88 (3): 339-411.

Assael H. (1987), *Consumer Behavior and Marketing Actions*, Boston, MA, USA.

Aubert-Gamet V. (1997), "Twisting Servicescapes: Diversion of the Physical Environment in a Re-Appropriation Process", *International Journal of Service Industry Management*, vol. 8 (1): 26-41.

Aubert-Gamet V., Cova B. (1999), "Servicescapes: From Modern Non-Places to Postmodern Common Places", *Journal of Business Research*, vol. 44 (1): 37-45.

Aylott R., Mitchell V. W. (1998), "An Exploratory Study of Grocery Shopping Stressors", *International Journal of Retail and Distribution Management*, vol. 26 (9): 362-373.

Babin B. J., Darden W. R. (1995), "Consumer Self-Regulation in a Retail Environment", *Journal of Retailing*, vol. 71 (1): 47-70.

Babin, B. J., Darden W. R., Griffin M. (1994), "Work and/or Fun: Measuring Hedonic and Utilitarian Shopping Value", *Journal of Consumer Research*, vol. 20 (4): 644-656.

Babin B. J., Chebat J., Robicheaux R. (2006), "Introduction to the Special Section on Retailing Research: The Mind and Emotion of the 21st Century Shopper", *Journal of Business Research*, vol. 59 (12): 1279-1280.

Bagnobianchi I. M. (2004), *Merchandising strategico. Pianificare il merchandising per i prodotti di largo consumo e misurarne l'efficacia*, Franco Angeli, Milan, Italy.

Bagozzi R. P., Gopinath M., Nyer P. U. (1999), "The Role of Emotions in Marketing", *Journal of the Academy of Marketing Science*, vol. 27 (2): 184-205.

Baker J., Grewal D., Parasuraman A. (1994), "The Influence of Store Environment on Quality Inferences and Store Image", *Journal of the Academy of Marketing Science*, vol. 22 (4): 328-39.

Baker J., Levy M., Grewal D. (1992), "An Experimental Approach to Making Retail Store Environmental Decisions", *Journal of Retailing*, vol.68 (4): 445-460.

Barr V. (2008), "The Dark Side", *Display & Design Ideas*, vol. 20 (10): 32-33.

Baule G. (2001), "Nuovi paradigmi del design della comunicazione" in Baule G. (Ed.), *Materiali per la società dell'informazione*, Edizioni Poli. design, Milan, Italy.

Beatty S. E., Ferrel M. E. (1998), "Impulse Buying: Modelling its Precursors", *Journal of Retailing*, vol. 74 (2): 169-191.

Bellenger D., Kargaonkar R. (1980), "Profiling the Recreational Shopper", *Journal of Retailing*, vol. 56 (3): 72-92.

Bellizzi J. A., Crowley A. E., Hasty R. W. (1983), "The Effects of Color in Store Design", *Journal of Retailing*, vol. 59 (1): 21-45.

Benetello M. (1990), "Il visual merchandising", in Sicca L. (Ed.), *Il marketing dell'azienda dettagliante moderna*, Cedam, Padua, Italy.

Berman B., Evans J. R. (2013), *Retail Management: a Strategic Approach*, Upper Saddle River, Prentice-Hall Inc, New Jersey, USA.

Berruti G. (1992), *Il merchandising*, Franco Angeli, Milan, Italy.

Bertozzi P. (1993), "L'allocazione dello spazio alle referenze", in Pellegrini L., Bertozzi P., Sabbadin E., *Il merchandising. Interazione tra marketing del distributore e del produttore nel punto vendita*, CESCOM, Egea, Milan, Italy.

Biffi A., Salviotti G. (2010), "Store information system: informazioni e tecnologie per la gestione delle piattaforme relazionali", in Castaldo S. and Mauri C. (Eds.), *Store Management. La gestione delle piattaforme relazionali*, III Ed., Franco Angeli, Milan, Italy.

Biner P.M., Butler D.L., Fischer A.R., Westergren A.J. (1989), "An Arousal Optimization Model of Lighting Level Preferences: An Interaction of Social Situation and Task Demands", *Environment and Behavior*, vol. 21 (1): 3-16.

Birren E. (1969), *Light, Color and Environment*, Van Nostrand Reinhold, New York, NY, USA.

Bitner M. J. (1992), "Servicescapes: The Impact of Physical Surroundings on Customers and Employees", *Journal of Marketing*, vol. 56: 57-71.

Bloch P. H., Ridway N. M., Sherrell S. L. (1986), "Consumer Search: An Extended Framework", *Journal of Consumer Research*, vol. 13: 119-126.

Bloch P. H., Ridway N. M., Dawson S. A. (1994), "The Shopping Mall as a Consumer Habitat", *Journal of Retailing*, vol. 70 (1): 23-42.

Borghini S. (2010), "Store design e servicescape. Il place della relazione con il cliente", in Castaldo S. and Mauri C. (Eds.), *Store Management. La gestione delle piattaforme relazionali*, III Ed., Franco Angeli, Milan, Italy.

Borghini S., Zaghi K. (2007a), "L'attaccamento ai luoghi commerciali. Viaggio nelle esperienze quotidiane e straordinarie dei consumatori", *Micro & Macro Marketing*, n. 1: 59-69.

Borghini S., Zaghi K. (2007b), "Il caso Epicenter", in Castaldo S. and Mauri C. (Eds), *Innovazione, experience, partnership. Casi di innovazione nel retail*, Franco Angeli, Milan, Italy.

Borja De Mozota B. (2008), *Design Management. La cultura del progetto al centro della strategia d'impresa*, Franco Angeli, Milan, Italy.

Bruner G. C. (1990), "Music, Mood and Marketing", *Journal of Marketing*, vol. 54: 94-103.

Brusantin M. (1983), *Storia dei colori*, Piccola biblioteca Einaudi, Turin, Italy.

Bucchetti V. (2004), "Segni e artefatti per lo shopping" in Bucchetti V. (Ed.), *Design della comunicazione ed esperienze di acquisto*, Franco Angeli, Milan, Italy.

Buchanan L, Simmons C. J., Bickart B. A. (1999), "Brand Equity Dilution: Retailer Display and Context Brand Effects", *Journal of Marketing Research*, vol. 36 (August): 345-55.

Carù A. (2007), *Consumo e marketing dei servizi*, Egea, Milan, Italy.

Carù A., Cova B. (2003), "Approche empirique de l'immersion dans l'expérience de consommation: les opération d'appropriation", *Recherche et Applications en Marketing*, vol. 18 (2): 47-65.

Carù A., Cova B. (2008), "Un approccio duale al marketing esperienziale : divertimento e approfondimento nell'immersione", Mercati e Competitività, vol. 4: 17-40.

Castaldo S. (2001), *Retailing & Innovazione. L'evoluzione del marketing nella distribuzione*, Egea, Milan, Italy.

Castaldo S., Mauri C. (2017) (Eds.), *Store Management. La gestione delle piattaforme relazionali*, III ed., Franco Angeli, Milan, Italy.

Castaldo S., Botti S. (1999), "La dimensione emozionale dello shopping", *Economia & Management*, n. 1: 17-37.

Castaldo S., Botti S. (2001), "Lo shopping esperienziale", in Castaldo S. (Ed.), *Retailing & Innovazione. L'evoluzione del marketing nella distribuzione*, Egea, Milan, Italy.

Ceccanti G. (1997), *Sorgenti informative di mercato per i processi decisori d'impresa. Schema introduttivo al seminario*, Università degli Studi Milano-Bicocca, Italy.

Ceppi G. (2004), "Shopping experience: acquisto o perdita di esperienze" in Bucchetti V. (Ed.), *Design della comunicazione ed esperienze di acquisto*, Franco Angeli, Milan, Italy.

Chadwick P. (2003), "POP Dos and Don'ts", *Promotions & Incentives*, April: 45-7.

Chandon P., Hutchinson J.W., Bradlow E. T., Young S. H. (2009), "Does In-Store Marketing Work? Effects of the Number and Position of Shelf Facing on Brand Attentional Evaluation at the Point of Purchase", *Journal of Marketing*, 73 (November): 1-17.

Chebat J. C., Michon R. (2003), "Impact of Ambient Odors on Mall Shoppers' Emotions, Cognition and Spending: A Test of Competitive Causal Theories", *Journal of Business Research*, vol. 56 (7): 529-539.

Cicoria S. (2003), *La pubblicità sulla punta del naso*, Franco Angeli, Milan, Italy.

Clark I., Schmidt R. A. (1995), "Beyond the Servicescape: The Experience of Place", *Journal of Retailing and Consumer Services*, vol. 2 (3): 149-162.

Clarke J. S. and Holt R. (2016), "Vivienne Westwood and the Ethics of Consuming Fashion", *Journal of Management Inquiry* SAGE Vol. 25(2): 199 –213.

Codeluppi V. (1992), I consumatori, Franco Angeli, Milan, Italy.

Codeluppi V. (2000), *Lo spettacolo della merce*, Bompiani, Milan, Italy.

Codeluppi V. (2001), "Shoptainment: verso il marketing dell'esperienza", *Micro&Macro Marketing*, n.3, 403-412.

Collesei U. (1986), "Merchandising e comunicazione", in Lugli G. (Ed.), *Manuale di gestione delle imprese commerciali al dettaglio*, Franco Angeli, Milan, Italy.

Collesei U. (2000), *Marketing*, Cedam, Padua, Italy.

Cooper R., Bruce M. (1997), *Marketing and Design Management*, International Thomson Business Press, London, UK.

Cox K. (1964), "The Responsiveness of Food Sales to Shelf Space Changes in Supermarkets", *Journal of Marketing Research*, vol. 1 (2): 63-67.

D'Amico A. (2003), "Il consumatore va preso per il naso: opportunità e rischi del marketing olfattivo", *Congresso Internazionale Le Tendenze del Marketing*, Università Ca' Foscari, Venice, Italy.

Dalli D., Romani S. (2000), *Il comportamento del consumatore: teoria e applicazioni di marketing*, Franco Angeli, Milan, Italy.

Darley J. M., Glucksberge S., Kinchla R. A. (1998), *Fondamenti di psicologia*, in Anolli L. (Ed.), Il Mulino, Bologna, Italy.

De Grandis L. (1994), *Teoria e uso del colore*, Mondadori, Milan, Italy.

Del Chiappa G., Di Gregorio A. (2006), "Merchandising e innovazione tecnologica: tra marketing e organizzazione", *Congresso Internazionale Le Tendenze del Marketing*, Università Ca' Foscari, Venice, Italy.

De Luca P. (2000), "Gli effetti dell'atmosfera del punto vendita sul comportamento del consumatore: verifica empirica di un modello di psicologia ambientale", *Industria & Distribuzione*, vol. 2: 11-19.

De Luca P., Vianelli D. (2001), *Il marketing del punto vendita. Strumenti di gestione della densità e dell'affollamento*, Franco Angeli, Milan, Italy.

De Luca P., Vianelli D. (2003), "Coinvolgimento del consumatore e valutazione dell'atmosfera nel punto vendita", *Congresso Internazionale Le Tendenze Del Marketing*, Università Ca' Foscari, Venice, Italy.

Dennis C, Newman A., Michon R., Brakus J. J., Tiu Wright L (2010), "The Mediating Effects of Perception and Emotion: Digital Signage in Mall Atmospherics", Journal of Retailing and Consumer Services, 17 (3). 215-211.

Del Gatto S. (2002), "L'atmosfera del punto vendita quale strumento di differenziazione dell'insegna: una verifica empirica degli effetti della variabile olfattiva", *Congresso Internazionale Le Tendenze Del Marketing*, Università Ca' Foscari, Venice, Italy.

Diamond J., Diamond E. (1999), *Contemporary Visual Merchandising*, Prentice-Hall Inc., Upper Saddle River, NJ, USA.

Dion D. (1999), "A Theoretical and Empirical Study of Retail Crowding", *Advances in Consumer Research*, vol. 4: 51-57.

Dogana F. (1993), *Psicopatologia dei consumi quotidiani*, Franco Angeli, Milan, Italy.

Donovan R. J., Rossiter J. R. (1982), "Store Atmosphere: An Environmental Psychology Approach", *Journal of Retailing*, vol.58 (1): 34-57.

Donovan R. J., Rossiter J. R., Marcoolyn G., Nesdale A. (1994), "Store Atmosphere and Purchasing Behavior", *Journal of Retailing*, vol. 70 (3): 283-294.

Dorfles G. (1962), *Simbolo comunicazione consumo*, Saggi 303, Einaudi, Turin, Italy.

Driss F. E. B., Hafsia H. B. L., Zghal M. (2008), "L'impact d'un éclairage additionnel dans un point de vente sur les réactions comportamentales du consommateur", *La Revue de Sciences de Gestion*, vol. 229: 41-49.

Eichorn B. J. (1996), "Selling by Design: Using Lifestyles Analysis to Revamp Retail Space", *American Demographics*, October, vol.18 (10): 44-48.

Fabris G. (2003), *Il nuovo consumatore: verso il postmoderno*, Franco Angeli, Milan, Italy.

Fady A., Seret M. (1991), *Le merchandising, techniques modernes du commerce de detail*, Vulbert, Paris (Italian translation: Il merchandising, Etas Libri, Milan, 1992).

Ferraresi M., Schmitt B. H. (2007), *Marketing esperienziale*, Franco Angeli, Milan, Italy.

Fiocca R. (2017), *Impresa e Valore*, Franco Angeli, Milan, Italy.

Fisher G. N. (1992), *Psychologie sociale de l'espace*, Privat, Pratiques Sociales, Toulouse.

Flack J.A. (2002), "Putting Up with POP", *Marketing Week*, 11 April: 33-4; Special Report, Food Service POP (1998), *POP Times, The New Publication of Point of Purchase Advertising, Display and Packaging*, April: 32-44.

Floch J. M. (1995), *Identités visuelles*, Puf, Paris, France.

Friskney D. (2007), "Digital Billboards: A Growing Opportunity for the Display Business", *Information Display*, April: 8-9.

Fung A., Tai S. (1997), "Application of an Environmental Psychology Model to In-Store Buying Behavior", *The International Review of Retail*, Distribution and Consumer research, vol. 7 (4): 311-337.

Gallucci F. (2007), *Marketing emozionale*, Egea, Milan, Italy.

Gardner M. P. (1985), "Mood States and Consumer Behavior: A Critical Review", *Journal of Consumer Research*, vol. 12 (3): 281-300.

Gardner M. P., Siomkos G. J. (1986), "Towards a Methodology for Assessing Effects of the Store Atmospherics", *Advances in Consumer Research*, vol. 13 (1): 27-31.

Genzini F., Costantino G. (1998), "Il punto vendita: ruolo centrale o marginale nell'immediato futuro?", *Trade Marketing*, vol. 22: 127-139.

Giacoma Caire G. (2009), *Visual Merchandising*, Creative Group, Milan, Italy.

Gifford R. (1988), "Light, décor, arousal, comfort and communication", *Journal of Environmental Psychology*, vol. 8: 177-189.

Golinelli G. M. (2000), *L'approccio sistemico al governo dell'impresa*, Vol. I e II, Cedam, Padua, Italy.

Gombrich E. (1960), *Arte e illusione*, Saggi 354, Einaudi, Turin, Italy.

Goss J. (1993), "The "Magic of the Mall": An Analysis of Form, Function, and Meaning in the Contemporary Retail Built Environment", *Annals of the Association of American Geographers*, vol. 83 (1): 18-47.

Grandi R. (Ed.) (1994), *Semiotica al marketing, Le tendenze della ricerca nel marketing nel consumo, nella pubblicità*, Franco Angeli, Milan, Italy.

Grandinetti R. (1993), *Reti di marketing. Dal marketing delle merci al marketing delle relazioni*, Etas, Milan.

Guéguen N., Jacob C., Lourel M., Le Guellec H. (2007), "Effect of Background Music on Consumer Behavior: A Field Experiment in an Open-Air Market, *European Journal of Scientific Research*, vol. 16 (2): 268-272.

Gustafson P. (2001), "Meanings of Place: Everyday Experience and Theoretical Conceptualizations", *Journal of Environmental Psychology*, vol. 21 (1): 5-16.

Hall J. D., Vecchia E. M. (1990), "More Touching Observations-New Insights on Men, Women and Interpersonal Touch", *Journal of Personality and Social Psychology*, vol. 59 (6): 1155-1162.

Häubl G., Trifts V. (2000), "Consumer Decision Making in Online Shopping Environments: The Effects of Interactive Decision Aids", *Marketing Science*, vol. 19 (1): 4-21.

Herrington J. D., Capella L. M. (1996), "Effects of Music in Service Environments: A Field Study", *Journal of Services Marketing*, vol. 10 (2): 36-41.

Hidalgo M. C., Hernàndez B. (2001), "Place Attachment: Conceptual and Empirical Questions", *Journal of Environmental Psychology*, vol. 21 (3): 273-281.

Hillesland J., Maise J. N., Rudolph T., Gisholt O. (2012), *Fundamentals of Retailing and Shopper Marketing*, Prentice Hall, Pearson Education, Switzerland.

Hoffman D., Novak T. (2011), "Marketing Communication in a Digital Era", *Marketing Management*, vol. 20 (3): 37-42.

Hoffman D., Novak T. (2012), "Toward a Deeper Understanding of Social Media", *Journal of Interactive Marketing*, vol. 26 (May): 69-70.

Holbrook M. B. (2000), "Millennial Consumer in the Texts of Our Time: Experience and Entertainment" *Journal of Macromarketing*, vol. 20 (2): 178-192.

Holbrook M. B., Hirschman E. C. (1982), "The Experiential Aspects of Consumption: Consumer Fantasies, Feelings and Fun", *Journal of Consumer Research*, vol. 9 (2): 132-140.

Hornik J. (1992), "Tactile Stimulation and Consumer Response", *Journal of Consumer Research*, vol. 19 (3): 449-458.

Hui D. B., Bateson J. E. G. (1990), "Testing a Theory of Crowing in the Service Environment", *Advances in Consumer Research*, vol. 17: 866-873.

Hui M. K., Dube L., Chebat C. J. (1997), "The Impact of Music on Consumers' Reactions to Waiting for Services", *Journal of Retailing*, vol. 73 (1): 87-104.

Inman J.J., Russell S.W., Ferraro R. (2009), "The Interplay Among Category Characteristics, and Consumer Activities on In-Store Decision Making", *Journal of Marketing*, 73 (September): 19-29.

Itten J. (1961), *Arte del colore*, Il Saggiatore, Milan, Italy.

Iyer E. S., Ahlawat S. S. (1987), "Deviations from Shopping Plan: When and why do Consumers not Buy as Planned", *Advances in Consumer Research*, vol.14: 246-249.

Jackobson R. (1978), *Lo sviluppo della semiotica*, Bompiani, Milan, Italy.

Jarboe G. R., McDaniel C. D. (1987), "A Profile of Browsers in Regional Shopping Malls", *Journal of the Academy of Marketing Science*, vol. 15 (1): 46-53.

Jones M.A., Reynolds K.E., Weun S., Beatty S.E. (2003), "The Product-Specific Nature of Impulse Buying Tendency", *Journal of Business Research*, vol. 56 (7): 505-11.

Joy A., Sherry J. (2003), "Speaking of art on Embodied Imagination: a Multisensory Approach to Understanding Aesthetic Experience", *Journal of Consumer Research*, vol. 30 (2): 259-282.

Kacen J. J., Hess J. D., Walker D. (2012), "Spontaneous Selection: The Influence of Product and Retailing Factors on Consumer Impulse Purchases", *Journal of Retailing and Consumer Services*, vol. 19 (6): 578-588.

Kandinsky W. (1926), *Punto, linea, superficie*, Biblioteca Adelphi, Milan, Italy.

Kargaonkar P. K. (1981), "Shopping Orientations, Importance of Store Attributes, Demographics and Store Patronage: A Multivariate Investigation", *Akron Business & Economic Review*, vol. 12: 34-38.

Kellaris J. J., Moses A. B. (1992), "The Experience of Time as a Function of Musical Loudness and Gender of Listener", *Advances in Consumer Research*, vol. 19 (1): 725-730.

Kellaris J. J., Kent R. J. (1991), "Exploring Tempo and Modality Effects on Consumer Responses to Music", *Advances in Consumer Research*, vol. 18 (1): 243-248.

Kehnove P., Desrumaux P. (1997), "The Relationship between States and Approach or Avoidance Responses in a Retail Environment", *The International Review of Retail, Distribution and Consumer Research*, vol. 7 (4): 351-368.

Kociatkiewicz J., Zostera M. (1999), "The Anthropology of Empty Spaces", *Qualitative Sociology*, vol. 22 (1): 37-50.

Kotler P. (1973), "Atmospheric as a Marketing Tool", *Journal of Retailing*, vol. 49, Winter: 48-64.

Kozinets R. V., Sherry J. F. Jr., Storm D., Duhachek A., Nuttavuthisit K., DeBerry-Spence B. (2002), "Themed Flagship Brand Stores in the New Millennium: Theory, Practice, Prospects", *Journal of Retailing*, vol. 78 (1): 17-29.

Kozinets R. V., Sherry J. F. Jr., Storm D., Duhachek A., Nuttavuthisit K., De-Berry - Spence B. (2004), "Ludic Agency and Retail Spectacle", *Journal of Consumer Research*, vol. 31 (3): 658-672.

Kumari K.B., Venkatramaiah S.R. (1974), "Effects of Anxiety on Closure Effect Disappearance Threshold (Brain Blood, Shift Gradient) ", *Indian Journal of Clinical Psychology*, vol. 1 (2): 114-120.

Langrehr F.W. (1991), "Retail Shopping Mall Semiotics and Hedonic Consumption", *Advances in Consumer Research*, vol. 18 (1): 428-433.

Law D, Wong C., Yip J. (2012), "How does Visual Merchandising Affect Consumer Affective Response?: An Intimate Apparel Experience", *European Journal of Marketing*, 46 (1): 112-33.

Lazarus R. S. (1991), *Emotion and Adaptation*, Oxford University Press, New York, USA.

Lee W. (1961), "Space Management in Retail Stores and Implications to Agriculture", in Dolva W. K., *Marketing keys to profits in the 1960's*, American Marketing Association, Chicago, USA.

Lefevre H. (1974), *La production de l'espace*, Anthropos, Paris, France.

Levy S. I., Weitz J. (2004), *Retailing Marketing*, McGraw-Hill, New York, NY, USA.

Lewison D. M. (2002), *Retailing*, Prentice-Hall, NJ, USA.

Li H., Daugherty T., Biocca F. (2002), "Impact of 3-D Advertising on Product Intention: The Mediating Role of Presence", *Journal of Advertising*, vol. 31 (3): 43-57.

Liljenwall R., Maskulka J. (2002), *Marketing's Powerful Weapon: Point of Purchase Advertising*, Point of Purchase Advertising International, Washington, DC, USA.

Lillis C., Markin R., Narayana C. (1976), "Social – Psychological Significance of Store Space", *Journal of Retailing*, vol. 52 (1): 43-54.

Lucas G. H., Bush R. P., Gresham L. G. (1994), *Retailing*, Houghton Mifflin, Boston, USA.

Lugli G. (1988), *La gestione dello spazio espositivo nel libero servizio*, Franco Angeli, Milan, Italy.

Lugli G. (1993), *Economia e politiche di marketing delle imprese commerciali*, Utet, Turin, Italy.

Lugli G. (2011), *Neuroshopping*, Apogeo, Milan, Italy.

Lugli G., Pellegrini L. (2002), *Marketing distributivo*, Utet, Milan, Italy.

Lugli G., Ziliani C. (2004), *Micromarketing. Creare valore con le informazioni di cliente*, Utet, Turin, Italy.

Lyn I. Y. (2004), "Evaluating a Servicescape: The Effect of Cognition and Emotion", *International Journal of Hospitality Management*, vol. 23 (2): 163-178.

Maclaran P., Brown S. (2005), "The Center cannot Hold: Consuming the Utopian Marketplace", *Journal of Consumer Research*, vol. 32 (2): 311-323.

Maclaran P., Stevens L. (1998), "Romancing the Utopian Marketplace", in Brown S., Doherty A. M., Clarke B., *Romancing the market*, Routledge, London, UK.

Mandelli A., Accoto C. (2012), *Social Mobile Marketing*, Egea, Milan, Italy.

Magne S. (1999), *Essai de mesure de l'attitude esthétique du consommateur envers la forme-design du packaging et d'une variable explicative, la sensibilité esthetique personnelle: une application au Design de couvertures de livres*, tesi di dottorato in Scienze Manageriali, Università di Toulouse 1, ESUG.

Maille V. (2001), "L'influence des stimoli olfactives sur le comportement du consommateur: un état de recherche", *Recherche et Applications en Marketing*, vol. 16 (2): 51-75.

Manzo L. C. (2003), "Beyond House and Haven: Toward a Revisioning of Emotional Relationship with Places", *Journal of Environmental Psychology*, vol. 23: 47-61.

Marcolli A. (1971), *Teoria del campo 1, Corso di educazione alla visione*, Editrice Sansoni, Florence, Italy.

Marion G. (1989), *Les images de l'entreprise*, Les Editions d'Organisation, Paris, France.

Markin R.J., Lillis C.M., Narayana, C.L. (1976), "Social-Psychological Significance of Store Space", *Journal of Retailing*, vol. 52 (1): 43-54.

Marsciani F. (2004), "Percorsi nel punto vendita tra gesti e sensibilità" in Bucchetti V. (Ed.), *Design della comunicazione ed esperienze di acquisto*, Franco Angeli, Milan, Italy.

Masson J. E., Wellhoff A. (2005), *Il merchandising: come avere successo nel commercio moderno*, Franco Angeli, Milan, Italy.

Mattila A. S., Wirzt J. (2001), "Congruency of Scent and Music as a Driver on In-Store Evaluations and Behavior", *Journal of Retailing*, vol. 77 (2): 273-289.

Mazursky D., Jacoby J. (1986), "Exploring the Development of Store Images", *Journal of Retailing*, vol. 62 (2): 145-165.

Mc Donnell J. (2002), *Sensorial Marketing for Those who can Wait no Longer*, Convegno sul marketing sensoriale, Sophia Antipolis, Nice, France.

Mehrabian A., Russell J. A. (1974), *An Approach to Environmental Psychology*, MIT Press, Cambridge, MA, USA.

Milgram P., Takemura A., Utsumi A., Kishino F. (1994). "Augmented Reality: A Class of Displays on the Reality-Virtuality Continuum", *Telemanipulator and Telepresence Technologies*, SPIE, Vol. 2351.

Milliman R. E. (1982), "Using Background Music to Affect the Behavior of Supermarket Shoppers", *Journal of Marketing*, vol. 46 (3): 86-91.

Milliman R. E. (1986), "The influence of background music on the Behavior of Restaurant Patrons", *Journal of Consumer Research*, vol. 13 (2): 286-289.

Mills K. H., Paul J. E. (1988), *Applied Visual Merchandising*, Prentice-Hall Inc., Englewood Cliffs. NJ, USA.

Mitchell D. J., Kahn B. E., Knasko S. C. (1995), "There's Something in the Air: Effects of Ambient Odor on Consumer Decision Making" *Journal of Consumer Research*, vol. 22 (2): 229-238.

Morace F., Terzi A., Tomassini N. (1990), *Iperspesa: vendere e comprare nel duemila*, Lupetti & Co, Milan, Italy.

Morgan T. (2011), *Visual Merchandising. L'allestimento degli spazi commerciali*, Logos, Modena, Italy.

Moro W. (1987), *Didattica della comunicazione visiva*, La Nuova Italia, Florence, Italy.

Morrin M., Ratneshwar S. (2000), "The Impact of Ambient Scent on Evaluation, Attention, Memory for Familiar and Unfamiliar Brands", *Journal of Business Research*, vol. 49 (2): 157-165.

Morrin M., Ratneshwar S. (2003), "Does it Make Sense to Use Scents to Enhance Brand Memory?", *Journal of Marketing Research*, vol. 40 (1): 10-25.

Mulhern F. J. (1997), "Retail Marketing: From Distribution to Integration", *International Journal of Research in Marketing*, vol. 14 (2): 103-124.

Munsell A. (1913), *A Color Notation*, Boston, MA, USA.

Napolitano M., De Nisco A. (2003), "La rappresentazione dell'identità di marca attraverso i luoghi d'acquisto: la brand experience e i flagship store", *Industria&Distribuzione*, vol. 2: 13-30.

Panza R. (2013), *Manuale di progettazione per la grande distribuzione. Strategie, immagine e format per nuovi consumatori*, Franco Angeli, Milan, Italy.

Park C.W., Iyer E., Smith D.C. (1989), "The Effects of Situational Factors on In-Store Grocery Shopping Behavior: The Role of Store Environment and Time Available for Shopping", *Journal of Consumer Research*, vol. 15 (4): 422-32.

Pasquinelli C. (2004), *La vertigine dell'ordine*, Baldini Castoldi Dalai, Milan, Italy.

Pastoureau M. (1987), *L'uomo e il colore*, Giunti, Florence, Italy.

Patterson M. L., Powell J. K., Lenihan M. G. (1986), "Touch Compliance and Interpersonal Affects", *Journal of Nonverbal Behavior*, vol. 10 (1): 41-50.

Pechmann C., Stewart D.W. (1990), "The Effects of Comparative Advertising on Attention, Memory, and Purchase Intentions", *Journal of Consumer Research*, vol. 17 (2): 180-91.

Pegler M. M. (1912), *Visual Merchandising & Display*, 6th Edition, Fairchild Publications, New York, NY, USA.

Pellegrini L. (1993), "Merchandising e rapporti di canale" in Pellegrini L., Bertozzi P., Sabbadin E., *Il merchandising. Interazione tra marketing del distributore e del produttore nel punto vendita*, CESCOM, Egea, Milan, Italy.

Pieters R., Wedel M. (2007), "Informativeness of Eye Movements for Visual Merchandising: Six Cornerstones", in Wedel M. and Mahwah R. P., *Visual Marketing: From Attention to Action*, Lawrence Erlbaum Associates, NJ: 34-72.

Pine B., Gilmore J.H. (1999), *The Experience Economy: Work is Theatre & Every Business a Stage*, Harvard Business School Press, Boston, USA (Italian translation (2000); *L'economia delle esperienze*, Etas, Milan, Italy).

Piron F. (1989), *A Definition and Empirical Investigation of Impulse Purchasing*, Unpublished Dissertation, University of South Carolina, USA.

Proshansky H. M., Fabiani A. K., Kaminoff R. (1983), "Place - Identity: Physical World Socialization of the Self", *Journal of Environmental Psychology*, vol. 3: 57-83.

Provenzano A. (2012), *Visual Merchandising. Dal marketing emozionale alla vendita visiva*, Franco Angeli, Milan, Italy.

Ragone G., (Ed.) (1992), *Sociologia dei fenomeni di moda*, Collana Comunicazione e Società, Franco Angeli, Milan, Italy.

Raghubir P., Valenzuela A. (2006), "Center-of-Inattention: Position Biases in Decision-Making", *Organizational Behavior and Human Processes*, 99, 1: 66-80.

Raghubir P., Valenzuela A. (2008), *Center-of-Orientation: Effects of Vertical and Horizontal Shelf Space Product Position*, working paper, Baruch College, City University of New York.

Ravazzi C. (2002), *Visual merchandising: per sviluppare la vendita visiva nei punti vendita di ogni tipo e dimensione*, Franco Angeli, Milan, Italy.

Ravazzi G. (2000), *Marketing nel punto vendita*, Franco Angeli, Milan, Italy.

Ravizza D. (2011), *Progettare con la luce*, Franco Angeli, Milan, Italy.

Reite M. (1990), "Touch, Attachment and Health: Is there a Relationship?" in Bernard K. E., Brazelton T. B. (Eds.), *Touch: the foundation of experience*, International Universities Press, Madison, CT, USA.

Relph E. (1976), *Place and Placelessness*, Pion Ltd, London, UK.

Rizzi B., Milani S. (2013), *Visual merchandising e visual marketing*, Franco Angeli, Milan, Italy.

Rogers D. S., Gamans L. R., Grassi M. M. T. (1992), *Retailing: New Perspectives*, The Dryden Press, Harcourt Brace College Publishers, New York, NY, USA.

Rook D. W. (1987), "The Buying Impulse", *Journal of Consumer Research*, vol. 14 (2): 189-199.

Rook D.W. e R.J. Fisher (1995), "Normative Influence on Impulse Buying Behavior", *Journal of Consumer Research*, vol. 22 (December): 305-13.

Rook D. W., Hoch S. J. (1985) , "Consuming Impulses", *Advances in Consumer Research*, vol. 12: 23-28.

Rook D.W., Gardner M. P. (1993), "In the Mood: Impulsive Buying Affective Antecedents" *Research in Consumer Behavior*, vol. 6: 1-28.

Russell M. G. (2010), "Point of Purchase Engagement Boots Perception and Purchase", *American Academy of Advertising Conference Proceedings*: 161-168.

Sabbadin E. (1991), *Merchandising, packaging e promozione: le nuove dimensioni della concorrenza verticale*, Franco Angeli, Milan, Italy.

Sabbadin E. (1993), "Classificazione dell'assortimento, layout e category management", in Pellegrini L., Bertozzi P., Sabbadin E., *Il merchandising. Interazione tra marketing del distributore e del produttore nel punto vendita*, CESCOM, Egea, Milan, Italy.

Sansone M., Scafarto F. (2003), "Il ruolo comunicativo del punto vendita nel "sistema moda", *Congresso Internazionale Le Tendenze Del Marketing*, Università Ca' Foscari, Venice, Italy.

Schmitt B. H. (1999), *Experiential Marketing: How to Get Customers to SENSE, FEEL, THINK, ACT and RELATE to Your Company and Brands*, The Free Press, New York, NY, USA.

Schmitt B. H., Simonson A. (1997), *Marketing Aesthestic*, The Free Press, New York, NY, USA.

Semprini A. (1993), *Marche e mondi possibili*, Franco Angeli, Milan, Italy.

Sherry J. F. Jr (1998), *Servicescapes: The Concept of Place in Contemporary Markets*, AMA, Chicago, IL, USA.

Schewe, C.D. (1988), "Marketing to our Aging Population: responding to Physiological Changes", *The Journal of Consumer Marketing*, vol. 5 (3): 61-73.

Sicca L. (1990), *Il marketing dell'azienda dettagliante moderna*, Cedam, Padua, Italy.

Silvestrelli S., Gregori G. (1998), "Un ruolo dell'agente di commercio nei moderni canali di distribuzione", *Sinergie*, vol. 47: 197-226.

Soscia I. (2001), "Semiotica e comunicazione in store", in Castaldo S. (Ed.), *Retailing e Innovazione*, Egea, Milan, Italy.

Soscia I. (2009), *Emozioni & Consumo*, Egea, Milan, Italy.

Spangenberg E. R., Crowley A. E., Henderson P. W. (1996), "Improving the Store Behavior", *Journal of Marketing*, vol. 60 (2): 67-70.

Srivastava R.K. (2009), "Measuring Brand Strategy: can Brand Equity and Brand Score be a Tool to Measure the Effectiveness of Strategy?", *Journal of Strategic Marketing*, 17 (6): 487-97.

Summers A. T., Hebert R. P. (2001), "Shedding some Light on Store Atmospherics. Influence of Illumination on Consumer Behavior", *Journal of Business Research*, vol. 54 (2): 145-150.

Stern B. (1998), *Representing Consumers: Voices, Views, and Visions*, Routledge, New York, NY, USA.

Stokols D., Shumaker S. A., (1981), "People in Places: A Transactional View of Settings", in Harvey J. (Ed.), *Cognition, Social Behavior and the Environment*, Erlbaum, NJ, USA.

Stone G. P. (1954), "City Shoppers and Urban Identification: Observation on the Social Psychology of City Life", *American journal of Sociology*, vol. 60 (1): 36-45.

Sundar S. S., Kalyanaraman S. (2004), "Arousal, Memory, and Impression-Formation Effects of Animation Speed in Web Advertising", *Journal of Advertising*, vol. 33 (1): 7-17.

Sutherland I. (1968), "A Head-Mounted Three-Dimensional Display", *AFIPS Conference Proceedings* No.33, Fall Joint Computer Conference.

Tauber E. M. (1972), "Marketing Notes and Communication: Why do People Shop?" *Journal of Marketing*, vol.36 (1): 46-59.

Testori M. (2015), *Shopper Marketing*, Franco Angeli, Milan, Italy.

Tirelli D. (2009), *Digital signage. L'immagine onnipresente*, Franco Angeli, Milan, Italy.

Thompson K. E., Chen Y. L. (1998), "Retail Store Image: a Means-End Approach", *Journal of Marketing Practice*, vol. 4 (6): 161-173.

Trevisan M., Pegoraro M. (2007), *Retail Design*, Franco Angeli, Milan, Italy.

Trevisani D. (2001), *Psicologia di marketing e comunicazione: pulsioni d'acquisto, leve persuasive, nuove strategie di comunicazione e management*, Franco Angeli, Milan, Italy.

Tuan Y. (1977), *Space and Place: the Perspective of Experience*, University of Minnesota Press, Minneapolis, MN, USA.

Tuci C. (2008), *La vendita visiva*, Franco Angeli, Milan.

Turley L. W., Milliman R. E. (2000), "Atmospheric Effects on Shopping Behavior: A Review of the Experimental Evidence", *Journal of Business Research*, vol. 49 (2): 193-211.

Twigger - Ross C. L., Uzzell D. L. (1996), "Place and Identity Processes", *Journal of Environmental Psychology*, vol. 16 (3): 205-220.

Underhill P. (1999), *Why we Buy: The Science of Shopping*, Orion Business Books, London, UK (Italian translation: *Shopping mania*, Sperling & Kupfer Editori, Milan, Italy, 2006).

Van der Lans R., Rik P., Wedel M. (2008), "Competitive Brand Salience", *Marketing Science*, vol. 27 (5): 922-31.

Varela F., Thompson E., Rosch E. (1991), *The Embodied Mind: Cognitive Science and Human Experience*, MIT Press, Cambridge, MA, USA.

Vitta M. (1996), *La visione del negozio*, in Micheli S., "Progettare negozi: cinema, restaurant, shop", Almea, Florence, Italy.

Wedel M., Pieters R. (2008), "A Review of Eye-Tracking Research in Marketing", *Review of Marketing Research*, 4: 123-47.

Weitzl W., Zniva R. (2010), "The In-Store Antecedents and Consequences of

Perceived Shopping Value for Regularly Purchased Products", European Retail Research, vol. 24 (1): 121-148.

Westwood V. and Kelly I. (2014), *Vivienne Westwood*, Picador, London, UK.

Wilson R. T., Till B. D. (2008), "Airport Advertising Effectiveness", *Journal of Advertising*, vol. 37 (1): 59-72.

Yalch R., Spangenberg E. (1990), "Effects of Store Music on Shopping Behavior", *Journal of Service marketing*, vol. 4 (1): 31-39.

Yim M. Y., Yoo S., Sauer P., Seo J. (2013), "Hedonic Shopping Motivation and Co-Shopper Influence on Utilitarian Grocery Shopping in Superstores", *Journal of the Academy of Marketing Science*, DOI: 10.1007/s11747-013-0357-2.

Yim M. Y., Yoo S., Till B., Eastin M. (2010), "In-Store Video Advertising Effectiveness", *Journal of Advertising Research*, vol. 50 (4): 386-401.

Yoo C., Park J., MacInnis D.J. (1998), "Effects of Store Characteristics and In-Store Emotional Experiences on Store Attitude", *Journal of Business Research*, vol. 42 (3): 253-263.

Zaghi K. (2006), "Il Merchandising e la store atmosphere" in *Distribuzione e Sales in Enciclopedia di Management*, vol. 13, Egea, Milan, Italy.

Zaghi K. (2010), "Il Visual Merchandising", in Castaldo S. and Mauri C. (Eds), *Store Management. La gestione delle piattaforme relazionali*, III Ed., Franco Angeli, Milan, Italy.

Zaghi K. (2008), *Atmosfera e visual merchandising: ambienti, relazioni ed esperienze*, Franco Angeli, Milan, Italy.

Zaghi K. (2013), *Visual Merchandising e relazioni di canale*, Franco Angeli, Milan, Italy.

Zantorello L. (2005), "Marketing dell'esperienza: quali approcci possibili?", *Micro & Macro Marketing*, vol. 2: 177-195.

Zeithaml V. (1988), "Consumer Perceptions of Price Quality, and Value: A Means-End Model and Synthesis of Evidence", *Journal of Marketing*, vol. 52 (3): 2-22.